BUILDING THEIR OWN WALDOS

Building Their Own Waldos

*Emerson's First Biographers and the
Politics of Life-Writing in the Gilded Age*

by ROBERT D. HABICH

28 March 2011

*For Terry King,
with gratitude for the
support of my work —

Bob*

UNIVERSITY OF IOWA PRESS
Iowa City

University of Iowa Press, Iowa City 52242

COPYRIGHT © 2011 BY THE UNIVERSITY OF IOWA PRESS

www.uiowapress.org

Printed in the United States of America

Design by Teresa W. Wingfield

The University of Iowa Press is a member of Green Press Initiative
and is committed to preserving natural resources.

Printed on acid-free paper

Library of Congress Cataloging-in-Publication Data

Habich, Robert D., 1951–
Building their own Waldos: Emerson's first biographers and the politics of
life-writing in the Gilded Age / by Robert D. Habich.
p.   cm.
Includes bibliographical references and index.
ISBN-13: 978-1-58729-962-9 (pbk)
ISBN-10: 1-58729-962-3 (pbk)
ISBN-13: 978-1-58729-963-6 (e-book)
ISBN-10: 1-58729-963-1 (e-book)
1. Emerson, Ralph Waldo, 1803–1882.   2. Emerson, Ralph Waldo,
1803–1882—Criticism and interpretation—History.   3. Authors, American—
Biography—History and criticism.   4. American prose literature—History and
criticism.   5. Biography as a literary form.   I. Title.
PS1631.H28 2011
814'.3—dc22
[B]
2010033753

For Brenda

CONTENTS

ACKNOWLEDGMENTS

WRITING A NARRATIVE BASED in archival sources is like assembling a jigsaw puzzle without having the box it came in: you don't know till the end what the picture looks like, and you're never quite sure you have all the pieces. While writing this book I have incurred a number of debts to those who have helped me to complete the puzzle. For permission to use and quote from archival material in their collections, I wish to thank the Bentley Historical Library and the Special Collections Library, both of the University of Michigan; the Concord Free Public Library; the Library of Congress; the Dedham (Massachusetts) Historical Society; Archives and Special Collections, Dickinson College, Carlisle, Pennsylvania; the Fruitlands Museum, Harvard, Massachusetts; the Special Collections of Glasgow University; the Houghton Library, Harvard University; the Arthur and Elizabeth Schlesinger Library on the History of Women in America, Radcliffe Institute for Advanced Study, Harvard University; the Indiana State Library; the Massachusetts Historical Society; the Centre for Writing, Publishing and Printing History in the Special Collections, University of Reading, England; and the Watkinson Library, Trinity College. In addition, the following institutions were generous in providing information and access to their collections: the Andover-Harvard Divinity School Library; the Beverly (Massachusetts) Historical Society; the library of the Boston Museum of Fine Arts; the Boston Public Library; the British Library; the Rare Book and Manuscript Library, Columbia University; the Harvard University Archives; the Indiana Historical Society; the Jefferson County (Wisconsin) Historical and Genealogical Society; the Manchester Central Library, England; the Burrage Library, Olivet College, Michigan; the Phillips Library, Peabody Essex Museum, Salem, Massachusetts; and the Walworth County (Wisconsin) Historical Society. It is a pleasure to thank those archivists who have gone out of their way to share their expertise and help me locate material, particularly Leslie Perrin Wilson, Curator, William Munroe Special Collections, Concord Free Public Library; Leslie A. Morris, Curator, Modern Books and Manuscripts, Houghton Library, Harvard University; Peter Drummey, Stephen T. Riley Librarian, Massachusetts Historical Society; Michael Volmar, Curator of Collections, Fruitlands Museum; and Michael Bott, Curator, and Verity Andrews, Archives Assistant, Special Collections, University of Reading. Some of the material in this book appeared in earlier form as my essays "Holmes, Cabot, and Edward Emerson and the Challenges of Writing Emerson's Biography in the 1880s," in *Emerson Bicentennial Essays*, ed. Ronald A. Bosco and Joel Myerson (Boston: Massachusetts Historical Society, 2006), 3–32, and "Channing Remembers Emerson: Visits to Concord in 1870 and 1877," *New England Quarterly* 73 (2000): 495–506. I thank the Massachusetts Historical Society and the *New England Quarterly* for permission to reprint revised sections of those essays.

All students of Emerson owe a debt of gratitude to the Emerson family members who have over the years preserved and made accessible a treasure trove of material for scholarly use. I am particularly grateful to Margaret Emerson Bancroft of the Ralph Waldo Emerson Memorial Association and Professor Beatrice Forbes Manz of the Forbes Family Archives Committee for graciously sharing their knowledge. No Emersonian could ask for a better sounding board than my pals in the Ralph Waldo Emerson Society; I particularly thank Phyllis Cole, Len Gougeon, and Wes Mott. Ronald A. Bosco and Joel Myerson, our premiere scholars of Emerson's texts and times, have been unfailingly generous with their expertise and encouragement. To Robert N. Hudspeth I owe a special debt for teaching me how to do this work—and why. Conversations with my colleagues on the literature faculty at Ball State University, including Patrick Collier and Rai Peterson, improved this book and kept the ideas alive. I benefited from the thoughtful suggestions of the readers at the University of Iowa Press, including one who later revealed himself as Scott E. Casper, the author of outstanding work on American biography. Over the years a series of doctoral research assistants at Ball State University have been dutiful in checking facts and tracking down leads, including Jeff Ramsay, Laura Swartz, Maria Staton, David DiSarro, and Monica Robison. The staff of the University of Iowa Press, especially Holly Carver, Joe Parsons, and Charlotte Wright, have been supportive and good-humored throughout the book-making process. Jennifer Hope of Mesa Verde Media Services has copyedited the text with care and intelligence. To all, my sincere thanks.

This publication was produced in part with generous support from Ball State University, Muncie, Indiana, Office of the Provost, Dr. Terry King. I am grateful to the Sponsored Programs Office at Ball State University, directed by James L. Pyle, Kristi Koriath, and Robert J. Morris, for providing financial and logistical support at various times for travel and summer grants; to the Office of the Provost, Ball State University, for a special assigned leave with pay that allowed me to work in England; and to the National Endowment for the Humanities, Division of Research Programs, for a Summer Stipend. I was fortunate to participate in the American Antiquarian Society's 2004 Summer Seminar on the History of the Book, a wonderful immersion in print culture that broadened my knowledge of nineteenth-century publishing and enabled me to try out ideas in a congenial setting with the AAS's welcoming and knowledgeable staff. A visiting faculty exchange through the European Teacher Education Network at the Escola Superior de Educação do Instituto Politécnico in Porto, Portugal, deepened my understanding of American literary history with an international audience of students and faculty colleagues.

Few researchers are lucky enough to have professional librarians by their sides, and none is as fortunate as I am. Brenda Yates Habich has been a source of patience, smart advice, and loving support throughout the making of this book, and for this, as for all the other riches she brings to my life, I am more grateful than I can say.

Building Their Own Waldos

Conductors of newspapers and magazines should promptly advertise that no "reminiscences" of EMERSON are wanted, and that writers of such reminiscences will be treated with the utmost rigor of lawlessness in case they present themselves in editorial offices.
— *New-York Times*, MAY 2, 1882

IN LATE 1884, just past his seventy-fifth birthday, Oliver Wendell Holmes took stock of the two years of work on his recently completed biography of Ralph Waldo Emerson. On the positive side, he had come to better appreciate Emerson's complex thought and writing, even feeling some "vibrations" of spirituality from working on the project; and his publisher, Houghton, Mifflin, anticipated sufficient sales to help secure Holmes in his retirement. But the work had left him exhausted: "I did not know how difficult a task I had undertaken in venturing upon a memoir of a man whom all, or almost all, agree upon as one of the great lights of the New World."[1]

Holmes's comment points out the challenge faced by all of Emerson's early biographers: how to represent a figure whose subversive individualism had been eclipsed in his later years by his celebrity, making him less a representative of his age than a caricature of it—the "Sage of Concord" who embodied the Gilded Age virtues of gentility, piety, moderation, and sensibly progressive thinking. For a biographer, Holmes sighed, it was like writing about "an unpredicted Messiah."[2]

Those issues of biography and celebrity lie at the heart of this book. The decade of the 1880s witnessed the wholesale reinterpretation of American Renaissance writers like Margaret Fuller, Nathaniel Hawthorne, and Henry David Thoreau, as new biographers sought to reconcile Romantic authors with the tastes and thinking of the Gilded Age and to stabilize models of national identity during a period of sudden multiculturalism. But reinterpretations of Emerson also resulted from a conscious, sometimes incompatible set of agendas by family, friends, and publishers; from technological and social challenges to the definitions of biography; and from the deliberate decisions, personal needs, and political preferences of his biographers. Holmes's sardonic observations about Emerson's celebrity, and about the complications of writing his life, had actually become commonplace long before he wrote them. Just a few days after Emerson's death on April 27, 1882, the writer for the *New York Times*, quoted above, anticipated with surprising irreverence the "shower of libelous reminiscences" sure to follow:

> It will appear that Mr. Emerson has acted as private literary godfather to every poetical and philosophical imbecile in the country, and it will only remain for some particularly malicious person to charge him with having had a pecuniary interest in every idiot asylum where the treatment of new poets and precocious philosophers is made a specialty.[3]

Acerbic though it was about the abuses of great men—and the self-serving nature of those who claimed their friendship—in its prediction of the sheer volume of biographical attention shortly to be paid to Emerson, the *Times* article got it just right. What's more, the *Times*'s suggestion that Emerson would be appropriated in uniform, culturally useful ways quickly became apparent. Even before his death, the sanctification of Emerson had begun, and after it the trend continued. As H. L. Kleinfield puts it, "Whether for purity, nobility, inspiration, or self-reliance, Emerson was praised in continually mounting crescendo for two decades."[4] For generations of readers, admirers, even detractors, he was the Sage of Concord, the Wisest American, the embodiment of "Man Thinking," the "apostle of light."[5]

But not everyone who wrote of him treated Emerson's life as seamlessly iconic. Six months after the great Transcendentalist's death, commenting on what was already a barrage of articles, essays, appreciations, memorials, testimonials, recollections, and appraisals, William Henry Channing, a family advisor and one of his oldest surviving friends, pointed out another difficulty in writing Emerson's biography:

No two observers saw the same man. Unchangingly faithful to his own spirit, as he was, he yet presented ever new phases to the persons he met, according to their quality. And each onlooker saw that side only which his own vision was fitted to discern. . . . One is inclined, therefore, to whisper in the ear of his critics: Beware how you judge this whole-souled brother.[6]

As Channing predicted, the continuing revaluation of Emerson's life and work over the past century and more testifies to the problems of seeing him "whole-souled," even (maybe especially) for those who knew him best. But the *Times* writer had a point, too. Those who knew him least well often constructed him according to certain predictable, reductive patterns, sandpapering his individuality in their zeal to create a smooth and idealized Sage of Concord. In the years just following his death, Emerson's biographical presence vacillated between idolatry and idiosyncrasy.

Neither option was what the Emerson family had planned. For years they had struggled—as had Emerson himself—to control the public understandings of his life, or at least to manage the less responsible ones. The family appointed a literary executor in 1875, James Elliot Cabot, who later became their official biographer, and they judiciously limited other biographers' access to the trove of manuscripts, drafts, lecture notes, journals, letters, account books, and other documents we now know to be crucial to understanding Emerson as a person and as a writer. Their efforts to create an authorized biography, however, were to no avail. By the end of the decade, as Channing had predicted, Emerson's public identity was being constructed in multiple venues. Among them were the six competing full-length biographical studies that form the core of this book. These were written by his friends and a member of his family: George Willis Cooke, a minister most recently from Indianapolis who considered himself a disciple (*Ralph Waldo Emerson*, 1881); the English reformer and newspaper mogul Alexander Ireland, a friend for half a century (*In Memoriam*, 1882, later titled *Ralph Waldo Emerson*); a Southern abolitionist then residing in London, Moncure D. Conway, who called Emerson his "spiritual father and intellectual teacher"[7] (*Emerson at Home and Abroad*, 1882); the poet and medical professor Oliver Wendell Holmes (*Ralph Waldo Emerson*, 1885), who, with Emerson, was a member of Boston's gathering of literary elite, the Saturday Club; Cabot, the authorized biographer, an architect and amateur philosopher with unlimited access to Emerson's unpublished papers (*A Memoir*, 1887); and Emerson's son Edward, a physician and painter whose father had passed over him as literary executor in favor of Cabot (*Emerson in Concord*, 1889).[8]

By the end of the 1880s, hundreds of others had inscribed their versions of Emerson on the public's collective memory, many of them faithfully reinforcing platitudes about his piety, wisdom, and moral example. The title of this book, however, an allusion to Emerson's most summative essay, is meant to suggest why these six early biographies are distinctive. "Build, therefore, your own world" is Emerson's famous exhortation near the end of *Nature* (1836), a testament to his belief in the subjectivity of knowledge and the absolute power of individual vision to transform reality. The six biographies written during the 1880s are built versions of Emerson's life that reflect the interior and exterior worlds of their creators; they were constructed not by strangers or readers or casual acquaintances but by his intimates, to whom he was not "The Sage of Concord" or "The Wisest American" but "Mr. Emerson," occasionally "Waldo," or in Edward Emerson's case, "Father."[9] In their detail, length, and depth these six biographies test and refute Emerson's one-dimensional reputation. In their depictions of Emerson they differ from each other as widely as their authors do. To Cooke, Emerson was a Christian mystic; to Ireland, a social reformer and citizen of the world; to Conway, a principled activist; to Holmes, a detached artist; to Cabot, a practical ethicist; and to his son Edward, the family man and good neighbor in Concord. How these biographies were constructed, why, by whom, and to what effect, are the subjects of this book.

— I —

My study begins with a central question: during a period of massive appropriation of Emerson as cultural icon, how can we account for the varied versions of him by the biographers who knew him best? In theoretical terms, the question is a nonstarter. Biography may be the least theorized of all literary genres; but certainly the drift of conversations about both aesthetics and narrative over the past century has made it increasingly difficult to argue for anything *but* subjectivity on the part of life-writers. As Paul Ricoeur claims in his discussion of historical narrative, problematic differences in values and context inevitably confound our understanding of other human beings and make any retrospective narrative at best a sympathetic approximation of the past. Ricoeur, who wryly calls this condition "incomplete objectivity," in fact applauds informed subjectivity as a function of the historian's expertise, a combination of good judgment and constructive imagination.[10] Susan Tridgell has recently taken a similar view in *Understanding Our Selves: The Dangerous Art of Biography* (2004), where she labels biographical objectivity a "myth" and condemns both the "Positivist approach" to life-writing, which aims for scientific exactitude, and the "Idealist approach," which holds out the hope for a perfect biography while simultaneously condemning the genre for failing to meet what is in the end an impossible standard. Biography, Tridgell argues, is not a "transparent container of facts" but a constructed argument. Just as individuals constantly redefine themselves, so biographers always engage in "limitless redescription" of their subjects.[11] For the study of biography, subjectivity involves the intermingling of author and subject, the creation of an other according to the needs and circumstances of the self, the biographer's vision and "quality," to use Channing's terms.

While this subjectivity is generally conceded by successful practitioners of the genre such as Robert D. Richardson Jr., who cheerfully compares the biographer's illusions to the magician's,[12] critics like Stanley Fish tend to dismiss the entire enterprise as a "bad game" in which order is fabricated and logic imposed by self-indulgent biographers condemned to "substitute their own story for the story of their announced subject." Biographies "don't mean anything in particular, or can mean anything at all," Fish maintains.[13] If Fish's indictment dominates contemporary critical discussion, perhaps it is because there is more history on its side. Profound suspicions that biography was a manipulative, subjective art have existed since the 1880s. Fueled by three decades of encroachment by photography as an alternative—some say more objective and less mediated—form of representation, condemnation of the subjectivity of life-writing was as rampant as the debates over its ethics, form, and purpose. In 1883, Margaret O. W. Oliphant, a prolific English novelist and sometime biographer herself, identified three types of biographers—family members, disciples, and cynics—then admitted that she trusted none of them, hamstrung as they were by their own prejudices and the demands of a genre she accused of systematically desecrating the dead.[14] *Literary* biography was especially suspect. Authors as different as Charles Dickens and Horatio Alger burned their papers lest they fall into the hands of unscrupulous biographers; George Eliot famously dismissed biography as "something like the uncovering of the dead Byron's club-foot."[15] At the same time, biographers were struggling with their own roles, as the aims of the genre underwent a fundamental shift, beginning around mid-century, from an emphasis on didacticism and a subject's representativeness, to a concern with character analysis and a subject's individuality. By the 1880s, Scott E. Casper argues, torn between these two contradictory dictates, American life-writers occupied "multiple biographical worlds" and felt constrained to choose among them.[16]

It is clear, in short, that the theory, practice, and critical history of biography all support the expectation that biography is a subjective, constructed genre, and thus we should not be surprised that lengthy, serious biographies of Emerson—especially by those who knew him fairly well—would differ widely in their depictions of him. But neither subjectivity nor the practical history of the genre alone is sufficient to explain the six early biographies, for if all biographers are subjective and untrustworthy, why was it that the other writers of Emerson were so uniform in their depictions of him, and so widely trusted? Modern critical attention to Emerson's depiction and reputation are similarly unhelpful in explaining the variations. Indeed, virtually every study of Emerson's early biographies has assumed instead a kind of uniformity among them that is quite at odds with Channing's early perception of an Emerson who "presented ever new phases" to his biographers—and at odds with the evidence of the books themselves.

Ronald A. Bosco observes of Emerson's biographers that they find in Emerson what they are looking for.[17] Much the same can be said for the biographers' critics and historians, who have tended to frame their analyses in terms of ideology and culture as they seek an Emerson who is meaningful to his times, and to ours. Among the most thoughtful of these explanations is offered up by Randall Fuller, whose *Emerson's Ghosts* (2007) acknowledges in Gilded Age culture not a monolithic "gentility" but a conflicting set of cultural anxieties—theology was threatened by science, personal autonomy was challenged by the development of the corporation, traditional definitions of domesticity "suffered from strain and tension." Thus Emerson's "new and often contradictory meanings" multiplied at the same time as his "widespread sanctification." This biographical elasticity made Emerson culturally useful without requiring his being consistent, Fuller argues, and the various biographies in the 1880s and 1890s shared a commitment to Emerson as an ideological standard-bearer while differing about the cultural capital of his life. Holmes, for instance, according to Fuller, "enshrine[d] Emerson as a cultural ideal set against the threatening forces of rapid industrialization," while Cabot presented Emerson outside a social context as "an example of philosophical equipoise" who modeled practical wisdom during an age of intellectual uncertainty.[18]

Other recent critics and historians, while somewhat less nuanced than Fuller, offer similar explanations for the way Emerson was idealized, and in due course sanctified, by his culture. In *Individualism and Its Discontents: Appropriations of Emerson, 1880–1950* (1997), Charles E. Mitchell places the early biographies in a "tradition of Emerson worship" in the late nineteenth century. Mitchell notes the inherent dangers of self-reliance and nonconformity and examines how the biographies transform Emerson into an embodiment of Gilded Age ideals of behavior and character: civility, sanity, cleanliness, piety, and benevolence. Together, Mitchell concludes, the biographies constitute a "collective portrait" of an Emerson whose purity of thought and high moral tone "represented the timeless and universal values that the genteel critics counted on to preserve the unity and order of American culture."[19] T. S. McMillin, in *Our Preposterous Use of Literature* (2000), also sees in the biographies of the 1880s an "early example of the detranscendentalization of Emerson" in favor of a culturally safer and more pragmatic emphasis on his life at the expense of his work. In their "re-membering" of Emerson, calling up the man for the ideas, Emerson's early biographers become in McMillin's aggregate formulation "Waldo, Inc.," committed to a common project "to promote harmony, symmetry, benignity, and stability in the face of the displacing (inharmonious, asymmetrical, malignant, destabilizing) qualities inherent to the increasing incorporation of American culture."[20]

— II —

What unites the existing scholarship on Emerson's early biographies is its attention to the formative influence of culture and ideology. As Fuller aptly puts it, "The Emerson who emerges in late-nineteenth-century biographies, commemorative poems, and solemn frontispiece portraits is almost always a cultural ideal capable of acculturating and even improving individuals while at the same time justifying, and on occasion critiquing, institutional interests."[21] In this book I do not discount such readings; rather, I hope, my argument builds upon them, tests them, and in some ways extends them by applying to the biographical enterprise an expanded view of ideology grounded in circumstance. In its classic economic formulation by Louis Althusser, ideology is both pervasive and coercive, demanding "submission to the ruling ideology for the workers, and . . . the ability to manipulate the ruling ideology correctly for the agents of exploitation and repression." This is surely what we mean when we talk of the appropriation of Emerson—his status as a cultural representative, his compelling appeal as a Gilded Age model, his comfortably iconic stature as the reconciler of cultural extremes. For Althusser, however, "ideology" is marked by both imagination and materiality. If ideology "represents the imaginary relationship of individuals to their real conditions of existence," Althusser is quick to point out how ideology, though it originates in the imaginary, evidences itself in the material and demonstrates itself in individual choice.[22]

The approach much favored in Emerson studies by the early twenty-first century, to measure his cultural authority by his congruence with the ideologies of his times and ours, is powerful, productive, and perceptive. But when considering texts and how they come about, especially a textual situation as complicated as the one that gave rise to Emerson's early biographies, it gives us limited interpretive traction. Adept at describing what Emerson's image became, for a number of reasons it is less useful when accounting for how it became so. First of all, the cultural approach both assumes and implies an ideological coherence that has been challenged by most historians of the Victorian era. As John Tomsich points out in his study of Gilded Age politics, "gentility" as a concept was largely reactive, a hedge against economic and social instability, and had more to do with conduct than content—a "clear set of standards to govern public behavior" in a world of shifting standards, gentility was at best a loose and flexible ideology nimble enough to hit moving targets. Even during the Gilded Age itself, the connotation of the word "genteel" migrated from politeness and poise to the kind of dandified overrefinement that led to George Santayana's dismissive use of the term in "The Genteel Tradition in American Philosophy" (1911).[23] Second, ideological and cultural approaches can too easily ignore salient personal differences among the biographers or dismiss the conditions in which they wrote as incidental to the larger narratives they seem to confirm. In point of fact Emerson's early biographers shared very little except that (1) they knew Emerson and chose to write about him and (2) we today know virtually nothing about them and why they did so. Only Holmes survives in modern memory; it is tempting to view the rest of them as some vaguely affiliated biographical committee made up of somber, cigar-smoking clubmen. But to do so is to ignore their significant personal, competitive, political, and economic differences and the extraordinary variations among their relationships to Emerson himself. Third, some of the most influential episodes in the creation of Emerson's early biographies defy easy, or any, cultural or ideological interpretation: a publisher's venture into pornography, a celebrated poet's need for a more secluded retirement home, a family's attempts to emerge from the shadow of its patriarch, a teenager's infatuation with literary heroes, a son's attempts to simultaneously defy and please his father, two daughters who asserted their father's humanity and won, the birth of children and the loss of them, the theft and recovery of an author's correspondence. To understand the influence of these snippets of human drama is to recognize the role of circumstance, vocation, family dynamics, personal finances, petty jealousies, quiet self-effacement, and psychological need in the early creations of Emerson. That the work of biographers is a richly human pursuit may be too obvious to state, but it is everywhere illustrated, I hope, in the pages that follow.

And finally, a concern for the ideological and cultural significance of Emerson's biography assumes that the biographers were more or less unconscious scribes whose motives, were we to know them, matter far less than the cultural work they did. In this book I proceed instead from the assumption that cultural agents have agency, and I believe that the story of Emerson's biographers bears that assumption out. It is certainly possible to recognize the ideological resonance of a figure like Emerson while also recognizing the operation of what historian David Hackett Fischer has termed "contingency" ("something that may or may not happen") in how that figure was constructed. Biographies evidence the choices of their makers, and it is productive to see them, as Fischer sees the coming of the American Revolution, as "a series of contingent happenings, shaped by the choices of individual actors within the context of large cultural processes."[24] Emerson's early biographers may or may not have been fully aware of the cultural implications of their work. But they were without doubt consciously, explicitly, and anxiously aware of themselves *as biographers* during a decade when the popularization of photography, the development of celebrity culture, the availability of competing information technologies, a brisk transatlantic conversation about the moral purposes and appropriate forms of life-writing, competition among literary houses, widening audiences, the emergence of modern ideas of psychology, and a general "craze for biographies" (as the London *Spectator* called it in 1888) all encouraged biographers to rethink their task. What's more, as writers of *Emerson's* life they confronted the additional difficulty of saying something new about a saintly figure much in the news, the "unpredicted Messiah," as Holmes called him. Forced to carve out new rhetorical territories for themselves, Emerson's early biographers provide us a rich, unstudied episode in the politics and commerce of life-writing borne out by a wealth of documentary evidence, correspondence, business records, account books, notes, drafts, and other manuscripts, most included here for the first time. If the biographers reflect, confirm, and question some Gilded Age beliefs and values—and I think it is clear that they do—they also lived in a world where those ideologies were manifested in conditions of readership, commerce, production, technology, private and family agendas, personal needs, and generic redefinitions—a complex of forces that Richard H. Brodhead calls a "culture of letters"[25] and that I refer to as the politics of the genre of biography. To chart the biographers' responses to these material circumstances, as I do in the following pages, is not to deny the pull of ideology but to put a face on it, recognize its materiality, and track its footprints in the world of human affairs.

— III —

A brief example, much more fully developed in chapter 3, may suggest the importance of factoring generic politics into the construction of Emerson's reputation. Let us put side-by-side two suggestive facts: (1) in his 1882 biography, *Emerson at Home and Abroad*, Moncure Daniel Conway departed from the traditional depictions of Emerson by emphasizing his social activism and personal warmth, and (2) the book got little attention when it appeared and is virtually ignored today.[26] The apparent explanation for this failure is that conservatively genteel Gilded Age readers were uninterested in a politically radical or emotionally engaged Emerson and therefore ignored a book depicting him that way. There is, however, an alternative explanation in the circumstances of the book's publication, an explanation more commercial than cultural, more documented than presumptive, and less dependent upon assumptions about the sway of ideology—an explanation grounded in material and commercial circumstances that reveal what Virginia Woolf called in biography "the creative fact; the fertile fact; the fact that suggests and engenders."[27] Readers ignored Conway's book; here's why:

Conway was a transatlantic literary entrepreneur (while living in London he arranged for the English publication of Howells, Whitman, and Twain) who enjoyed a fractious relationship with English publishers. Prolific but often sloppy in his scholarship, with a reputation for bombast, Conway tended to write fast and ask questions later. But *Emerson at Home and Abroad*, it turns out, was his most deliberate book and the most heavily and self-consciously revised of the early biographies. Drafted twelve years earlier as "Emerson and His Friends," an introduction to a proposed (and eventually abandoned) English collection of Emerson's occasional essays, it was later re-envisioned as a book called "Concordia" that would capitalize on Conway's reminiscences of the town he claimed to be his "second birthplace," and finally reshaped (and retitled) at the last minute as *Emerson at Home and Abroad*, apparently to generate market appeal on both sides of the Atlantic. A revealing portrait of a relational and grounded Emerson, the book is lively, anecdotal, and idiosyncratic—very "Conwayish," some reviewers sneered. Had it found a suitable publisher in 1882, it might easily have altered the iconic trajectory of Emerson's constructed reputation. But around 1880 Conway and his publisher had a falling-out over a perceived discrepancy in royalties, and Conway brought his revised Emerson biography instead to Macmillan of London, which was rapidly becoming the most distinguished literary house in England. Unfortunately for him, Macmillan rejected Conway's manuscript—twice: in its original version because it included too little about other Concord writers and in a revised version because it now included too much. With time running out, other biographies already entering the market, and bridges burning behind him in the publishing world, Conway settled for a smaller, more commercial firm in London. This English edition was poorly advertised and appeared late in the holiday season; his American publisher was on his way out of business; and Conway's biography of Emerson, repeatedly rewritten for a changing audience and the perceived demands of the market, met with dismal sales, at home and abroad. Probably the most authentic book he ever wrote, Conway's *Emerson* was a casualty not of ideology but of commercial neglect.

— IV —

In this book I reconstruct the activities of Emerson's first biographers and contextualize them in the contested definitions of the genre in the 1880s, the collateral influences of other representational media such as photography and portraiture, the economics of publication in later Victorian America and England, published and unpublished commentary about the biographies, and the individual agendas of biographers, family, publishers, and friends, who balanced competition and collaboration with each other as they strove to build their own versions of Waldo Emerson. Chapter 1 charts the changing landscape of biography in the 1880s and recounts the attempts by Emerson's family and friends to direct his construction. Chapters 2, 3, 4, and 5 narrate the efforts of his early biographers, singly or in pairs, and analyze the biographies themselves. Chapter 6 examines the fate of the books and their makers and speculates on their value today.

By focusing in this way on the contexts of genre, commerce, family agendas, and the world of print culture, I hope to accomplish several things. First, I tell for the first time the complete story of the six biographers and their work. For three of them—Cooke, Ireland, and Edward Emerson—there is no other extended biographical study, and for Holmes and Conway, existing biographies all but ignore their work on Emerson. Second, by reconstructing from extensive archival evidence the motives, activities, and reception of Emerson's six early biographers from 1881 to 1889, my book recenters the making of Emerson's reputation in situation as well as ideology, in genre as well as culture. A narrative about the making of narratives and a biography of biographers, this book informs our knowledge about the process of Emerson's canonization and shows in detail how the biographers struggled to negotiate public perceptions of a figure already steeped in celebrity, at once revered as a saint and dismissed as a disengaged idealist. The biographers' unique and diverse approaches—as well as the compelling stories of their own lives as practicing writers—both confirm and challenge Emerson's reputation as the Sage of Concord, just as their relationships with Emerson, his family, their publishers, and the reading public challenge the too easy depiction of the biographers themselves as ideologically homogenous and interchangeably genteel.

Third, I hope to show the interpretive possibilities of circumstance, genre, and commerce on Emerson's biographies. Textual constructionists have legitimized the marriage of scholarship and hermeneutics in ways that I hope this study profits by. Jerome J. McGann, for instance, has argued persuasively for textuality as "a social condition of various times, places, and persons."[28] While I value more heavily than McGann does the importance of authorial intentionality, or at least awareness, the story of Emerson's biographies seems to me to confirm McGann's definition of texts as "complex networks of communicative exchanges" among author, reader, and publisher.[29] As an examination of the "textual condition" of Emerson's biographical construction, this book traces a rich case study in the making of literary reputation and offers a detailed historical example in the world of print culture of the revolution in life-writing and celebrity that coincided with the decade of Emerson's death. Nowhere else in American literature do we find such a deliberate, documented, and suggestive episode in the making of biographies, albeit one whose story has remained almost completely untold until now.

By the end of the nineteenth century, the patterning of Emerson's life anticipated by the 1882 New York Times writer had in fact occurred, in ways that were perhaps predictably iconic. However, the six biographers who knew him best recognized the variety of the man, and as Channing predicted, each saw and defined him according to his individual needs and situation and the demands of the literary marketplace. We can appreciate their contribution to Emerson's reputation only by looking, in the terms much favored by the biographers themselves, at their inner, outer, and private lives and by coordinating their work with the intellectual, commercial, and literary contexts in which it was performed. By 1900, the preconditions were set for reading Emerson (the man and his work) as ideological and impersonal. For better or for worse, that iconic reputation was fixed for most of the next century. But a Waldo Emerson far more multidimensional, whole-souled, and—dare I say it?—*contemporary* emerges from the work of his earliest biographers. This book tells the story of their books.

ABBREVIATIONS

AI   Alexander Ireland (1810–1894)
Conway *EHA*   Conway, Moncure D. *Emerson at Home and Abroad.*
                    Boston: James R. Osgood and Co., 1882; London:
                    Trübner, 1883.
Cooke *RWE*   Cooke, George Willis. *Ralph Waldo Emerson: His Life,
                    Writings, and Philosophy.* Boston: James R. Osgood and
                    Co., 1881; London: Sampson Low, Marston Searle, &
                    Rivington, 1882.
E in C   Emerson, Edward Waldo. *Emerson in Concord: A
                    Memoir.* Boston and New York: Houghton, Mifflin, 1889.
EmLet   *Letters of Ralph Waldo Emerson.* Ed. Ralph L. Rusk and
                    Eleanor M. Tilton. 10 vols. New York: Columbia Univer-
                    sity Press, 1939, 1990–1995.
ETE   *The Letters of Ellen Tucker Emerson.* Ed. Edith E. W.
                    Gregg. 2 vols. Kent, OH: Kent State University Press,
                    1982.
EWE   Edward Waldo Emerson (1844–1930)
GWC   George Willis Cooke (1848–1923)
Holmes *RWE*   Holmes, Oliver Wendell. *Ralph Waldo Emerson.*
                    American Men of Letters Series. Boston and New York:
                    Houghton, Mifflin, 1885.
Ireland *RWE*   Ireland, Alexander. *Ralph Waldo Emerson. His Life,
                    Genius, and Writings. A Biographical Sketch.* London:
                    Simpkin, Marshall, 1882.

JEC   James Elliot Cabot (1819–1903)
JMN   *The Journals and Miscellaneous Notebooks of Ralph
          Waldo Emerson*. Ed. William H. Gilman, et al. 16 vols.
          Cambridge, MA: The Belknap Press of Harvard Univer-
          sity Press, 1960–1982.
MDC   Moncure Daniel Conway (1832–1907)
Memoir   Cabot, James Elliot. *A Memoir of Ralph Waldo Emerson*.
          2 vols. Boston and New York: Houghton, Mifflin, 1887.
OWH   Oliver Wendell Holmes (1809–1894)

BUILDING THEIR OWN WALDOS

ONE

A Genre in Transition

Biography in the 1880s

IN NOVEMBER 1877 James Elliot Cabot received a letter from Edward Waldo Emerson, asking him to write his father's biography. Cabot had already agreed some two years earlier to serve as Emerson's literary executor, making sense of the mountain of manuscript drafts, journals, lectures, notebooks, and letters that constituted Emerson's literary legacy. Working closely with family, especially with Emerson's elder daughter Ellen, he had put several volumes into shape, including one, *Letters and Social Aims*, that Emerson himself admitted was more "Mr. Cabot's book" than his own. Edward's latest request could not have been welcome, for Cabot was unpracticed as a biographer and had already devoted several years to a task he accepted without pay, a favor for a man he admired and a family to whom he was related distantly by marriage. For his part, Edward found it a difficult request to make, as witness the worked-over rough draft of his letter that survives with the fair copy. But there was no time to waste, for the family had a "strong suspicion" that two other men were "already collecting materials for that purpose." "Father shudders at the thought that these persons should do the work," Edward confided to Cabot, and the family was eager to make an "arrangement that would please him and thus to be able in the simplest way to forestall any future application by them for help and material."[1]

The two unsuitable biographers, never named, were most likely Moncure D. Conway and Frank Sanborn, both well known to the Emersons. As early as 1872, just after a devastating fire gutted the Emerson home and in the midst of a debacle over a proposed English edition of his uncollected works, Waldo Emerson told the family how he "dreaded" Conway's or Sanborn's getting hold of his papers, and he had already cautioned his friend Thomas Carlyle to steer clear of Conway, who couldn't keep his facts straight.[2] Now, in 1877, two family advisors—Edward's draft of the letter identifies them as William Henry Channing and Henry James Sr.—were urging the Emersons to "take some steps" to secure a proper biographer.[3] As Edward recalled long afterward, even before the fire his father had "wistfully" mentioned Cabot as someone who could "deal with his manuscripts when he was gone" but thought the favor too great to ask.[4] Clearly, the steady, businesslike Cabot was the early frontrunner as the steward of Emerson's papers, and years afterward every one of the Emerson children acknowledged Cabot's work with undisguised gratitude. Cabot's transition from executor to biographer was a logical, if momentous, progression of events.

Cabot's reply to the family's request in 1877 points out some personal and generic issues that inform not only the construction of Emerson's image after his death but also the larger enterprise of biography in the Gilded Age. He accepted the invitation with unfeigned trepidation: honored to be asked to write Emerson's biography, he felt unfit for the task but was "willing to undertake to collect the material for the right man whenever he shall appear."[5] Four years later he reiterated those doubts, in a letter to Ellen Tucker Emerson:

> I do not expect to write anything that could be considered a biography or a full account of your Father—should I survive him. . . . At any rate, I am not the person to do it. What I expect to undertake if the case arises is to put in shape what information is at hand & can be got from his journals & mss. to supplement the accounts that the public already have.[6]

As Ellen reported back to her sister Edith Emerson Forbes, Cabot's demurral had the family worried, but they were confident he would stay the course. "Only he wants us to understand that he doesn't call it a biography which last, he thinks, needs a perspective of fifty to a hundred years."[7]

What seems to be at most a semantic disagreement over the word "biography" is in fact much more than that, especially when we realize how cagey some of Emerson's other early biographers also were when describing what they were doing. Cooke insisted that his 1881 *Ralph Waldo Emerson: His Life, Writings, and Philosophy* was biographical "only because light may be thrown upon his books by the events of his life" and that "little effort has been made to open [Emerson's] personal history."[8] Ireland claimed that his 300-page book was "nothing beyond a Biographical Sketch—Emerson seen through the eyes of those who knew him best."[9] Holmes located Emerson's real life in his works, leaving for the biographer merely "those human accidents which individualize him in space and time,"[10] and Edward Emerson unapologetically vowed to "pass lightly over" public events and achievements and instead tell "the story of my father."[11] To be sure, for convenience readers and reviewers commonly referred to these books as "biographies," just as we do today, and it may have partially been modesty that led Emerson's early biographers to prefer "memoir" or "sketch" or "annals," terms with less ambitious suggestions of personal recollection, anecdote, or chronology. But the fact is, Cabot and the others specifically resisted the term (only Ireland used the word "biography" in the title of his *Ralph Waldo Emerson*), and most placed explicit limits on their roles as biographers. Their anxiety ought to give us pause. While life-writing reached a high point in England and the United States during the last half of the nineteenth century, definitions and expectations of it as a genre were undergoing a significant shift in the 1880s. Emerson's early biographers wrote in response to some very personal circumstances and agendas, but at the same time they were responding to a vigorous Anglo-American debate over the shape of biography itself.

— I —

Sir Leslie Stephen, the first editor of the *Dictionary of National Biography*, wrote that the Victorian era suffered from a "commemorative instinct" that manifested itself in narratives of conventional lives that served to stabilize genteel ideologies like civic responsibility, progressive thinking, and domestic constancy. Stephen sardonically dismissed the subjects of these humdrum biographies as a "long procession of the hopelessly insignificant."[12] But in truth there was nothing insignificant about biography itself in the later Victorian era, which saw an explosion of projects like the *DNB*, the Lives of the Lord Chancellors, the Lives of the Lord Chief Justices, the English Men of Letters series, and many others.[13] As A. O. J. Cockshut points out, Anglo-American biography in the nineteenth century took as its informing principle the creation of the heroic, and by the later Victorian period heroism was put to service defending ideologies of marriage, gender, religion, nationalism, imperialism, capitalism, and race.[14]

This complex cultural work, and the sheer number of biographies published during the Victorian period, strained the definitions and expectations for life-writing; by the decade of Emerson's death, biography was a genre under fire. Here is a representative salvo from the Boston *Literary World* in May 1885:

> The biography of the present, not to mention the unworthy subjects which occasionally find their way into its realm, has become more or less diluted with egoistic puerilities, insipid sentimentalities, and not-to-be-exposed privacies.[15]

The "true and legitimate end" of biography, to reveal the heroic, had been co-opted by sensationalism and a fetish for intimacies—whether a great artist "was possessed of good table manners, had a clear complexion, or even loved pie!"[16] Until the reading public demands more substantial fare than this, warned the *Literary World*, the "heroic age" would be held hostage by popular biographers, a "deluge of mere money-making, insipid, literary personalities."[17]

It was a daunting prospect, surely, but not a new one. As early as 1854 a tongue-in-cheek essay entitled "Biographical Mania" in *Tait's Edinburgh Magazine* railed against the glut of life-writing being published at that time: "it is diluting our literature; it is caricaturing religion; it is dwarfing science; and it is addling the brains of village politicians."[18] On a more serious (if elitist) note, the essay pinpointed an increasing commonness among biographical subjects that deprived biography of its moral force. "Biography, instead of confining itself, as once was the case, to the apex of the pyramid, now nestles itself at the base, and really, on some occasions, it grubs at the foundations of the edifice."[19] It became a frequent refrain in the Anglo-American debate about biography, this notion of commonness; to many, life-writing had degenerated into mere gossip or an exhausting recitation of the trivial, and it seemed as though the reading public couldn't get enough of it. In 1888 the London *Spectator* labeled biography a full-blown "craze."[20] The genre itself was undergoing a profound reconfiguration.[21]

Paul Murray Kendall notes two competing urges in the late nineteenth century that affected the genre of biography: the urge to assemble, organize, and disseminate information, on the one hand, and the urge for privacy, on the other.[22] In part the redefinition of biography represented a struggle between these urges: the more private the life, the greater the challenge to get at its truth. For biographers in the United States, especially literary biographers, the issue of privacy may be grounded in somewhat different cultural circumstances. During the nineteenth century, as an increasingly commercialized society sorted out vocation from avocation, the national agenda both demanded and shaped the development of a professional class of authors. If literary biography did cultural work by making an author's life exemplify the particular "genius" of the nation that produced it, the promotion of public image also carried with it, for writers such as Walt Whitman, the need to guard, and sometimes to falsify, their private lives. (We are reminded of Thoreau's famous complaint in *Walden* about the "men-harriers" who poked about in his cupboard and inspected his laundry.[23]) What Richard D. Altick calls the Victorian "passion for privacy"[24] inevitably came in conflict with biography's cultural mandate, to validate ideologies of nationality, gender, and race by making public the lives of representative men and women.

Just how sensitive these issues had become is brought into sharp relief by the infamous case of James Anthony Froude, who in 1881 began publishing his landmark biographical work on Thomas Carlyle. An accomplished but highly controversial English historian (his 1872 American lecture tour was cut short after threats on his life by the Irish Catholic community), Froude (1818–1894) was Boswell to Carlyle's Johnson, a trusted companion, protégé, and literary executor. Froude's biographical work came in a rush in the early 1880s, just following Carlyle's death: an edition of Thomas Carlyle's blunt *Reminiscences* (1881), which included an intimate portrait of his wife and their marriage; an edition of Jane Welsh Carlyle's equally personal *Letters and Memorials* (1883); and, from 1882 to 1884, *Thomas Carlyle: A History of the First Forty Years of His Life, 1795–1835* and *Thomas Carlyle: A History of His Life in London, 1834–1881*. Drawing on the "letters, diaries, memoirs, [and] miscellanies" Carlyle entrusted to him, Froude cast the "Sage of Chelsea" as a brilliant prophet, flawed husband, and guilt-ridden misanthrope, easy to admire but as Froude would later admit, very hard to love.[25]

Victorian readers were not amused. As Froude recalled it, he was greeted with "a violence of censure for which I was wholly unprepared," vilified in the press as an opportunistic turncoat, and subject to a vicious smear campaign.[26] The normally staid *North American Review*, for instance, called the *Reminiscences* a "waste-basket of a great man's spleen" and likened reading it to "serving round a famous man's spittoon."[27] Charles Eliot Norton, who would edit the Emerson-Carlyle correspondence and reedit the *Reminiscences*, grumbled privately about Froude's "artfully malignant" treatment of the Carlyles and the "gross indelicacy" of his biographical disclosure:

> I could not have believed, even of Froude, bad as I thought him, a
> capacity for such falseness, for such betrayal of a most sacred trust, for
> such cynical treachery to the memory of one who had put faith in him.[28]

Froude died in 1894, convinced to the end that his honesty had paid Carlyle the highest respect (and, ironically, also convinced in his final delirium that his enemies would use his manuscripts against him[29]). But generations of friends and family members soldiered on, prolonging and escalating the debate over the nature of biography with the vigor and longevity of a Dickensian lawsuit. The posthumous publication in 1903 of Froude's apologia, *My Relations with Carlyle*, with its inflammatory claim that Carlyle was impotent, called forth another round of Froude-bashing. Well into the twentieth century, Lytton Strachey recalled stories of Froude's "strange melancholy" and reported, tongue firmly in cheek, the rumors that his eyes glowed a Satanic red.[30]

Froude's case illustrates the personal cost of writing the "new biography," a lesson not lost on Emerson's biographers. Their connections with Froude are remarkable. Ireland, Cooke, and Conway all knew him personally. So did Emerson himself; he had met Froude on his trip to England in 1848 and would join other literary dignitaries at a commemorative dinner in New York to kick off Froude's 1872 American lecture tour. Cabot found himself in precisely the same predicament as Froude with regard to Emerson's papers but would sturdily distance himself from Froude's bare-knuckle approach to his subject. Norton, Froude's chief American antagonist, was one of the Emerson family's most trusted advisors from the 1870s on. The varied agendas of Emerson's early biographers would reflect their apprehensions about the debate over the genre of biography that Froude's case crystallized—a debate centering on privacy, accuracy, disclosure, morality, and the responsible relationship of subject and biographer.

Scholars and historians have advanced a variety of explanations, too numerous for more than a survey here, for the dramatic change in biography as a genre around the time of the Froude debacle: shifting conceptions of "the heroic," the struggle between candor and prudence, cultural anxieties about "domesticity, love and work in the construction of literary masculinities."[31] The consensus is that Victorian-era life-writing was more prolific than skillful, more reverential than literary. Paul Murray Kendall dismisses Victorian life-writing as "pseudobiography"[32]; Richard D. Altick laments that American literary biography before the 1920s "affords little scope to the would-be chronicler of lively episodes, and even less satisfaction to the critic."[33] As Nigel Hamilton sums it up in his recent history of biography,

Victorian biography was "respectful, prolific, unimaginative, ponderous—and pure." Hamilton distinguishes biography from the "biography-styled fiction" popularized by Dickens, the Brontës, and Gaskell in England and Hawthorne and Melville in the United States. Reputation, Hamilton argues, was of paramount importance in the Victorian world, and privacy was the means to preserve it; but a culture committed to privacy was also intrigued by violations of it. Thus to Victorian biographies fell the task of maintaining reputations and to Victorian fiction the opportunity for destroying them by exposing lives of both virtue and vice.[34]

To the list of challenges to late-nineteenth-century biography I would add competition from another way of representing human personality: photography. The name alone—"light writing"—suggests photography's connection with literature, just as its other contemporary name—"sun painting"—connects photography with the other visual arts. From its tentative beginnings in 1839 as the delicate daguerreotype, the photograph had by the 1880s achieved a ubiquitous presence in American culture, "a radically useful and omnivorous tool for recording reality" that transformed the way Americans saw the world around them.[35] No less a confirmed rationalist than Oliver Wendell Holmes enthused that photography could capture the "latent soul" of its subject.[36] Thanks to consumer demand and technological ingenuity, by the 1880s photography was becoming easier, cheaper, and more natural.[37]

The result was what the New York Times called in 1884 a "camera epidemic,"[38] which joined biography as one of the decade's defining passions. Photography and biography influenced each other in several important ways. Collecting photographs of famous people, which sold for as little as a penny apiece, became an enormously popular fad, especially in American cities.[39] One New York dealer in 1883 reportedly offered more than 50,000 photographs of noted people—"actors, actresses, authors, lecturers, soldiers, preachers, statesmen, and politicians."[40] Of the celebrity authors, the most salable in 1882 were Twain, Harte, Bryant, Longfellow, and Emerson.[41] At the same time, photography transformed periodicals into visual media. While earlier "illustrated" magazines like Harper's and Leslie's included artwork, they were confined technologically to various forms of engraving—woodcuts, zincographs, chalk plates—that rendered not a photograph but a drawing of one. The late 1870s, however, saw the development of a halftone engraving process capable of transferring photographs to print, and in March 1880, the New York Daily Graphic carried the first newspaper halftone photograph.[42]

Photography's capabilities for accuracy, objectivity, and inclusiveness of detail presented new challenges to other representations of human lives. Traditional portraiture in oil, for instance, now seemed a contrived, mediated version of reality, thanks to a widely held belief that photography removed human error and bias from the act of representation.[43] For the biographer, a portraitist in words, the photograph and the newspaper would forever change the way subjects were depicted, as biographers suddenly found themselves writing about people the public already knew and competing with other forms of representation more timely than the book (newspapers and magazines) and arguably more accurate (the photograph). Add to this competitive pressure the generic stress fractures that forced difficult choices for biographers—the tensions between reverence and revelation, character and personality, the private and the public, interpretation and documentation. And finally, factor in the peculiar difficulties for Emerson's earliest biographers, whose subject was already well known to the public with a reputation already beginning to crystallize into iconography. Cooke, Ireland, Conway, Holmes, Cabot, and Edward Emerson faced the challenge of negotiating new demands of the genre as well as accommodating the personal and commercial demands of creating salable representations of Emerson in a glutted and highly competitive marketplace.

— II —

The rise of alternative biographical venues fed the vigorous debate over some central questions about life-writing, including some very practical matters for biographers themselves. Was the purpose of biography reverence or disclosure? Was the biographer an artist who shaped the presentation of lives or—as Leslie Stephen put it in 1893—merely "the connecting wire" who put the subject at one end of the "literary telephone" and the reader at the other?[44] Would shorter, more popular biographies break what Edmund Gosse later called the "big-biography habit"?[45] And how would competition for readers and the rise of the big literary houses like Houghton, Mifflin and Macmillan further commercialize and commodify the writing of biography?

For Emerson's early biographers in particular, this unsettled reconsideration of the form and practice of life-writing was complicated by a growing tendency in post–Civil War America to dismiss the movement Emerson was most associated with, Transcendentalism, as naively out of step with new scientific and social realities. By the time of Emerson's death, the "New

School" was increasingly seen as passé: disengaged, irrelevant, childlike, even comic. Witness this newspaper item from the middle 1880s:

> Mr Alcott told the Concord Summer School of Philosophers that "Actuality is the Thingness of the Here." The information almost paralyzed them. For years they had been laboring under the misapprehension that the hereness of the actuality is the thing.[46]

Even more sober sources were writing off Transcendentalism. In his 1879 study of Nathaniel Hawthorne, Henry James recalls the Transcendentalists as harmless naïfs who "played at a wonderful game" but "appeared unstained by the world, unfamiliar with worldly desires and standards, and with those various forms of human depravity which flourish in some high phases of civilization."[47] Similarly, an article on "Mr. Emerson's Philosophy" in the *Nation* in 1881 pronounced the movement "the delight of a small and diminishing body of enthusiasts, the object of a contemptuous but not unkindly ignorance on the part of the rest of the world."[48]

At least partly as a result of this dismissal, America in the 1880s witnessed the reconsideration of the Transcendental writers and their circle, all of them now aging or dead—Hawthorne, Fuller, Thoreau, and especially Emerson—in a conscious attempt to rescue individual Transcendentalists from the derision that affected the movement as a whole. Thomas Wentworth Higginson's biography *Margaret Fuller Ossoli* (1885), for instance, was intentionally a corrective to the 1852 *Memoirs of Margaret Fuller Ossoli* by Emerson, James Freeman Clarke, and William Henry Channing—a book, Higginson charged, that "leaves her a little too much in the clouds."[49] Thoreau, largely dismissed in his lifetime as an imitator of Emerson, an "unfeeling hermit," or a mere nature writer,[50] was rehabilitated beginning in the 1870s by what Gary Scharnhorst has called "Thoreau's posthumous revival": the promotion of Concord as a literary mecca and "the reinvention of Thoreau as a sort of crackerbarrel philosopher"—a concerted effort by Houghton, Mifflin to market his writing.[51] Thoreauvian defenders such as Henry S. Salt tried to rehabilitate Thoreau's reputation by disassociating him from the more easily ridiculed aspects of Transcendentalism. As Higginson attempted to reverse popular opinion about Fuller's antisocial eccentricities, so Salt painted Thoreau in 1890 as principled, practical, and optimistic, no Transcendental freeloader but a hardworking enemy of time idly spent.[52] As the acknowledged if reluctant spokesperson for Transcendentalism in America, Emerson would need a similar makeover.

Emerson's early biographers, in short, were working under a number of daunting constraints:

> The genre was undergoing a redefinition driven in part by commercial considerations and in part by competing purposes.
>
> Biographers themselves enjoyed a checkered reputation as ghoulish violators of the dead, with Froude's vilification a chilling reminder of the social costs of transgressing the very permeable boundaries that separated respectful inquiry from biographical voyeurism.
>
> Emerson's growing visual and media presence, which was already transforming him into a larger-than-life icon, complicated attempts to say something new about him.
>
> Each of the biographers could lay claim to knowing certain aspects of Emerson especially well, though each was also aware of significant lacunae in their knowledge, competencies, and sympathies.
>
> The expansion of biographical venues—from commercial "mug books," cheap paperbacks, and periodicals to dignified biographical series suitable for shelving—testified to an expanding commercial market for life-writing that commodified the process and demanded some accommodation, at least, to the expectations of readers.
>
> Emerson's family, invested in the responsible stewardship of his reputation, exercised caution in releasing the unpublished letters, journals, account books, and literary manuscripts they had already purposefully reserved for their chosen executor's use and in which they had commercial as well as familial interest.
>
> In Channing's terms, no biographer could see Emerson "whole-souled" without filtering him through their experience, motives, needs, and personal situations.

Clearly, to write Emerson's life in the 1880s was fraught with problems. The conscious attempt to rehabilitate his Transcendental past provided an additional one. His transformation from the latest formulator of infidelity in the 1830s to the benign Sage of Concord a half-century later may be remarkable, but it was not accidental. What his 1880s biographers shared with each other, and with other biographers of the Transcendentalists, was a need to detranscendentalize Emerson by distancing him from philosophical extremism and redeeming him as an exemplary American. Their task was to assert Emerson's centrality to the nation's intellectual life without overstating his leadership of the rapidly discredited Transcendental movement.

It was a difficult needle to thread, for to depict Emerson as a disengaged saint dismissed him as surely as painting him as a Transcendental idler. Emerson's early biographers tried to preserve his relevance but not his extremism, his personality without his idiosyncrasies, his individualism along with his representativeness. As their stories will show, their efforts were largely ineffective in stemming Emerson's iconization, in ways that reveal much about biography, biographers, Emerson himself, and the politics of reputation and commerce that shaped what we know of him. Despite the efforts of his early biographers, Emerson emerged from the 1880s well on his way to what Robert D. Richardson Jr. has called his "vast, unfortunate, and self-perpetuating reputation" as passionless, cerebral, and ultimately safe[53]—the iconic, saintly "Wisest American," about whom one fin-de-siècle admirer could say, "His whole life, however closely examined, shows no flaw of temper or of foible. It was serene and lovely to the end."[54]

TWO

An Act of Wholesome and Pure-hearted Admiration

Emerson's First Biographer, George Willis Cooke

IN 1918, TO COMMEMORATE his seventieth birthday, the Free Religious Association of Boston hosted a reception for George Willis Cooke[1] at the Unitarian Building on Beacon Street. It was a mild April afternoon, punctuated with light rain, and the turnout was good—some two dozen ministers attended, and many old friends, including Edward Waldo Emerson,[2] to honor the man one attendee called a "preacher, scholar, writer, lecturer, historian, courageous pioneer and prophet."[3] Cooke had been an active lecturer for four decades; he wrote the most comprehensive history of American Unitarianism and a half-dozen books on the New England Transcendentalists; he was at work on an ambitious study entitled *The Social Evolution of Religion* (1920). And he remained a tireless activist for what he called "collectivism" in religious and economic thought. But despite a lifetime spent championing progressive causes, Cooke always fit uneasily into the institutions of liberalism and had gotten none of the public recognition traditionally given to American religious thinkers: no honorary degrees, few invitations to speak at the major denominational meetings, no calls to the pulpit at what are today called the "tall steeple churches" of prestige and influence.[4]

Forty years earlier, in 1878, Cooke's fate would have been hard to anticipate. But already, early in his career, there were signs of an uncomfortable relationship with religious institutions that would lead him to sympathize with Emerson's writings—and in time, to become Emerson's first biographer. In 1878 Cooke was preaching at the Unity Church (a Unitarian congregation) in Indianapolis, his fourth parish in six years. Based upon what we know of his prior service as a minister in rural Wisconsin and Michigan, it is clear that his would be no conventional Unitarian ministry, even by the very flexible standards used to measure liberal Christianity at that time. Cooke must have felt some pressure to succeed in Indiana, at the age of 30, married with two young daughters; nevertheless, he would last only two years there, and by early 1880 he had relinquished his pulpit to head to New England, specifically to Concord, Massachusetts, to meet his hero Ralph Waldo Emerson.

— I —

Cooke's experience in Indianapolis enacts a pattern of rebellion and retreat that marks the history of Unitarianism beyond the Alleghenies at least since the 1820s, when the American Unitarian Association first sent emissaries to the Midwest in hopes of securing a foothold in a religious climate weakened by sectarian fighting.[5] What's more, it reflects some specific religious and cultural tensions of its place and time, as well as Cooke's growing admiration for Emerson. Cooke brought to Indianapolis a long history of liberalism and an educational wanderlust that foreshadowed his peripatetic career as a minister. Born in rural Comstock, Michigan, on April 23, 1848, he spent two years in the college preparatory program at Olivet College in Michigan[6] (1866–1868) and two more years (1868–1870) at the Jefferson Liberal Institute in Wisconsin, a struggling school sponsored by the Universalists and destined to collapse financially in less than a decade.[7] In 1870 he was off to the Meadville (Pennsylvania) Theological School, finishing a short course as a "certificated undergraduate" two years later.[8] Following stints at Sheboygan (eight months) and Sharon, Wisconsin (three years), he became the minister of the First Unitarian Church in Grand Haven, Michigan, in February 1876.

Under Cooke's leadership the Grand Haven congregation grew in size, and he was unanimously called to settle there. As he told his lifelong confidante and fellow minister Jabez T. Sunderland, with the tentativeness that often characterized Cooke's relationships with his congregations, "I guess I've been growing in the liking of the people, and they begin to think I may be all right. I am inclined to think we are doing well here at present. I hope so."[9] But Cooke's liberalism went down hard in Grand Haven, within his congregation and outside it, and he got an early lesson in sectarianism that would color his denominational affiliation for the rest of his career:

We have had much to contend with—have much opposition from other churches here. And this opposition is bitter, underhanded and mean. For instance, we are called Spiritualists in disguise. . . . Some are afraid I am too radical &c. The Universalists in the Society are afraid of me—of course they always oppose all which is not universalism.[10]

He began work on two ambitious series of lectures, one called "Workers, Lenders and Beggars," the other on what would become his lifelong obsession, the evolution of religious beliefs.[11] But his daily pastoral work was uninspiring to him. He told Sunderland, "I'm too much of a student for it—and am too anxious to do a different work than is needed here."[12] By the spring of 1878, with his writing stalled and his annual salary stuck at a meager $1,000, Cooke was desperate for a change. He wrote Sunderland from Grand Haven, "What I shall do I don't yet know. I want to go East, am almost settled in my own mind to do so. What had I better do? You know I have never liked it here & I like the shape of things still less now. . . . What can you suggest? What can I do East?"[13] An Eastern pulpit would have to wait, however. After considering an opening in Denver, Cooke reluctantly accepted the invitation to preach in Indianapolis. He had "little if any expectation of settling there," dreaded uprooting his family again, and considered the move "largely an experiment."[14] Nonetheless, in late October 1878 he arrived at Indianapolis's Unity Church.[15]

During Cooke's Midwestern ministries, he found himself making public choices about two inflammatory issues, one intellectual, the other denominational. The intellectual issue was that most animating question for Gilded Age thinkers: whether science, particularly evolutionary science, was compatible with or opposed to religion. The denominational issue was the so-called "Western Unitarian Controversy" spearheaded by the Rev. Jenkin Lloyd Jones, like Cooke a Wisconsin farm-boy and a product of Meadville, where he and Cooke may have crossed paths. (Jones was graduated in 1870.) Jones promoted a creedless "ethics based" religion rooted in social action and civic improvement; to his opponents, Jones threatened to deny the Christic quality of Unitarianism altogether and to cut the denomination off from its historic roots in theism. As the most charismatic figure in the Western Unitarian Conference, Jones "encountered friction from the American Unitarian Association (AUA) because of his independent course and friction within the WUC because of his theological radicalism."[16]

Cooke's independence of mind (with Jones and Sunderland he founded the progressive magazine *Unity*, which was published from 1878 through

1965) and his lack of any personal connection to the institutions of Eastern liberalism inevitably drove him toward the more radical positions on these two issues. On the first, he championed a complementary view of evolution and religion in line with the Free Religious Association.[17] On the second issue, Cooke allied himself with the radical Jonesite wing of the WUC and announced its positions as the foundation of his ministry in Indianapolis. In an "Open Letter in Behalf of Unity Church and Its Teachings," undated but likely circulated in 1879, Cooke outlines a creedless alternative for those "liberals" dissatisfied with their present denominations. "In place of a doctrinal conformity we seek a heartier and a more helpful fellowship in character. Our first aim is to make man better in this world." Hopeful, rational, socially aware, the Unity Church retreated from the anti-theism of Jones—"To us God is goodness and love, to be trusted and obeyed"—yet maintained a fundamentally reformist focus: "It is our earnest wish to make our church a practical center of benevolence, reform and study, where the aim shall be to go about the extinguishment of the world's evils."[18]

Despite Cooke's anxiety about his Indianapolis appointment, his first year there was promising. He had an ally in the minister at the Plymouth Congregational Church, Oscar Carleton McCulloch (1843–1891), who arrived in Indianapolis about the same time as Cooke and was busy organizing charities, championing working class rights, and battling a host of industrial evils. While Cooke must have felt overshadowed by the dynamic McCulloch, he immersed himself in McCulloch's social programs, becoming in early 1879 a vice-president of the Indianapolis Benevolent Society (which McCulloch organized and named himself president of) and helping later in the year to inaugurate a "Charity Organization Society."[19]

Buoyed by this activity, even the reserved Cooke could muster some enthusiasm for his prospects at Indianapolis, at least early on. "Our Unity church is doing splendidly and is gaining every week," he wrote to Sunderland three months after his arrival in Indiana. "The field here is a hard one, I can tell you, & it seems almost impossible to make an impression."[20] But by the middle of 1879 his optimism was already giving way to an almost unrelieved list of complaints that mirrors his situation in Grand Haven: low salary (a pressing consideration, since Lucy Nash Cooke would soon become pregnant with their third child), overwork, resistance to his liberalism. He resolved to "try it another year, but it will be a piece of hard work and with slow returns."[21] Once again, Cooke felt unappreciated. He had begun another lecture series, a reworking of his earlier "social science" lectures now entitled "Workers, Beggars and Criminals: Studies of Some Pressing Social Problems" delivered on Sunday evenings at the Indianapolis Opera House.[22] Though the series was well attended, his congregation's response is indicated by a tepid report from the Unity Church secretary, who recorded that the lectures "have been but a slight drain, if any, upon the resources of the society."[23] The spring of 1880 brought family tragedy. The Cooke daughters, Mabel and Florence, contracted measles and passed the disease to their mother, who became seriously ill and miscarried. Despondent at work and at home, "spiritually worn out," Cooke offered his resignation.[24] As he later told Sunderland, "All my hopes about Indianapolis proved delusive, and I have been too discouraged and depressed for the last six months to write to any one. I trust my experience there will be profitable, but it has surely taken out of me a good deal of hope and courage."[25]

Stopping in Indianapolis on a lecture tour early the next year, Bronson Alcott learned (perhaps from McCulloch, with whom he visited) that Cooke had "attempted to build up a True Church" but "failed of gaining any wide support."[26] Likely Cooke's ministry was also a casualty for more prosaic reasons: his zealous attacks on other creeds, time spent lecturing rather than pursuing his pastoral duties, an abstruse intellectualism that seemed not to fire the interest of his congregation—or, as he referred to them in tellingly impersonal language, "the people to whom I speak on Sunday (in a Unitarian Church)." Cooke was an uninspiring public speaker who, according to Sunderland, "never descended to story-telling, to jokes or extravagances of language for the sake of effect."[27] Moreover, Cooke threatened the religious politics of a city that boasted 82 churches in 1880[28] by blatantly trying to loot the membership rolls of other denominations. As he said boldly in his "Open Letter" of 1879, "If all who think and believe as we do in this city would come over and help us[,] ours would be by far the most powerful church here."[29] The result was just the opposite. Indianapolis's fledgling Unitarian Society, established in 1868,[30] was already struggling financially when Cooke arrived a decade later, and his activism made things worse. After Cooke left his pastorate in 1880, the post went unfilled, and the building became home to the Ninth Presbyterian Church (Colored).[31] The Indianapolis city/county historian pronounced in 1884: "Two denominations that at one time were quite prominent, the Universalist and Unitarian, have disappeared altogether in the last few years as distinct sects."[32]

Small wonder that in the midst of his collapsing ministry Cooke would be drawn to another Unitarian iconoclast who also questioned creeds as "corpse-cold" systems of belief. Cooke's growing disenchantment with sectarianism and the routine of pastoral care, his interest in science and faith in human improvability, even his self-conscious attempts to make a career as a lecturer, all betoken a modeling of Emerson's life and beliefs. In fact, Cooke's long foreground in Emersonianism had begun years earlier, in the late 1860s, when as a student in the Jefferson Liberal Institute he first came in contact with Emerson's essays in the home of a local manufacturer and attorney named Dempster Ostrander,[33] whose brother served on the school's executive board.[34] Dempster Ostrander (1834–1907),[35] with his unlikely combination of interests in poetry, social reform, and fire prevention insurance theory, may well have provided the young Cooke his first flesh-and-blood example of an intellectual Renaissance man whose accomplishments spanned the literary, the progressive, and the practical. Cooke would dedicate his Emerson biography to Ostrander, "a true friend, and a genuine lover of books, in whose library I first read and learned to love the essays of Emerson."[36]

Thanks to Ostrander's tutelage, Cooke had a long familiarity with Emerson's writings by the time he arrived in Indianapolis, and about a year later he made what is apparently his first attempt to contact Emerson himself. On October 17, 1879, Cooke wrote an effusive letter to Emerson, thanking him for the continuing inspiration of his work:

> Permit me to express my own great satisfaction in your books, to acknowledge the great help they have given me for years, and at this time the strengthening of faith in the spiritual side of life. They have helped, too, to liberate me from the forms of the church and to find liberty in regard for the moral integrity of the universe.[37]

The preceding summer, Cooke continued, as his ministry in Grand Haven was collapsing, he had returned in earnest to Emerson's writings, seeking a way to reconcile the competing intellectual and religious claims of his times, and finding it. Cooke would later affirm Emerson's "loyal and inspired interpretation of science, ethics and religion as one, all resting on the same facts and laws."[38] Those views, Cooke told Emerson in the letter, were an "off-set" to evolutionism yet complementary to it, emphasizing "the ethical side" of the "great problems of life and nature."[39]

Cooke concluded his letter with a series of questions that suggest how much the younger man valued Emerson's counsel: "Do you regard Christianity as in any way final, or only one step towards a true ethics and religion? To what extent may we rely on the methods of Idealism in contrast with those of science?"[40] The aging Emerson was incapable of addressing these issues, and no response to Cooke's letter survives. But Cooke apparently needed none, for he already considered himself a disciple. Soon after writing to Emerson, Cooke began what he described to Emerson as "a course of lectures out of your writings" to impress upon his Indianapolis congregation the "ethical side of things."[41]

This lecture series was surely the one Cooke announced in a handbill distributed in the fall of 1879, eight talks "on the origin and growth of Religious beliefs." Cooke offered the first two on November 9 ("The Reign of Natural Law: Its Nature, Limits and Consequences") and November 30 ("The Ultimate Truth in the God-Idea"), leaving the other six to be scheduled later at intervals of two or three weeks: "Matter and Mind: Their Nature and Relations," "The Knowable: Its Modes of Manifestation and Its Limits," "The Genesis of Religion, and Its Fundamental Nature," "The Special Causes of Religious Conceptions, as Soul, God, Hereafter, Prayer, &c.," "The Origin and the Sanctions of Morality," and "The Laws According to Which Religions Develop." The purpose of this ambitious series, Cooke announced, was "to ascertain whether there is any natural and necessary basis for religion."[42] It would be followed by a second series on the development of Judaism and by a third, "a somewhat full one," on the origin of Christianity.[43] How much these lectures owed to Emersonian ideas remains a matter of speculation. None of the lectures survives, and Emerson's name is not mentioned among the dozen thinkers to whom Cooke pays homage in his prospectus. Cooke may well have shortened the series or abandoned it altogether, for by February 15, 1880, he was lecturing instead on capital punishment.

Clearly, though, the lectures indicate a broadening of Cooke's interests beyond the strictly pastoral, as well as an expansion of his geographic horizons, audience, and sense of his own vocation. Increasingly he was turning his attention to a life of letters, becoming a contributor to the Indianapolis *Saturday Herald*, the city's self-proclaimed literary paper. It was in the *Herald* that his first foray into Emersonian criticism appeared in February 1880, in a piece that inaugurated Cooke's relationship with the Emerson family as well as his career as a commentator on New England thought and letters. The issue was a topical one. In Emerson's final years, critics made smug claims about his supposed abandonment of "pantheism" and retreat to orthodox Protestantism, charges made especially vigorously by Rev. Joseph Cook, a Harvard and Andover graduate[44] who in his lectures claimed that Emerson's change of heart occurred as a result of his hearing Cook's own preaching.[45] The question of his philosophical and religious consistency would later become a concern for all of Emerson's early biographers; in 1880, though, two years before Emerson's death, the matter was more personally sensitive to his family, because it intruded into the private world of an aging man whose celebrity subjected his every word and gesture to public scrutiny. (Part of the argument for his supposed "retraction" of Transcendentalism was Emerson's attendance at Sunday church services in Concord and the saintly look on his face.) Edward Emerson came to his father's defense in a letter first printed in the *Indianapolis Journal* for February 22, 1880, and later noticed in the Boston *Commonwealth* and re-printed, with commentary, in the *Index* (March 4) and the *Saturday Herald* (March 6).[46] According to Edward, Waldo Emerson had indeed met Joseph Cook and heard him preach, but claims of Emerson's supposed "conver-sion to orthodoxy" were "in every respect incorrect": "He has not joined any church, nor has he retracted any views expressed in his writings after his withdrawal from the ministry."[47] Ellen Emerson, who was embarrassed by the fuss and "hate[d] to have the family appear to rush into print about the matter," still noted with some pride to her sister Edith how her father "liked to have the truth told" (*ETE*, 2:373).

Into this fray came George Willis Cooke, whose lengthy defense of Em-erson appeared in the *Herald* even before Edward's did, on February 14, 1880.[48] With characteristic pedantry, including footnotes and citations to Emerson's work, Cooke argues at length that Emerson "held steadily to the same great opinions from first to last," to wit, opposition to creeds and reverence for "an Infinite Soul that fills all the bounds of being."[49] That these two beliefs precisely mirror Cooke's own is significant for under-standing his affinity with Emerson, his sense of discipleship, and eventu-ally his writing of Emerson's biography. More immediately important for Cooke's career as a biographer, however, the article brought him to the attention of the Emerson family. The nature of that early relationship is cloudy. Someone in the family (likely Ellen) surely opened Cooke's Oc-tober 1879 letter and might have recalled his interest. On the other hand, Ellen's formal locution in a letter to Edith of March 4, 1880—"Have you seen Rev. George W. Cooke on Father?" (*ETE*, 2:373)—suggests she did not know him well, if at all, until later in 1880. While the opportunity for a face-to-face meeting would not occur for several months, certainly by the spring of 1880 George Willis Cooke's name would have been increasingly familiar to the extended Emerson household, thanks to his spirited part in a debate over a bellwether issue not only for the family but for the shifting genre of biography—the extent to which one's private life was fair game for those who would read into it facts of mind and character.

The timing and nature of Cooke's relationship at this time to Emerson, his family, and his friends are significant, because by early 1880 Cooke seems already to have had in mind a more-or-less complete plan for his Emerson biography. Considering hindrances caused by his responsibilities as a minister, his active lecture schedule, and his relative isolation from libraries, actually writing the book while living in Indianapolis would have been nearly impossible without relying on resources in New England. The *Saturday Herald* for February 14, 1880, months before Cooke left Indianapolis, announced that he had "nearly completed a book to be called 'A Study of Emerson.'"[50] The announcement lists twenty-nine chapters, eleven of which match closely the ones in the completed 1881 book. Cooke's book might have been in partial draft, merely blocked out in chapters, or in an even less advanced stage; news of it certainly came from Cooke himself, whose account of his progress might have been exaggerated. Regardless, his plans for completing the project were firmer by late February 1880, when the *Herald* announced, "Rev. Geo. W. Cooke goes to Boston in a week or two to collect material for the final revision of his book on Emerson. He will spend several weeks there, and arrange for the publication of his book, which a well-known Boston house has indicated a desire to publish on very favorable terms."[51]

It was a busy and productive visit East in the spring of 1880, with Cooke reading diligently at libraries in Concord, Cambridge, and Boston and trying to establish a toehold in New England's literary community. He contributed an essay on Emerson's literary methods—which reappears in his *Ralph Waldo Emerson*—for a special May 22 issue of the *Literary World*, joining such well-known Concord insiders as Bronson Alcott and Frank Sanborn, along with aging members of the wider Transcendental circle including Thomas Wentworth Higginson, Frederic Henry Hedge, and Walt Whitman. Once again, however, tragedy dogged him. Cooke returned briefly to Indianapolis in late May to find his children sick again, his wife an invalid, and the always tentative prospects of his Indianapolis ministry in a shambles. As he later put it, "every promise made me there was violated."[52] Cooke formally severed his relationship with Unity Church as of June 1, 1880,[53] and returned to Massachusetts, leaving his family in Indianapolis until he could secure a position elsewhere. The *Herald* announced his plan to "spend the summer in Concord, Connecticut [sic], where he will finish his 'Life of Emerson.'"[54]

That summer Cooke attended the second annual session of Bronson Alcott's Concord School of Philosophy, which ran from July 12 through August 14 in the newly built Hillside Chapel behind Orchard House, just down the Lexington Pike from the Emerson house. There, Cooke immersed himself in New England Transcendentalism. The 1880 session, heavily weighted toward lectures on Platonic and Hegelian philosophy, included many of the surviving members of the Transcendental circle: Alcott himself, of course, but also Hedge, William Henry Channing, Cyrus A. Bartol, and Elizabeth Palmer Peabody.[55] Others in attendance included Franklin Benjamin Sanborn, who would rival Cooke as a chronicler of the Transcendentalists, and Louisa May Alcott, who worshipped Emerson but had little patience for the airy speculations of her father's school.[56] Cooke found their conversation and recollections immeasurably valuable for his work on Emerson. As he told Sunderland in a letter of August 27: "Have been very busy here this summer and have collected many notes of value."[57] Emerson himself attended the Concord School, reading his lecture "The True Gentleman" to an audience Cooke estimated at 200 or more.[58] He and Lidian even hosted a Sunday evening gathering at Bush for townsfolk and participants at the school. We can only imagine Cooke's excitement that remarkable evening as he watched the aging Emersons arrange chairs in the parlor and shake hands with their guests. Waldo introduced remarks by Channing, Bronson Alcott, and Peabody by rapping a doorframe and announcing, "Some of our friends have something to say to us, and we shall be glad to have them begin."[59]

For Cooke, the Concord School was a crash course in the personalities and ideas of Transcendentalism. As he told Sunderland: "Am at the School of Philosophy in pursuance of a better knowledge of Emerson. Shall stay here most of the summer. The school is dogmatic to a great degree, but there are some very good lectures, and I expect much help in my work."[60] Cooke was moved by Channing's passion, instructed by the impromptu "parlor gatherings" (where discussion topics ranged from prehistoric man to education for girls), and thrilled to hear the illuminating conversations and reminiscences about Thoreau, Hawthorne, and Fuller. By the same token, he was disheartened by what he perceived as the school's "propagandism." "It has a system to elucidate, a dogma to defend, a creed wrought out to teach," he complained in a series of reports to the *Christian Register*. Cooke particularly resented the "constant spirit of contempt toward scientific methods" by lackluster speakers without the "breadth of insight" to fully understand the complementary relationship between science and faith. An irate Elizabeth Peabody, who claimed to speak for "everybody else who was present throughout the sessions, with whom I have conversed about them," answered Cooke's ad hominem attacks by defending both the liberality of the school and the quality of its speakers.[61] Clearly, though he considered himself a Transcendentalist sympathizer, Cooke would be no intellectual pushover. Nevertheless, he had situated himself geographically and intellectually in the movement that would define his scholarly career, and his work on the Emerson biography cemented for him the disparate philosophical tendencies that had torn at him in Indianapolis and confirmed views he had long felt himself. He told Alcott that "writing the Life of Emerson converted him to Idealism—to which he is temperamentally inclined."[62]

— II —

Despite his summer in Concord—or perhaps because of it—Cooke felt himself an outsider. In the fall of 1880, while living in Boston, he continued to search for a pastorate. "Can you do anything to smooth the way for me?" he had pleaded with Sunderland over the summer. "I have no friendly influence here."[63] Cooke was learning the cost of independence. The American Unitarian Association offered him little support in his search for a position, and Rush R. Shippen, its executive secretary, warned Cooke that "a man writing a book about Emerson wasn't fit to occupy a Unitarian pulpit."[64] His only prospect was the tiny rural community of Harvard, Massachusetts—long ago the site of Alcott's ill-fated Fruitlands community—which offered him a pulpit at $600 a year, not nearly enough.[65] At last, on December 1, 1880, Cooke began a "connection" (his carefully chosen word) with the Third Parish Church in West Dedham, Massachusetts, southwest of Boston and an easy ride to Concord. The arrangement offered Cooke more than location. "Supplying the pulpit" on Sundays, rather than taking on the full duties of a settled minister, left his weekdays free for writing.[66]

Cooke worked diligently to expand and revise his biography of Emerson during the spring and summer of 1881. In April he sent the entire manuscript to Edward Emerson for review, along with some questions. Edward agreed to help,[67] but may not have done so, for he was busy preparing for a long trip to California. After a few weeks he passed along the manuscript to his sister Ellen and asked her to mail it back to Cooke. Instead, she read it herself and returned it in May with her own detailed corrections and comments.[68]

Ellen Emerson's long letter to Cooke provides us the best glimpse into his developing relationship with the Emerson family and their involvement with the book that would be published in the fall of 1881 as *Ralph Waldo Emerson: His Life, Writings, and Philosophy.* Ellen's critique of the draft was full and unflinching. Impatient with inaccuracies, she corrects Cooke on at least ten occasions where he misstates the facts: locations of ancestral homes, her father's response to the Battle of Bull Run, the audience's reaction to his faltering performance at the Phi Beta Kappa oration in 1867 ("the applause was kind, it was not ardent"), and the like. But worse, in Ellen's view at least, Cooke had fundamentally misinterpreted texts, influences, and Emerson's reading—errors of judgment she was well equipped to spot after years of working with Elliot Cabot and Edward on her father's papers. For instance, in a comment on Cooke's chapter 9, "Lectures and Essays," she writes:

> [T]he account of his reading surprised us all very much, and, making allowance for forgetfulness even, I think not without reason. There is no doubt that he always valued St Augustine's Confessions, but the box story is incredible. He & Mother are sure that Boehme was never a favourite, and both deny any acquaintance with the "Way to Christ." He did read Jacob Behmen, and it must be that which was meant by your informant. Tauler he never would read, a little was too much for him, the book looks perfectly new still. He may have read Eckhardt, he says he did not[.] I never heard him mention the name.

Two rather remarkable observations stand out in this passage and show up elsewhere in the letter as well. First, Ellen was fact-checking Cooke's manuscript against her father's and mother's memories, making it the only biography to have benefited from Waldo Emerson's direct intervention, however limited his abilities may have been by 1881. Second, Cooke was getting some of his information secondhand, from an unnamed "informant" not wholly in agreement with the family's take on things. Ellen concluded her letter affably enough, with thanks for "the opportunity you have given us to look over the book" and an appreciation for the complexity of Cooke's undertaking: "It is interesting to me to see how much work & care you have spent over it, and with these points corrected, I think there is no fault to find with it." But she (and presumably her parents) were dismayed over how easily Cooke accepted the word of others on major interpretive points. At times in the letter her impatience with him is palpable:

> In Chap. II, p. 16 [page 23 of the finished book], you say he studied under Dr Channing's supervision. This is a mistake. He never had any more connection with Dr Channing than that [sic]. He went to see him once or twice, to consult him and once Dr Channing lent him a book. All that passage will have to be revised, as it is all written under this wrong impression. I continually wonder where you got your informa-

tion of this kind much of which is new to me, some of it I know to be true, some true enough, and what I am pretty sure is false I shall mention.[69]

Just where *did* Cooke get his information? Who were his "informants"? The participants at the 1880 Concord School augmented Cooke's knowledge with firsthand information during their conversations and would surely have answered Cooke's inevitable questions. To fill in other gaps in his knowledge, Cooke was diligently canvassing Emerson's surviving acquaintances in 1880. Some had little to offer, like Lydia Maria Child;[70] others had no time to answer, like William Henry Channing,[71] who presumably had talked with Cooke in person at the Concord School. Still, Cooke found a variety of "informants" cooperative and helpful. Foremost among them was Bronson Alcott, who noted in his journal how much of Cooke's book "was taken from my lips. My diaries were also gleaned by him."[72] Cooke also wrote to Frederic Henry Hedge, one of Emerson's oldest living friends, who would later help Elliot Cabot understand Emerson's early years (*ETE*, 2:414–415). Intriguingly, Cooke claimed in his article for the *Herald* to have, in late 1879, sent a "friend of the writer's [that is, of Cooke], who went to Concord specially to collect information for him" and interviewed Emerson himself at his home about his supposed conversion to orthodoxy. According to Cooke, Emerson told this unnamed visitor, "My views . . . are to be found in what I have written" and then pointed his "long, farmer-like hand" to one of his bookcases.[73] While the episode smacks of the apocryphal, the level of detail lends some credibility to this eyewitness account, which Cooke repeats in the introduction to *Ralph Waldo Emerson*. If the family never mentioned the episode, neither did they deny it, even when combing Cooke's manuscript for errors. Cooke's emissary remains unidentified.

Cooke's progress on the biography raised once again the issue of who owned Emerson's public reputation, as it was raised in 1877, when the family arranged for James Elliot Cabot to write the authorized version of Emerson's life. They did so then in order to forestall having to cooperate with other biographers. Ironically, in February 1881, they found themselves in precisely that situation. Their legal advisor James B. Thayer warned that "it was high time Mr C[abot]'s biography should be announced since G. W. Cooke is writing to Mr Hedge to engage his assistance in his" (*ETE*, 2:414–415). Apparently the Emerson family did not share Thayer's sense of urgency, for they waited more than a year to comply, the earliest public announcement of Cabot's biography appearing in print around June 1882, shortly after Waldo's death.[74] Indeed, while Cooke completed the draft of his biography, Cabot worried Edward and Ellen by seeming to abandon his. In a reiteration of his earlier objection, Cabot claimed he was not the man to write a biography but only to collect the material for one.[75] As Ellen reported later to her sister, Cabot's quibbles seemed at worst to be harmlessly semantic. "I don't see that he is likely to disappoint us at all" (*ETE*, 2:414–415). But the doubts came at an awkward time. As Cabot waffled, Cooke wrote, his relationship with the Emersons becoming increasingly cordial. Ellen provided him a photograph of her father from the mid-1850s, approved by Lidian Emerson and Frank Sanborn for use as a frontispiece. (Cooke chose a more staid 1870s portrait instead.) She consulted Cabot about Emerson's reading of Boehme and asked Rockwood and Elizabeth Hoar about the accuracy of the portrait of Emerson lecturing that now hangs in the Concord Free Public Library, all presumably in answer to questions from Cooke.[76]

While the family extended its cooperation, the sticking point for Cooke was still access to Emerson's unpublished papers—his lectures, poems, notebooks, correspondence, and journals. In the preface to *Ralph Waldo Emerson: His Life, Writings, and Philosophy*, Cooke would thank Emerson "for the use of such of his writings as have been quoted, that are not contained in his published volumes" (Cooke *RWE*, viii), phrasing that suggests an insider's privilege for Cooke. Reviewers of the book would later pick up on that wording, a number of them suggesting that a primary virtue of Cooke's study was its inclusion of new material. The Boston *Commonwealth*, for example, claimed for Cooke's study "the presentation of many hitherto unpublished papers of its subject" and listed as "new matter, not in Mr. Emerson's volumes": the Concord address on the death of Lincoln; the comments at the dedication of the Minute Man statue in 1875; the welcoming remarks at Kossuth's 1852 visit to America; and selections from Emerson's addresses on woman's suffrage, Scott and Burns, emancipation, the Concord Public Library, and Charles Sumner.[77] In fact, every one of these had appeared in newspapers or magazines prior to 1881, though not technically in Emerson's "volumes."[78] To be fair, in an age before libraries routinely archived old periodicals, biographers performed a valuable conservative function by reprinting and summarizing fugitive pieces. Still, Cooke's careful wording in the preface was self-serving, if not actually deceptive, because it lent authority to Cooke's work and a cachet to his relationship to the family. Claiming insider knowledge and previously unknown information was (and is) a common gambit for biographers, and the strategy was not discouraged by publishers eager to claim for their products something new and salable. Sunderland's verdict on the matter—that much of the material in Cooke's biography was "otherwise not accessible" to readers—comes closer to the mark.[79] Despite the misleading suggestion in his preface, Cooke used not a word of Emerson's that had not been published before.

Nor was the family always willing for him to use even previously published material that might compromise the commercial value of the ongoing Riverside Edition. Ellen was as firm as she could muster when she spotted in Cooke's manuscript mentions of two unpublished Emerson lectures available at that time only in newspaper summaries, "The Superlative" and "Historic Notes on Life and Letters in Massachusetts" (later "New England"). Of the latter lecture she wrote to Cooke on May 5, 1881:

> He [that is, her father] read it only on condition that no reporter should be allowed in the Hall, and was shocked to find that there was a report in the papers immediately. He hoped that it would pass unnoticed and would have been very sorry to hear of its being taken up and incorporated in a book. Now he cannot care any longer, but I have the feeling about it, he always has had. I do not command its suppression, you may take the feeling for what you think it is worth, and act as you think best.[80]

Ellen's rhetoric was pathetic, subtle, and effective: without "command[ing]" that he do so, the family hoped Cooke would honor not only their wishes but also the failing Waldo's. In his book Cooke accommodated Ellen's criticisms with some cagey rewording. For example, he prefaces his comments on Eckhart's influence with the disclaimer "though Emerson has not studied Eckhart" (Cooke *RWE*, 276), and he deletes the statement that Emerson studied under Dr. Channing, preferring instead to say, "Emerson eagerly embraced the essential spirit of Channing's teaching" (Cooke *RWE*, 23). But on the issue of the two unpublished lectures, he complied, omitting both of them from his book.[81] The episode illustrates how deeply committed the family remained to protecting Cabot's exclusive access to Emerson's unpublished papers. After all, Cabot, Ellen, and Edward were still piecing together texts and deciding what to include in the Riverside Edition of Emerson's *Collected Writings*. Cooperative yet protective—it was a difficult policy for the family to maintain as Emerson's celebrity increasingly opened his life to public scrutiny.

As he polished the draft of his biography, Cooke continued preaching at West Dedham, evidently with success, for in March 1881 the congregation called him to settle there permanently.[82] Characteristically (though inexplicably, given his desperate finances), Cooke refused the offer, agreeing instead to continue supplying the pulpit on Sundays but not to take on the workaday schedule of a settled pastor.[83] Turning down one agreement, however, he accepted another. On August 1, 1881, he signed a contract with James R. Osgood and Company of Boston to publish *Ralph Waldo Emerson: His Life, Writings, and Philosophy*. He would receive 10 percent royalties based on a retail price of $2.50.[84] Likely Cooke devoted his vacation month to ironing out the last-minute details, reading proof, and seeing the book through the press. On October 5, one thousand copies were printed, and the Boston *Daily Advertiser* announced that the book was "published this day" on October 19, 1881. According to the advertisement, the biography was "issued by Permission and Approval of Mr. Emerson and his Family."[85]

— III —

The book's tripartite subtitle gives a misleading picture of the proportions actually devoted to Emerson's "life, writings, and philosophy." Cooke's literary analyses, though apt, are less important than the groundbreaking context he provides for Emerson, and fully half the book—the second half—is given over to topical discussion of his "philosophy" and influences. In a response, perhaps, to the excesses of the Concord School, Cooke argues that Emerson is no speculative philosopher, but belongs instead to the tradition of Christian mysticism. Christian mysticism posited an idealistic split between mind and body, idea and matter, and envisioned the individual's relationship to the Divinity as direct, intuitive, and intimate. As Cooke summarizes it:

> The idea of Eckhart and Emerson, as it is of Boehme, Schelling, Coleridge, and all others who accept the conclusions of mysticism, is that of the absolute oneness of the Universal Spirit, that there is but one essential being and life, that this life is present in all things, that man has his life in the Universal Spirit, that all his thinking is its expression through him. (Cooke *RWE*, 314)

Cooke does not deny Emerson's interest in the world of affairs; in fact, he sees Emerson as articulating a Social Darwinist vision of "the survival of those men and interests fittest to carry forward social order" (Cooke *RWE*, 341). Yet he treats Emerson primarily as an Idealist in a line of descent from the thirteenth-century heretic Meister Eckhart through the visionary mystics Jacob Boehme (or Behmen) and Emanuel Swedenborg. However valid Christian mysticism may have been for the interpretation of Emerson's writings, it was a potentially disruptive force in the creation of his reputation, for it recalled earlier claims for his airiness and arrogance, removed him from the relatively safe world of rationality, and placed him instead in the more nebulous realm of enthusiasm and intuition. Having situated Emerson intellectually in the company of heretics and visionaries, Cooke had all the more reason to minimize the unconventional or idiosyncratic where he could—in the biography.

The first 14 chapters of Cooke's study, the biography proper, are largely an account of Emerson's writing career—what he wrote, when—which is consistent with Cooke's promise to make the book "an introduction to the study of the writings of Mr. Emerson" (Cooke *RWE*, v). The biography itself is predicated upon an initially curious definition of the genre. As Cooke defined his purposes in the preface, his book would be "biographical only because light may be thrown upon [Emerson's] books by the events of his life. Little effort has been made to open his personal history. As with all such minds, most of what is truly biographical is in his letters and diaries. Yet the life of Mr. Emerson has been in his thoughts, and these are in his books" (Cooke *RWE*, v).

Thus Cooke immediately privileges "the life ... in his thoughts" over Emerson's "personal history," public books over private letters and diaries. By defining the "truly biographical" as "personal history" and then having little of that personal history to relate, Cooke as a biographer seems to be self-defeating. Indeed, his *Ralph Waldo Emerson* is sometimes short on even the most basic biographical information. Before its publication, Bronson Alcott anticipated that Cooke's book would be merely "annals," a year-by-year chronicle of Emerson's career as a writer; after he read it, he pronounced it "not a biography, but gathered material for one."[86] Alcott had a point: significant facts of Emerson's life are glossed over or ignored, while apparently extraneous ones receive more attention than modern readers are likely to need or tolerate. Opening the book, for instance, is a minutely detailed genealogy since the thirteenth century, maternal and paternal, which sets up Cooke's contention that Emerson inherited "the intellectuality and moral vigor of the one family, and the devoutness and mysticism of the other" (Cooke *RWE*, 14–15). His father's literary achievements are chronicled, as are the lives of Waldo's brothers, mother, and aunt Mary. But Waldo's marriages and nuclear family—indeed his entire domestic life, most of his activities in Concord, his travels, his friendships, and his growing involvement in social reform—are, for Cooke, all but invisible. Emerson's relationship to his first wife Ellen Louisa Tucker—by modern consensus the great passion of his life—receives only two sentences, one on the wedding, one on her early death (Cooke *RWE*, 34); his marriage to Lidian gets a single line (Cooke *RWE*, 38). Amidst two pages describing Emerson's house, his children are dismissed unnamed in a footnote: "Emerson has had four children, two sons and two daughters. One son died early, and the other is a much-respected physician in Concord. The older daughter is unmarried, and is the mainstay of the home. The other is married" (Cooke *RWE*, 190). Cooke's respect for family privacy verges on indifference. If Emerson's life was, as Cooke put it, "above reproach" (Cooke *RWE*, 200), its details were apparently beneath notice. In their place, Cooke substitutes the sort of iconic platitudes typical of the appraisals of Emerson by his life's end, retreating into absolutes about the loftiness of his "saintly life" (Cooke *RWE*, 201).

Was Cooke's preference for thoughts and books over biographical details and personal documents simply a manifestation of the general Victorian "passion for privacy," as Richard D. Altick calls it?[87] No doubt that was part of it. Like the Emersons themselves, who viewed attention like the Joseph Cook episode as an intrusion into family business, Cooke would have participated in a delicacy about public discussion of families and relationships, even the most oblique references to them.[88] Certainly Cooke the practical biographer could not have failed to notice even before the Froude debacle how writers increasingly were vilified as disloyal voyeurs for "grub[bing] at the foundations" of their subjects' private lives.[89] What's more, as T. S. McMillin and others have shown, a revivified but depersonalized "Sage of Concord" seemed to have satisfied a variety of cultural needs in late-nineteenth-century America. Still, ideological explanations cannot account for readers' vocal disappointment with the depersonalized Sage whom they supposedly were eager to accept. Zeitgeist has its limits. If Cooke exceeded even his age's tolerance for Emersonian hagiography, his reasons may have been as much circumstantial and generic as ideological.

For one thing, Cooke's focus on Emerson's *public* self reflected the practical limitations of his *private* knowledge. The plain facts are that

(1) Cooke had no access to the unpublished journals, letters, and diaries, the sources of what he admitted was "truly biographical" about Emerson, and

(2) as much as he portrayed himself as a disciple, Cooke's firsthand familiarity with Emerson was skimpy at best, less than two years' sporadic acquaintance after Emerson's illness had robbed him of all but the most fleeting remnants of his former power.

To his credit, Cooke did not write about what he didn't know. Then too, Cooke's biography appeared while Emerson was still alive, and he was sensitive to the family's privacy, having seen firsthand how the influx of pilgrims to Concord threatened the fragile decorum of village life. During the summer of 1880, Cooke's first in New England, the town was overrun with visitors drawn by the Concord School.[90] (Louisa May Alcott sardonically commented in her journal, "The town swarms with budding philosophers, and they roost on our steps like hens waiting for corn."[91]) Tourists thrilled to meet Emerson on the street, at the post office;[92] strangers showed up at his doorstep, expecting conversation that he could no longer sustain.[93] The intrusions must have struck the socially reserved Cooke as unspeakably rude.

If the practicalities of access and a sense of decorum kept Cooke from writing a "truly biographical" study of Emerson the man, so too did his ambivalence toward the value of the "personal." Cooke himself uses "the personal" in a variety of senses. Sometimes they are negative, as when he identifies "individual, personal, and selfish" actions that are opposed to obedience to "the universal ends of nature" (Cooke *RWE*, 304); other times, they are positive, as when he commends Emerson's "reserved personality, that is commanding, powerful, and charming" and "carries immense force" (Cooke *RWE*, 193). Though he found Emerson's verse deficient in craft, Cooke thought the poetry (much more so than the prose) "personal, touched always with his own emotions" and the best evidence of his inner life (Cooke *RWE*, 253). Yet except for "Threnody," which he glossed with a brief discussion of young Waldo's death, Cooke predictably preferred philosophical poems like "The Sphinx" (Cooke *RWE*, 253, 112, 251). This seeming ambivalence toward the biographically personal is perhaps explained by the distinction Cooke makes between the *personal* and the *characteristic*. In a central chapter entitled "The Man and the Life," he lists traits that he specifically calls "characteristic" of Emerson: diffidence, civic pride, broad sympathy to new ideas, hospitality, friendliness, guilelessness, and "a loyal love for truth" (Cooke *RWE*, 200). Against these aspects of Emerson's affective, inner life Cooke posits the outward manifestations of character that we might associate with his *personality*: reticence (Cooke *RWE*, 193), a hesitant manner of speaking (Cooke *RWE*, 264), warmth, frankness. Character was internal, essential, spiritual; personality was external, behavioral. Cooke was vitally concerned with the personal because it provided a behavioral correlative to the inner character. But he had no interest in the private or the idiosyncratic details of Emerson's life. And as for the nonliterary side of Emerson, his life was so cerebral and spiritual that "his outward life gives few events to record. The growth of his ideas, and of his influence, furnish nearly all the facts there are to his biography" (Cooke *RWE*, 107).

As this curious disclaimer suggests, Cooke's creation of an iconic Emerson derived from his definition of biography as a genre. As noted earlier, the "truly biographical" details resided in unpublished documents (that is, those we would call personal) and in poetry; Cooke had no access to the first and little interest in the second. Public achievements were certainly part of the mix for the biographer; but for Cooke Emerson's life had few of them. His preface several years later to a book on Victorian writers shows him to be consistent in his opposition to biographical "criticism," which he associates with fault-finding, the product of a "cold and analytic mind, incapable of sympathy and enthusiasm," a "mere waste of time." Instead of being judgmental, Cooke believed that the biographer's proper approach to authors was reverence, "wholesome and pure-hearted admiration" for their work, and attention to whatever is "most characteristic of their genius."[94]

What he found most characteristic of Emerson's genius was his "calm, rational, self-poised spirit" (Cooke *RWE*, 197). It is easy to read in this verdict a glib assertion of Gilded Age gentility, Emerson as pasteboard mask. But Cooke's portrait is not of a bloodless icon but of a complicated man who at once believed in "intuition and ecstasy" but viewed with contempt the "fervent heat of thought and excess of feeling" of friends like Margaret Fuller (Cooke *RWE*, 196–197). It was Emerson's control of emotion—not his denial of it—that accounted for his calmness. In the context of Emerson's developing reputation in the 1880s, his poise provided Cooke with a solution to the vexing problem of Emerson's Transcendental radicalism. As Emerson banked his own emotional fires, so he suppressed "the follies of the transcendental period, its wild excesses of feeling, of judgment, and of opinion" and distilled "dispassionately" the truth from "religious fanaticism" (Cooke *RWE*, 196–197). What Cooke called "poised" his age generally called "sane"—that is, balanced and therefore healthy. By excluding the private and idiosyncratic through his biographical lens, Cooke at once accommodated the practicalities of his situation as biographer and rescued Emerson from his Transcendentalist legacy.

— IV —

The only full-length study of Emerson and his work to appear while its subject was still alive, Cooke's *Emerson* capitalized upon public interest in a subject at the height of his celebrity. Still, the reviews were uneven, off-handed praise mixed with some damning indictments of Cooke's skills as a writer, and judging by the reaction of reviewers, Cooke's mystical Emerson was not the one readers wished to read about. Predictably, his friend Jabez T. Sunderland, who had seen parts of the book in proof sheets, promoted it in a prepublication notice as "admirably written, interesting and able."[95] Of the other reviews, one of the most positive appeared in the *Critic*, which called it "in all respects an admirable book," sufficiently detailed about Emerson's ancestry, "circumstances," and "practical labors" and most valuable for its exposition of his philosophy. Cooke writes "with judicious discrimination, warmed and illumined, but never blinded, by ardent sympathy."[96] Reviewers looking for an accurate rendition of Emerson's public self seemed to find Cooke's 14 chapters sufficient. Thus the reviewer for the New York *Daily Tribune* praises the book for subordinating the biographical to the expository: "A mere thread of personal biography runs through the chapters, and along this is strung the history of Emerson's writings and addresses." The *Tribune*'s reviewer called that strategy "perhaps the best that could have been adopted."[97] Nonetheless, while consistent with Cooke's intentions for the book, to concentrate on the work rather than the "personal history" of the author, verdicts like that skittered on the edge of damnation by faint praise, and Cooke could not have been flattered by the apparently well-meant remarks that "he does not aim at the display of critical sagacity, or elegance of style, or freshness of thought. It is to his credit that he has confined himself to the common sense function of exposition, and has rarely strayed into original comment."[98]

In other reviews as well, praise for the Cooke biography quickly petered out into neutrality. Frank Sanborn wrote Cooke soon after it appeared, applauding the effort but cagey about the product: "It seems to me exceedingly well done, from your point of view, and of real service to the old readers of Emerson as well as to the new generation. You have pursued your subject, (which though attractive, is a very difficult one) with devotion and appreciation, and if there were nothing in the book better than the industry it shows, I should commend it. But I find in it much more than that, and shall take occasion to say this publicly."[99] Some reviewers struggled to find something good to comment on before pointing out the book's weaknesses. A writer for the *Nation*, for instance, cited Cooke's thorough preparation, his clarity of expression, even the book's convenient size and typeface and "useful index" before unloading on Cooke with the same complaint about his bloodless depiction of Emerson that virtually every review of any length alludes to.

The great fault of the book is that it is not very interesting. It does not give enough of the attractive personal flavor of Mr. Emerson's home life or impress the reader sufficiently with his peculiar individuality as a man—omissions explainable in part, no doubt, by the courtesy due to a living friend, but nevertheless dulling the edge. The account of the philosophy is full and sound, but it has neither the contagious poetic fervor we expect from the disciple nor the incisive comment of the critic. Thus, with all its value, it is rather hard reading.[100]

The *Century Magazine* (February 1882) was even more blunt, calling the book "painstaking and business-like, though deficient in inspiration and insight" and dismissing Cooke as "far from being an ideal biographer."[101]

Cooke's response to these lukewarm verdicts does not survive, but they seem not to have dissuaded him from the genre, for in January 1882 Cooke contracted with Osgood to write another literary biography, this time of George Eliot, which would appear in 1883 with the identical subtitle: "Life, Writings, and Philosophy."[102] Less hagiographic than his *Emerson*, more attentive to personal issues and judgmental about Eliot's character, Cooke's *Eliot* suggests that he paid some heed to those reviewers who wanted him to be more rigorous in his evaluations.[103]

However they may have hurt Cooke's feelings, the mixed reviews of his *Emerson* did not hurt its initial sales. Osgood doubled the first printing, bringing out an additional one thousand copies by the end of 1881,[104] and by the summer of 1882, with interest surely spurred on by the news of Emerson's death in April, the book had completely sold out.[105] Yet there seems to have been no interest in another printing, and by the middle of 1882 Cooke was deeply occupied by his work on the Eliot book. It was due to the printers in July, and as he did with the Emerson biography, Cooke traveled to the source for information—Haslemere, Surrey, where Eliot and her common-law husband George Henry Lewes had purchased a cottage in 1876. Little is known of this brief trip to England except for Moncure Conway's mention of it: in March 1882 he and Cooke were in Surrey and visited Tennyson.[106] Cooke was back in the United States by the time of Emerson's death on April 27.

When the Eliot biography appeared, late in 1883, Cooke was already well into the research for his third book, a biographical and historical study of the *Dial* that would appear in two volumes in 1885 and would capitalize on his associations with the Transcendental group.[107] As always, Cooke was restive, and while he was increasingly successful in his literary career, his personal situation was getting worse. In March 1883, lightning destroyed the West Dedham church. Then in early summer, tragedy visited the family once again: nine-year-old daughter Mabel died of diphtheria on June 4, 1883, and Lucy Cooke, still frail from her miscarriage the year before, contracted the disease as well and was slow to recover. Struggling with the costs of rebuilding, the West Dedham congregation maintained Cooke's annual salary at $1,000 for several years, twice promising modest raises but never following through.[108] Another daughter, Marion (or Marian) W. Cooke, was born in November 1884,[109] straining even further Cooke's unchanging salary and his wife's frail health. Adding to Cooke's discouragement were the reviews of his Emerson biography, which raised again the doubts about his vocation that for Cooke were never far from the surface. He confessed to Sunderland late in 1883, after the publication of his *Eliot*:

> I hope it is a better book than the Emerson. I believe it is, tho' not so new in its biography, but more independent and original. . . . That I am not satisfied with it or this kind of work I need not tell you. Perhaps I shall never be satisfied with anything in this world—at least I have been but with very little so far. I would like to do more creative work, yet I have a passion for this sort of thing and a native capacity for it.[110]

Viewed from our perspective, Cooke sounds self-indulgently dramatic here, his litany of complaint all too familiar from his failed preaching career in the Midwest. Indeed, Cooke himself would admit years later that at age 35 he was something of a self-dramatizing pessimist, much to the annoyance of his congregation.[111] He was destined, after all, to become the most successful historian of his denomination, as well as an invaluable recorder of the Transcendentalist movement. But in 1883 his writing career spread out dark ahead of him. With money in short supply and family responsibilities weighing heavily upon him, Cooke began two new lecture series, one on Victorian writers (later published as *Poets and Problems*) and the other on the religious beliefs of American poets, which he delivered actively on New England lecture circuits over the next few years. Not surprisingly, given his literary commitments and his dissatisfaction with his salary, in 1887 he severed his connection with the West Dedham pulpit;[112] the congregation accepted his resignation on the same day he offered it, with any customary expressions of regret tellingly absent from the surviving church records.[113]

Over the next twelve years he preached at Lexington, Massachusetts, and Dublin, New Hampshire, before leaving the ministry for good in

1898 to devote himself to the great intellectual motifs of his life: the unity of world religions and the forward-thinking complex of ideas he called "collectivism"—peace, democracy, and women's rights in social policy and "co-operation, profit-sharing, socialization of labor, and federation of human effort" in economics.[114] Lucy Nash Cooke, suffering from arteriosclerosis, died in 1919 at age 71. She had been confined for a decade at the State Hospital at Danvers due to "mild insanity," according to her husband.[115] In 1923, on his seventy-fifth birthday, the ailing Cooke was married to a fellow Unitarian minister, Rev. Mary Leggett, who was among the first women to attend classes at Harvard's Divinity School.[116] He died a week later, on April 30, 1923.

Cooke's early work on the biography lent him a certain intimacy with the Emerson family, with whom he stayed in touch for the remainder of his long life. He was one of a hundred close friends invited to the private ceremony preceding Emerson's public funeral,[117] and in 1889 Edward Emerson asked the Cookes to attend a reading from his new book, *Emerson in Concord*.[118] During the centennial celebrations of Emerson's birth in 1903, Cooke was—typically—both a speaker and a chronicler. As for his biography of Emerson: in 1882 it was issued in London by Sampson Low, Marston Searle, & Rivington but was virtually ignored by English reviewers. The troubled firm of James R. Osgood and Company did not reissue the biography after it sold out in 1882, likely because it was then in competition with two other new books about Emerson's life. Through a series of business buyouts, by 1889 Houghton, Mifflin owned the rights to Cooke's *Emerson*, and in 1892 an enlarged edition of the book appeared with the Houghton, Mifflin imprint.[119] In this updated edition, Cooke added two chapters to his 1881 study, one a perfunctory account of Emerson's last years and the other a selection of "Tributes and Reminiscences." Coming fully a decade after Emerson's death, the expanded edition added nothing to the storehouse of recollections already published by that time and did nothing to respond to the criticism that the first version was tediously philosophical. Cooke left Emerson right where he found him, a religious mystic and "prophet of the soul" (Cooke *RWE*, 1892 edition, 407), and moved on to other scholarly and bibliographical projects.

Early in his writing career, Cooke confessed to Sunderland, "My interests are being more and more absorbed by books, this is not as I have wished to have it, but I do not see any other thing to be done now. I have grown to have some ambitions of this kind, and to look forward to doing something in time that will be really worth doing."[120] Had someone at Cooke's seventieth birthday celebration asked him to identify his magnum opus, he likely would have named his forthcoming *Social Evolution of Religion* (1920), representing as it did a half-century of study and contemplation and the culmination of a lifetime's engagement with progressive thought. But that book, dated, preachy, and dense, is as ignored today by readers as his final project was ignored by publishers—a book based on his 1897 lecture series "Woman's Place in the History of Humanity," which he tried in vain to get Houghton Mifflin to publish during the last years of his life. It is Cooke's first book, his biography of Emerson, that was most "worth doing," bolstered by Cooke's scholarly sense of accuracy that brings the book closer to objectivity than any of the other early biographies. But the life of his hero had a more personal meaning for the cerebral minister who saw Emerson's struggles mirrored in his own. Like the other early biographers, Cooke built the Emerson he needed, not just the one he knew.

THREE

Biographers and the Pornographer

Conway, Ireland, and "Emerson and His Friends"

— I —

Of all the early biographers, Alexander Ireland (1810–1894) knew Emerson nearly the longest but probably the least well. Theirs was an accidental friendship. Ireland was pressed into service at the end of Emerson's first European tour, in August 1833, when his host in Edinburgh, Dr. John Gairdner, backed out at the last minute due to the press of "professional duties" and Emerson was "handed over" to Ireland for a tour of the city (Ireland *RWE*, 140). The two talked of books and authors, including those Emerson had already visited, like Coleridge and Walter Savage Landor, and those he planned to meet before his trip ended, especially Wordsworth and Carlyle. A week or two later, Emerson wrote Ireland a long account of that visit and ended his letter with conventional sentiments that hint at Ireland's lack of self-confidence: "It will give me very great pleasure to hear from you, to know your thoughts. Every man that ever was born has some that are peculiar" (Ireland *RWE*, 151). As he would do with other young men of promise, Emerson encouraged Ireland to write down his ideas, most likely to keep a journal (Ireland *RWE*, 146). Ireland was smitten with his new friend, who struck him as urbane, sincere, and charismatic, full of "high thoughts and ripe wisdom":

> I must confess that the pregnant thoughts and serene self-possession
> of the young Boston minister had a greater charm for me than all the
> rhetorical splendours of Chalmers. His voice was the sweetest, the most

winning and penetrating of any I ever heard; nothing like it have I listened to since. (Ireland *RWE*, 142–143)

Emerson was 30 years of age during this first meeting, Ireland just 23, and it is clear from Ireland's detailed recollections that Emerson's was the more informed end of the conversation. But Ireland was no callow youth. Though he left school at age 15 to enter his father's business, he traveled in a lively intellectual circle in Edinburgh, and already he had begun the infatuation with authors and books that he would carry with him his entire life. At age 19 he had met Sir Walter Scott at Abbotsford, and he was busily reading Coleridge in his early 20s.[1] One of his close friends, Robert Chambers, was the secret author of the sensational evolutionary book *The Vestiges of the Natural History of Creation* (1845); Ireland himself would later become one of the four conspirators—his code name was "Alexius"—who arranged the book's printing and kept its authorship confidential for nearly 40 years.[2] If Ireland was "essentially a hero-worshiper," as a close friend put it, not a deep or introspective thinker, he was nonetheless very comfortable in the presence of literary figures like Emerson.[3] Over the course of their long lifetimes, they actually spent little more than a few weeks in each others' company and met but two more times—in 1847–1848, when Ireland arranged Emerson's British lecture tour, and in 1873, when Emerson and his daughter Ellen spent the final two days of their European visit in Ireland's Manchester home. But Ireland thought often of his famous friend, always with "affectionate reverence" for that early attention in 1833 (Ireland *RWE*, 129). "How the memory of that man lives in my soul!" Ireland wrote Conway 30 years later. "He has influenced me in many ways—more than I can tell! I wish I could see him or hear from him again."[4] For his part, Emerson seems to have remembered the relationship more tentatively. In late 1846, when Ireland wrote him to propose an English lecture tour, Emerson claimed to have been "reminded by your concise note . . . of our brief intercourse thirteen years ago, & which, it seems, has not yet quite ended."[5] Still, Ireland earned Emerson's gratitude for successfully organizing the tour, and Emerson praised him in a letter home to Lidian as "the king of all friends & helpful agents, the most active unweariable & unperturbable,"[6] a judgment he would repeat in *English Traits* (1856).[7]

Ireland has been all but lost in English literary history, though he numbered dozens of writers among his acquaintances. In those rare instances when he does show up, Ireland seems the stereotypical "Manchester Man,"[8] a type one recent historian of the city describes as "earnest, hardworking, self-righteous, a bit dull in matters of art and whimsy, morally concerned and puritanical in religion."[9] Carlyle would later call Ireland "a solid, dark, broad, rather heavy man; full of energy, and broad sagacity and practicality;—infinitely well affected to the man Emerson too."[10] But like characterizations of Manchester itself as "Cottonopolis" or the "Shock City" of the Industrial Revolution, the easy view of Ireland as a genial civic booster who collected literary friends fails to capture the complexity of this lifelong defender of Emerson or account for his biographical efforts, which spanned two decades.

Ireland came to Manchester in 1843 for commercial opportunities—his father's business had become, he said delicately, "unprosperous"—and for a new start in his personal life.[11] The year before, when Ireland was just 32, he had become a widower, his wife Eliza Mary Blithe of Birmingham having died in childbirth just three years into their marriage. Left to care for his two small children, Ireland was, in the recollection of a lifelong friend, "just emerging from the shadow of the sorrow that had so wrecked his domestic life" when he moved to Manchester.[12] Once there, Ireland quickly dove into the worlds of commerce and local politics.

There was plenty to occupy him. The machine manufacture of cotton and the completion of the Liverpool-to-Manchester Railway in 1830, with a London link by 1838, positioned Manchester as the industrial center of the north, and in an era of explosive urbanization all across England, the growth rate of its population rivaled London's.[13] With growth, of course, came the social ills that would become endemic in Western cities during the Victorian era. A cholera epidemic devastated Manchester in the 1830s; sewage ran openly into the water supply; the air was choked with coal smoke; and Mancunians who ventured into the Old City were daily reminded of the most shocking urban squalor. Friedrich Engels, who moved to Manchester at almost exactly the same time as Ireland did, described in *The Condition of the Working Class in England* "the filth and dilapidation of a district which is quite unfit for human habitation" and marveled that "such a district of at least twenty to thirty thousand inhabitants lies in the very centre of the second city in England, the most important factory town in the world."[14]

As Manchester's industrial ills grew, so did its reputation as a locus for radical politics. By the time of Ireland's arrival, the city had become a proving ground for Chartism, anti–child labor agitation, labor unionism, and especially the Questions of Free Trade movement, driven by the establishment in 1838 of Manchester's Anti–Corn Law Association by the activists Richard Cobden and John Bright. Free Trade vs. Interventionism dominated the debate over reforms in the 1840s. While Interventionists benefited from protectionist policies that restricted imports, Free Trade advocates held that Corn Law tariffs artificially inflated grain prices and thus magnified the suffering of the poor (by increasing the price of food) and diminished the competitiveness of manufacturers (who were pressured to increase wages). Predicated on the harmonious effects of laissez-faire capitalism, Free Trade was as much a social position as an economic one and defined political Liberalism during much of mid-nineteenth-century British history. So closely was Free Trade tied to the city that the concept became known as "The Manchester School of Economics." But the name was a convenient misnomer for a city that seethed with economic disagreement and class resentments.

Townsend Scudder, in his study of Emerson in England, points out that Ireland's "broad humanitarianism" led him to "enterprises which sought to check the evils that attended the rise of the new industrialism."[15] Ireland himself told Emerson cryptically that "a strange combination of circumstances" brought him to Manchester in 1843; but once there, he saw great opportunities "to do some good to my fellow-creatures."[16] His political idealism manifested itself in two very tangible ways. In 1846 he became publisher and business manager of the Manchester *Examiner*, a paper founded by Bright and others to advance economic reform and oppose the business interests of the rival Manchester *Guardian*. In a century when newspapers made little pretense of objectivity, the *Examiner* under Ireland's management was unabashedly a Cobdenite mouthpiece, advertising its purpose as late as 1880 in *Mitchell's Newspaper Press Directory* as the amelioration of the conditions of the working classes.[17]

Ireland's other venture is less obviously political to a modern eye. With the Public Libraries and Museums Act of 1850, Parliament authorized localities to raise revenue to construct library buildings. Ireland, already involved with populist educational ventures like the Mechanics Institute and the Manchester Athenaeum (where Emerson would lecture in 1848), became a director of the Manchester Free Public Library, one of the first in Britain to be opened under the new law. Though he was a book-lover and collector, Ireland's interest in the library was as political as it was literary, for public access to books and other printed material was seen as a key to the advancement of the working classes. The opening of the Manchester Free Public Library in 1852 was both a literary event—Dickens, Thackeray, and Bulwer-Lytton were among the celebrities who attended—and a political statement, albeit a mixed one. As Stuart Hylton notes in a modern history of Manchester, "Chartists hailed it as the 'dawn of a socialist paradise' because it extended knowledge to the people, while the business community said it showed the magnanimity of capitalism."[18] Innocuous as it may seem today, Ireland's support of the Manchester Free Public Library was a partisan political act fully in line with his belief in the nobility of working men and women. The interconnected realms of literature and politics would become the twin poles of Ireland's intellectual life.

Over the next decades Ireland's commitment to social justice and the well-being of the lower classes never wavered, though the fortunes of the *Examiner* declined. Hurt by competition from new local dailies and its support eroded by splits in the Liberal Party, the newspaper lost readership as Manchester's new rich became attracted to Conservatism in the late 1860s.[19] In 1872, with the ascendancy of the influential Liberal C. P. Scott to the editorship, the rival *Guardian* began encroaching upon the *Examiner*'s political base, and the *Examiner*'s influence—and along with it, Ireland's power as an advocate of working-class reform—fell into a steady, inexorable decline. Ireland ceased being the paid manager of the paper in 1881, living instead on his share of the paper's profits; but those declined severely, and in 1889 Ireland finally sold his interest in the *Examiner*.[20]

In the shifting allegiances of the political landscape, Ireland must have found his "natural happy optimism of disposition"[21] sorely tested—and just as likely, he valued even more Emerson's constancy, what he would in 1882 call Emerson's "steadfast belief in the ultimate sovereignty of righteousness and truth" (Ireland *RWE*, 180). Brian Harding has astutely observed how Ireland's enduring admiration for Emerson had much to do with Emerson's moral approach to the problems of modern industrial society, his ability to fuse art and spirituality in uplifting ways that endured regardless of the vagaries of political fashion: "in this American scholar Ireland believed he could recognise a religious conception of literature."[22] The bedrock of Ireland's relationship with Emerson was a shared confidence in the democracy of goodness that sustained the friendship even after the two men lost touch. By the mid-1860s, Ireland felt increasingly estranged from his most famous American friend.[23] But by then another Emersonian disciple had taken up residence in England, bringing with him a letter of introduction in Emerson's hand and reenergizing Ireland's interest in Emerson. Together, Ireland and Moncure Daniel Conway would undertake the arduous biographical project of recentering Emerson's life and legacy for the British reading public.

— II —

Conway's acquaintance with Emerson had begun accidentally, as did Ireland's, but it flourished with the same intensity that marked almost every other aspect of his life. The child of a prominent Virginia family that split over the issue of slavery, Moncure Daniel Conway (1832–1907) went north in 1847 to study at Dickinson College in Pennsylvania. By the age of 21 he had already undergone an agonizing spiritual conversion, studied law and abandoned it, embarked on the Methodist ministry and quit, flirted with secessionism and Quakerism, alienated members of his family with his antislavery views, and enrolled at Harvard's Divinity School, where he graduated in 1854 as a Unitarian minister.[24] Before giving up the name "Unitarian" in the early 1860s, he would serve congregations in Washington, D.C., where his radical antislavery views resulted in his ouster after two years, and from 1856 to 1862 in Cincinnati, where his progressively more unorthodox theological views polarized a church already schismatized over debates about Jesus's divinity and the historicity of miracles—the very issues that radicals like Emerson and Theodore Parker had enflamed a scant generation before. Modern scholars have seen an intellectual coherence in Conway's seemingly manic unorthodoxy—John d'Entremont calls it Conway's pursuit of "the spirit of dynamic free inquiry," his ability to "combine genuine tolerance with fierce commitment to principle."[25] His contemporaries often viewed Conway's intellectual wanderlust less charitably. "Conway is simply crazy—pure-hearted and cracked," said Thomas Starr King, a prominent Unitarian minister, in 1859. "It is too bad that our societies in responsible places should be fiddled on by such lunatics."[26] The American Civil War made it painfully difficult for him to balance family allegiance with principle. Two brothers served in the Confederate armies; Conway's mother and sister, both pro-Union, fled the South for Pennsylvania. By early 1862, while living in Boston and coediting with Frank Sanborn the abolitionist paper the *Commonwealth*, Conway began making plans to leave the country and lecture abroad on antislavery. On April 11, 1863, having solicited money for the trip from prominent abolitionists, he left his wife and two small sons, Eustace and Emerson, and sailed for England, Ralph Waldo Emerson's letter of introduction to Alexander Ireland in his pocket.

Conway was, by now, an intimate of Emerson and his family. He had first read Emerson in 1850 during what he called in his *Autobiography* a "spiritual crisis of whose import I was long unconscious," when his soul was "aimless, morbid, passionately longing for it knew not what." The story of Conway's discovery of Emerson is worth repeating, if not for its literal accuracy then for what it says about Conway's mythologizing of the older man's influence on him. In Conway's telling it goes as follows: Lounging by the Rappahannock River in Virginia, his flintlock and a copy of *Blackwood's* magazine by his side, Conway was startled by the sight of two mulatto children, naked and innocent, appearing out of the woods. Conway talked with them and, after they left, he "meditated more deeply than ever before on the condition of their race in America," then turned to his *Blackwood's*, which happened to be the number for December 1847. There, he came upon an article entitled "Emerson" and an extract from the essay "History" struck him "like an arrow"; it ended, "All that Shakespeare says of the king, yonder slip of a boy that reads in the corner feels to be true of himself." Though Emerson's words puzzled him, particularly the references to "self" rather than the more common "soul," their effect on Conway was galvanic:

> Whatever may have been the questionings, some revelation there was.
> A spiritual crisis, as I have said,—though it concerned only myself.
> Through a little rift I caught a glimpse of a vault beyond the familiar
> sky, from which flowed a spirit that was subtly imbreeding discontent
> in me, bereaving me of faith in myself, rendering me a mere source of
> anxiety to those around me. And what was I doing out there with a gun
> trying to kill happy little creatures of earth and sky? Was it for this I was
> born?[27]

He put aside his flintlock and rushed to a bookseller to find and read more Emerson.

This episode, often repeated as fact by later scholars, bears the stamp of Conway's signature self-dramatization; it strikes a modern eye as a verbal genre painting of the sort so loved by late Victorians, populated by stock characters and convenient moral props.[28] There is no doubting, however, how deeply Emerson shook Conway's old convictions and confirmed his new ones. A year later Conway wrote to Emerson, who responded by encouraging him to "let me sufficiently into your own habit of thought,"[29] and in May 1853 Conway, now a divinity student at Harvard, showed up unannounced at Emerson's doorstep in Concord with a letter of introduction from the former dean of the Divinity School, John Gorham Palfrey. Conway spent the day in Concord, dining with the family, walking to Walden Pond, and of course engaging in conversation. It was, Conway wrote in his journal that evening, "the most memorable day of my life:

spent with Ralph Waldo Emerson!"[30] Their friendship remained unbroken for nearly 30 years, the families close friends and for a while neighbors, when in 1862 they bought the Concord home vacated by Emerson's old minister, Barzillai Frost, at 235 West Main Street, an easy walk from the Emerson house.

When Conway left for England in the spring of 1863, Emerson recommended him to Ireland warmly if somewhat vaguely as "a man full of public & private virtues" whose mission was "to defend the cause of America" abroad.[31] Yet almost immediately Conway committed an outrageous public blunder that shook Emerson's—and almost everyone else's—confidence in him. Soon after his arrival in London Conway contacted J. M. Mason, the Confederate envoy to England, and suggested "on behalf of the leading antislavery men of America" that if the South would emancipate its slaves, abolitionists would pressure Lincoln to permit secession.[32] Mason, who had ample reason to discredit antislavery advocates, made the offer public. His crackpot status confirmed once again, Conway was censured by American antislavery groups.[33] While his professional reputation eventually recovered, residual suspicion about Conway's reliability lingered, in reviews of his books and even in the evaluations of his friends.

The humanitarian businessman Alexander Ireland and the peripatetic free-thinker Moncure Conway were an odd couple who would seem to be united by little more than their mutual admiration for Emerson. By the late 1860s, however, each had also become a relatively important player in the rapidly expanding arena of Anglo-American literary relations. Ireland now counted among his English friends Leigh Hunt, William Hazlitt, Thomas De Quincey, Tennyson, and Carlyle, and among his American friends Oliver Wendell Holmes, James Russell Lowell, and Nathaniel Hawthorne. Conway knew Thoreau, Walt Whitman, William Dean Howells, Mark Twain, the Alcotts, Henry James Jr., Henry Wadsworth Longfellow, and Lowell among the Americans, and in England Algernon Swinburne, John Stuart Mill, Robert Browning, Matthew Arnold, George Meredith, and James Anthony Froude.[34] As their political influence waned Ireland and Conway, both of whom had previously been men of affairs, also became increasingly men of letters, in a larger "culture of letters" (as Richard H. Brodhead calls it) that included publication, promotion, and the directing of literary taste. In 1870, they would be thrown together by their reverence for Emerson on a project to introduce English readers to his uncollected prose. Ultimately unsuccessful, it would begin their collaboration as Emerson's English biographers and lead to their separate biographies of him in 1882.

In the 1860s Conway had negotiated English publication contracts for his friends Whitman and Howells and helped to publish an English edition of Hawthorne's notebooks. Conway's partner on the Whitman and Hawthorne projects was John Camden Hotten (1832–1873), a London publisher known for his toughness and a willingness to take a chance on authors like Swinburne and Whitman, whose reputations ran to the scandalous.[35] By early 1870, Hotten and Conway were discussing another project: "going at the Emerson uncollected papers."[36] The plan, according to a newspaper announcement around this time, was "a complete edition, in two volumes, of the uncollected writings, essays, and lectures."[37] Dennis Welland has teased out the details of this aborted project, which involved Hotten, Conway, and Ireland, though differences remain among the principals as to who did what. According to Hotten's recollection several years later, in a letter to Conway, "The arrangement was that you were to collect—or assist in collecting—the scattered compositions & lectures of Mr Emerson, & write an Introduction to them for £50.0.0."[38] Conway recalled only the invitation to write the introduction[39] and insisted that it was Hotten "who ransacked magazines with his usual industry, and got hold of the old newspapers containing reports of lectures that had been delivered by Emerson during his earlier visits to England."[40] In any event, by February 1870 Conway and Hotten had the Emerson edition underway, and in early April Hotten invited Ireland to participate by helping to find fugitive notices of Emerson's English lectures. Ireland agreed, despite some reservations he shared with Conway about Hotten's "bad odour in the trade."[41]

Work on the Hotten edition proceeded quickly, with Conway and Ireland corresponding about it almost every day. Some version of Conway's biographical introduction, eventually called "Emerson and His Friends," was sent to the printer on April 19, 1870. Ireland read the proofs, offered his corrections and additions in June,[42] and added a long postscript about Emerson's first English visit in 1833. Both Conway and Ireland were privately apprehensive about the edition, with Conway wanting to be known only as its "Introduction-writer,—not an Editor or Collector—." Welland includes this quote from Conway's letter to Ireland in his article and also correctly points out the source of Conway's modesty: he was already uncomfortable about his involvement in a project Emerson knew nothing about.[43]

Not until July 1870 did Conway notify Emerson of the proposed edition; and when he did, the project came to an abrupt halt. Emerson wrote

Conway that he thought it "cruel" of Hotten to "drag out of darkness these rough papers of thirty years since."[44] At the least, Emerson wanted time to prepare a revised version of the selections. If not, he told Conway heatedly, "I shall denounce the book in the London papers."[45] Besides the question of authorial control, there was likely another issue adding to Emerson's distress: Hotten was a well-known publisher of Victorian pornography, a fact that none of the principals discussed in the surviving correspondence but one that could not have escaped their notice. Having at some pains redeemed his reputation in American letters by the 1860s, Emerson could ill afford now to hitch his wagon to the publisher of books like *Pretty Little Games for Young Ladies & Gentlemen* (1872) or *The Romance of the Rod.*[46] Just months after work on the projected edition began, both Ireland and Conway asked Hotten to suspend it until Emerson provided corrected copy. Hotten, whose right to publish Emerson in England was well within the copyright laws of the time, was unwilling to take the financial loss he had so far incurred with the printers and feared that any delay would allow another publisher to beat him to the punch. Nonetheless, he agreed to wait twelve months for Emerson's revisions. But 1871 came and went, with the overextended, aging Emerson increasingly distressed by the task hanging over his head. Conway asked Hotten to exercise "Xtian patience," promising that with Emerson "delay means a more painfully-wrought perfection in his work."[47] Then, in August 1872, Emerson's house burned, and a dispirited Emerson left Concord for a European tour. His work on the promised edition for Hotten was suspended indefinitely. Emerson's daughter Edith, her husband William Hathaway Forbes, and the American publisher James Osgood all appealed to Hotten to drop the matter;[48] Edward Emerson, studying medicine in London, visited Hotten personally and pleaded with him to give his father more time, in the interest of his health.[49]

By early 1873, it became clear that the Emerson edition was not to be and that the investment in it so far would be a loss. Hotten's only hope for recouping his losses was to publish Conway's and Ireland's biographical introduction, which Hotten had paid for and believed he owned: "I had understood that the memoir or introduction you wrote for our projected Emerson book was handed over & given to me for the great & unexpected expense I had been put to in printing it, and in printing the bulk of the book itself. The composition & correction of the Introduction will have cost from £15. to £18. so that *at any rate* it is saddled with this expense."[50] For their part, Conway and Ireland worried that the independent publication of their introduction while Emerson was living would give the appearance of "trying to coin a dear friend into money."[51] They proposed a compromise: in return for Hotten's guarantee not to publish the introduction, they would buy the printed sheets at cost and forgive the £50 fee he owed Conway and the £20 he owed Ireland. Hotten demurred. There were, he discovered, 1,000 printed copies of the introduction struck off two years ago. Why couldn't Conway and Ireland expand their work with essays on Hawthorne and Fuller and issue a separate book under Hotten's imprint?[52]

The disposition of "Emerson and His Friends" had reached an impasse when Hotten died suddenly on June 14, 1873. Hotten's successor, Andrew Chatto, handled the affair briskly a month afterwards: "With regard to the securing [of] your rights in the Emerson introduction," he wrote Conway, "very little is needed besides my guarantee that you are released from all claims on a/c of Mr. Hotten's estate and that all the copies printed shall be delivered to you. Should anyone dare to reprint it you could have an injunction against them at once. . . . You might also register the copy right at Stationers Hall in the name of Mr Ireland and yourself at a cost of 5/— —but this I do not consider necessary or advisable until the book is [actually?] published."[53]

As to the edition itself, Chatto was equally businesslike: "I am quite prepared to endorse Mr. Hotten's promise not to publish the edition of Emerson's uncollected works which he had made provided Mr Emerson will furnish as agreed the material for a new volume in lieu of it. I should like to be held free not to publish anything that I might consider likely to prove an unremunerable speculation."[54] A contract survives in the Chatto & Windus archives, endorsed by Conway on July 27, 1873. It stipulates that Emerson "shall consign and entrust to those who shall have the control of the said publishing business of the late J C Hotten, a volume of Essays now being prepared by the said Emerson, for publication in accordance with agreements entered into by the late J C Hotten," and that "the said M D Conway agrees to pay to the said Charlotte Hotten the sum of thirty pounds (£30) for the stock in hand of the said 'Introduction,' entitled 'Emerson and his Friends' or 1000 copies thereof, to cover all the expenses connected with with [sic] the printing and manufacture of the same, and to pay the further sum of forty five pounds (£45) in settlement of an account held by the said house of Jno C. Hotten against him."[55] The book Conway promised Hotten (and later Chatto) was eventually issued as *Letters and Social Aims*, substantially revised and selected by James Elliot Cabot. Published by Chatto & Windus in early 1876, it signaled an end to the unfortunate Hotten affair. Conway had successfully distanced himself from the publisher, at least in the eyes of the Emerson family, by depicting himself as the innocent dupe of a scheming businessman. "If I could have stopped the publication altogether I would have done so," he told Emerson disingenuously in July 1870; "The matter has troubled me exceedingly."[56] In gratitude for his "kind exertions . . . with regard to the Hotten book," Edward Emerson refunded Conway the £30 in printing costs he had paid Hotten's widow to retrieve the introduction.[57]

For the next decade both Ireland and Conway occupied themselves with other matters. Ireland, who had remarried in 1865, fathered five more children between 1866 and 1879. (The last of them was the composer John Nicholson Ireland.) As his newspaper's influence faded, Ireland capitalized upon his other career as a bibliophile, bringing out bibliographies of Hazlitt and Hunt in 1868 and building one of the most extensive private libraries in England. (Toward the end of his life, Ireland's collection numbered between 15,000 and 20,000 volumes.) Conway settled into the active expatriate life in London as a preacher and a professional author. Since 1866 he had been the minister at the progressive South Place Ethical Society, where he had free rein to develop his interests in world religions and write about the intersections of science, rationality, and spirituality. His literary career is marked with the variety of an author who writes for money—commissioned magazine articles, often about his travels; revisions of his discourses at South Place; collections like his widely reprinted *Sacred Anthology* (1874); forays into folklore and comparative religion like his *Demonology and Devil-Lore* (1879); and nontheological works as diverse as the children's book *A Necklace of Stories* (1880), a discourse on President Garfield (1881), and a hastily written biography of Thomas Carlyle (1881).[58] These were the happiest years in Conway's life, according to his biographer: "He had a transatlantic reputation, a comfortable living, satisfying work."[59] Though he visited Concord during his occasional trips to the United States, his biographical interest in Emerson was, if not forgotten, then at least buried under the weight of other duties. Both he and Ireland made good their early pledge not to capitalize upon their friendship with Emerson while he was alive.

— IV —

But all that changed after April 27, 1882. At the time of his death, Emerson's reputation in England was mixed and in transition, according to the most extensive study of the topic. As William J. Sowder notes, in *Emerson's Impact on the British Isles and Canada* (1966), early Victorian critics tended to applaud Emerson's antiestablishment views but considered his

Transcendentalism "either odious or the result of an eccentric personal preference, like eating pie for breakfast."[60] And due to their repugnance for his "pantheism," they "also rejected his political, economic, and social views."[61] Later Victorians remained uneasy over Emerson's religious opinions, except insofar as they could be aligned with conventional Christianity. Some opposed his "cavalier treatment of revelation, personal salvation, miracles, and belief in a future state,"[62] while others thought his optimism laughable. And it had long been fashionable among English *and* American critics to dismiss Emerson's poetry as artless restatements of the essays. There was an Emerson "revival" in the English periodical press from 1882 through the centenary of his birth in 1903, but it was driven by an academic interest in the man, not in his works, which were largely unread. The two-volume English edition of the *Complete Works of Ralph Waldo Emerson* (London: Bell & Daldy, 1866) sold poorly, even though at 6 shillings it was priced very competitively, according to Ireland—who made it his business to know such things. As Ireland himself put it, "It is too good a book for the ordinary herd of British readers."[63]

Of course, published reviews and book sales do not necessarily measure the full sentiment of English people toward Emerson. As Sowder points out, "Early enthusiasm for Emerson was a combination of the inspiration of his message and the inspiration of his presence."[64] In his lecture engagements Emerson found a ready audience among the working classes, and there were always among his supporters "the radicals, the freethinkers, the intellectuals . . . and the young."[65] By the early 1880s he had became an iconic figure among academics who may not have read him carefully, or at all. The fact remains, however, that his reputation in England had always been spotty. When Ireland and Conway began their efforts to publish separate biographies of Emerson, they were not simply working to inform English readers about the events of his life. Their books were an act of reclamation for a culture that had found Emerson's work offensive, obscure, or quaintly irrelevant.

In his chapter on Emerson's academic critics, Sowder unfairly criticizes both Ireland and Conway for rushing into print on the heels of their friend's death, Ireland "sensing a quick profit," Conway throwing together "the whole disorderly production" called *Emerson at Home and Abroad*.[66] To be sure, Ireland needed the money; at the age of 72 he was tired of the publishing business and would leave the management of the failing *Examiner* by the end of 1882.[67] But he was a newspaperman, and Emerson's lingering final illness was—thanks to the transatlantic telegraph—news. On April 29, 1882, the day after word of Emerson's passing reached England, Ireland published a memoir of him in the *Examiner*. A much-expanded edition appeared in book form five weeks later, as *In Memoriam. Ralph Waldo Emerson: Recollections of His Visits to England in 1833, 1847–8, 1872–3, and Extracts from Unpublished Letters* (London: Simpkin, Marshall, 1882).[68]

As its cumbersome title suggests, *In Memoriam* was divided into three parts. The first (pages 3–45), a thin biography of Emerson and an "appreciation" that draws from published commentary, is largely based on a reading of Cooke and on Conway's part of "Emerson and His Friends."[69] Sometimes the overlap is substantial and complicated, though not acknowledged. For instance, in writing of Emerson's mother, Ruth Haskins Emerson, Ireland (p. 4) quotes almost verbatim a paragraph from Cooke without attribution—and Cooke was himself quoting from an 1854 article in the *Christian Examiner*, which he does acknowledge (Cooke *RWE*, 16). Elsewhere, Ireland borrows from his own sections of the unpublished "Emerson and His Friends," which in turn are based upon his letter to Conway of June 23, 1870. For example, his description of Emerson's manner of lecturing appears on pages 135–136 of "Emerson and His Friends" and almost identically on pages 16–17 of *In Memoriam*. "Emerson is a legitimate product of Puritanism," a debatable point that Conway made in "Emerson and His Friends" (p. 11), shows up again on page 4 of *In Memoriam*, without quotation marks and unacknowledged, with only the verb tense changed. The point is not that Ireland was a plagiarist—the word meant little in the newspaper world of the nineteenth century, where columns were routinely filled with reprinted matter—but that Ireland's firsthand authority as a biographer was severely limited by his scant personal experience with Emerson himself. The biography is the most uneven and least personal section of Ireland's short first book, though at times we get glimpses of the bibliophile behind the biographer, as when he pauses in his discussion of Emerson's *Dial* pieces to add, "A complete set of the four volumes is now an almost unattainable rarity. Even odd numbers of it fetch a high price" (p. 11).

The second section of *In Memoriam* (pages 49–70), "Recollections," recounts Emerson's three trips to England, as Ireland remembered them; more detailed than any other accounts of Emerson's visits, these are the most valuable sections of the book, for Ireland recalls not just the events but the impressions they made on him. The section is punctuated with vignettes—Emerson in the lecture hall, Emerson in conversation, Emerson in drawing rooms and at dinner—that reveal a Boswellian self-effacement in Ireland, the witness at Emerson's elbow who records in detail the actions of the Great Man. Something of this personal touch continues in the third section (pages 71–120), a miscellany of original correspondence between Emerson and Carlyle; letters from Emerson to Ireland; and reprinted recollections by others, usually from magazines and newspapers. The book concludes with a short bibliography of Emerson's published works and works about Emerson.

Ireland's *In Memoriam* went on sale in England on June 3, 1882, and sold out in three months (Ireland *RWE*, vii). "Not a copy of the book remains," he told Conway in September, "so there is a fair prospect of sale for a moderately-sized 2d edition."[70] In fact he was already planning that second, enlarged edition within a week of his first book's publication, writing Conway for more information, asking to see Edith Emerson Forbes's letters about her father's last hours, and inquiring about Elizabeth Peabody's mailing address. But interest in Ireland's *In Memoriam* was not as serious as he would have preferred. By August, he carefully reported to Conway, there had been 38 positive reviews of it; by late September, 45.[71] Their tenor overall had been less than enthusiastic. He complained, "How remiss the London Press has been in this matter. The 'Athenaeum' has a notice today—but it is a poor one, & does not in the least touch upon the more significant parts of the book. No pains have been taken to give the reader the gist of it. Had it been about Mrs Langtrey or some other actress of cracked reputation, & not about a world-noted man of thought, no doubt room would have been found for long reviews and extracts."[72]

As a matter of fact, as Sowder indicates, the reviewers were in the main complimentary, if honest about the limitations of Ireland's "scraps."[73] During the summer Ireland corresponded with Emerson's friends and family and received information from Edward Emerson, William Henry Furness, Oliver Wendell Holmes, Elizabeth Palmer Peabody (whose response to Ireland ran 14 pages), Charles Eliot Norton, and the British physicist John Tyndall, among others, to beef up the book and add the personal acquaintance with Emerson that Ireland lacked.[74] To Holmes, he described his intentions for the new edition:

> The thin 1st Edition of my [?] & most inadequate book went off in
> 3 months, & I was encouraged to propose a new edition, much en-
> larged throughout—I added largely to the Memoir, & also to my recol-
> lections of the subject of it, & also to the characteristic records at the
> end. Then, I so much admired your *eloge*, that I decided to appropriate
> it wholesale, as well as the narratives of Dr Ellis & Judge Hoar[.] In fact,
> the matter grew on my hands, & I felt I could compile a more worthy
> book than the 1st Edition—that I could present Emerson more vividly

to the reader, bring the reader more to the man, by letting him be seen through many different eyes.[75]

Still, Ireland recognized the limits even of the expanded book. As he told Conway while the second edition was being printed, "It pretends to nothing beyond a Biographical Sketch—Emerson seen through the eyes of those who knew him best—It may help others to understand him, & to read him."[76] Ireland reiterated the point in his preface:

> Wherever he has found a vivid presentment of Emerson, the author has not hesitated to make use of it, and to incorporate it in his sketch, in order to add to the completeness of the picture. In this respect he has been but "a gatherer and disposer of other men's stuff." His object throughout has been to present a likeness of Emerson as true as he can make it—to the fidelity of which not merely his own opportunities of observation, but also the faithful reports of friends and life-long associates have contributed. (Ireland *RWE*, ix)

Ralph Waldo Emerson. His Life, Genius, and Writings (London: Simpkin, Marshall, 1882) was published on November 1, 1882, and bore the subtitle "A Biographical Sketch," the only incidence of the word "biography" in any title of the early lives of Emerson.[77] Referred to on the title page and in the preface as a "second edition, largely augmented" of *In Memoriam*, at 338 pages it was nearly three times the size of Ireland's first book. Ireland made use not only of the material sent him by Emerson's American friends and relatives but also of the wealth of reminiscences appearing in the press during the months after Emerson's death, which he reprinted freely. The result was a book that substantially expanded Ireland's first biography. As he puts it in the preface, with his businessman's eye for value, the biographical section increased from 47 to 129 pages; the recollections of Emerson's English visits, from 25 to 41 pages; the "miscellaneous characteristic records," from 34 to 92. Along with these expanded sections he reprinted addresses given by Holmes, Rockwood Hoar, and George E. Ellis at the May meeting of the Massachusetts Historical Society and selections from a memorial tribute by William Henry Channing published in October 1882.[78] The date of this last essay shows how Ireland scrambled to include the most current material he could find, adding to the book even while it was in press. He was also acknowledging old debts, identifying more fully his quotations from Cooke and including because "I consider it due to my friend"

(Ireland *RWE*, 213) a short, laudatory sketch of Conway's life along with the full text of Emerson's 1863 letter of introduction.

In expanding his earlier book, Ireland attempted to include some additional personal information about his subject. Whereas *In Memoriam* hurries in a single paragraph from Emerson's birth to his entrance into Harvard, in *Ralph Waldo Emerson* Ireland pauses to show young Waldo in grammar and Latin schools, already modeling the poetic and bookish man he would become (Ireland *RWE*, 6–8). (A letter from Furness, which Ireland quotes extensively, recalls a little boy who rarely played: "He lived always from the earliest in a serene world of letters" [Ireland *RWE*, 8].) Emerson's Harvard years are fleshed out with details about classmates, professors, reading. His marriage to Ellen Tucker—remarkably, it was not mentioned in *In Memoriam*—is noted, though Emerson's grief at her death is never connected to his resignation from the Second Church in 1832, a fact the widower Ireland could hardly have overlooked. But this newfound emphasis on Emerson's personal history lasts only until Ireland turns to Emerson's public career as a writer and lecturer in 1834; thereafter, the biographical sketch becomes a bibliography in prose, a chronological history of Emerson's writings and public lectures and their circumstances and reception. So thoroughly does Ireland abandon his attention to the personal after the 1830s that Emerson's final four years are compressed into a single paragraph in which Ireland domesticates Emerson with boilerplate platitudes: "He had never lost his inherent love of dignified simplicity in domestic life," "all children loved him," "his old age was serene, and the sweetness and gentleness of his character were more and more apparent as the years rolled on" (Ireland *RWE*, 97). As did others who wrote of Emerson's decline, Ireland makes the point that Emerson even in his dotage retained the power to entrance with his conversation. "Those who ever had the good fortune to hear him, in the free intercourse of his own study, will not soon forget the charm of his conversation and the graciousness of his demeanor" (Ireland *RWE*, 97–98). Ireland, of course, reports all this at second hand, never having set foot in Emerson's house or touched American soil. After the mid-1830s the details of Emerson's personal life—not his private life, but the personal events that distinguish him as a person from others—occupy less and less of Ireland's attention, even in the expanded version of the biography; he frequently gets the facts wrong (claiming that Emerson was graduated from the Divinity School, for instance, or misidentifying his first wife as "Helen Tucker") and rarely shows any interest in even the most rudimentary psychological motives.

In many ways, Ireland's focus on the public Emerson is the honest response of a man who did not finally know his subject's life very well. As he admits, he needed the testimony of others to bring Emerson to life, except for his detailed personal portraits of Emerson in England, where Ireland was on certain ground. Still, his purposes seem to lie elsewhere. As his digressive tribute to Conway suggests, Ireland saw biography as a venue for defending those whose reputations had suffered, and Emerson's in England, as already discussed, was in need of rehabilitation. Compared to *In Memoriam*, *Ralph Waldo Emerson* is not just a longer biography: it is a deeper one that makes an implicit argument for Emerson's value. But deeper where? What value? Ireland finds it less in the emotional and familial: Emerson's family is mentioned and dismissed in the first paragraph of the book, his marriage to Lidian sandwiched into a chronology of lecture appearances in 1835 (Ireland *RWE*, 19), the death of young Waldo reduced to a one-sentence preface to a quote from the poem "Threnody." Nor does Ireland show much understanding of the philosophy of the man he calls "the most original and independent thinker and greatest moral teacher that America has produced" (Ireland *RWE*, 1–2, 19); in fact, he consciously distances himself as a biographer from Emerson's ideas—"It would be out of place in a biographical sketch like the present to attempt to explain Emerson's philosophy" (Ireland *RWE*, 124). Transcendentalism is dismissed in two pages with long quotes from Frothingham and the *Harvard Magazine*, and Ireland prefaces even that abbreviated discussion with a list of disarming caveats: Emerson "propounded no system," founded no school, "has not discovered the secret of the universe" but shows an unwavering "faith in God, in spiritual laws, [and] in the moral law of the universe" (Ireland *RWE*, 124–125). Ireland's Emerson is a decidedly safe thinker, conventional, even tedious in his philosophical abstractions—much like Ireland himself.

Instead, Ireland shows Emerson's true value to be his "practical, unerring sagacity" (Ireland *RWE*, 102), the application of his philosophy to his personal behavior that revealed his *character*. If Emerson is a great moral teacher, Ireland argues, it is through his example, not his ideas—and by focusing on Emerson's exemplariness Ireland returns to the personal details that were most of interest to him: not matters of family and relationships that Ireland seemed to consider private, but Emerson's practical activities in the real world of public affairs. In the section entitled "Characteristic Episodes," and indeed throughout *Ralph Waldo Emerson*, Ireland chooses from among the multitude of existing reminiscences those that illustrate Emerson's plain-speaking honesty, his "good sense" in the face of "imbecilic" radicalism, his refusal to push his opinions on others, the way he combined loftiness of thought with shrewd observation, his ability (in the words of Edwin Whipple) to be "as good a judge of investments on earth as he was of investments in the heaven above the earth" (Ireland *RWE*, 301, 115, 101–102). These are matters of character, revealed in personal actions. Even his poetry, much maligned in England for its inattention to form and meter, reveals his true character: according to Hedge's testimony, its "utter spontaneity" is "but a mode of his sincerity" (Ireland *RWE*, 105). No obscure mystic or dangerous pantheist, Emerson is revealed as direct, pious, tolerant, a realist, a moderate, and an activist humanitarian—the "Sage of Concord" reborn as the "Manchester Man." And his character, far from threatening, leads him to support what for Ireland were the signature social reforms of his times: antislavery and Free Trade (Ireland *RWE*, 59–63, 95–96). While reviewers treated Ireland's book as a useful miscellany, in fact Ireland's selection was not miscellaneous at all but deliberate, returning again and again to Emerson as socially relevant and philosophically nonthreatening. In doing so, Ireland challenged the prevailing view of Emerson's achievement, translating it into terms that were not only compatible with Ireland's own politics but also a corrective to the critical disconnect that characterized views of Emerson in England—that is, a dangerous, somewhat irreligious philosopher who offered no practical solutions. Ireland argued just the opposite.

The publication of Ireland's expanded biography coincided with a wealth of memorializing articles, reminiscences, sermons, and evaluations that followed Emerson's death, as well as several other full-length studies of varying quality that distracted attention from Ireland's. Bronson Alcott's rhapsodic essay *Ralph Waldo Emerson: An Estimate of His Character and Genius in Prose and Verse* (Boston: A. Williams, 1882), itself a slight expansion of a work Alcott first published privately in 1865, appeared late in 1882; Joel Benton's influential *Emerson as a Poet* and Charles Eliot Norton's two-volume edition of the Emerson-Carlyle correspondence (*The Correspondence of Thomas Carlyle and Ralph Waldo Emerson, 1834–1872* [Boston: James R. Osgood, 1883]) were published very early in 1883. And Conway, as we shall see, would bring out his *Emerson at Home and Abroad* in America within weeks of Ireland's *Ralph Waldo Emerson* in the fall of 1882. With so much else to talk about, reviewers talked little about Ireland's "second edition." As with *In Memoriam*, the reviews were generally positive but cursory, praising the book as informative and a must-read for "all Emerson's admirers."[79] Sales of the expanded version were disappointingly flat, Ireland reported, everywhere but in Manchester.[80] In an attempt to drum up interest abroad, Ireland sent copies of the second edition to a dozen prominent Americans, including members of the Emerson family, Norton, Peabody, Alcott, Furness, and all five of the other biographers, each of whom he knew personally or through correspondence, but after waiting for weeks he received no acknowledgment from any of them.[81] He offered advance sheets to Harper & Company, then to Houghton, Mifflin; both houses turned him down. Frank Sanborn carried a copy of Ireland's book to the Emerson family and asked if they would approve its publication in the United States; they refused.[82] Neither of Ireland's Emerson biographies was ever published in the United States, nor was there any significant sale outside of the city of Manchester. Commercially, at least, the expanded edition proved to be a bad decision.[83]

The inconsistent reception of Ireland's biographical work, measured by both the sellout of the first edition and the relative failure of the second, may indeed be a comment on Ireland's skill at puzzling out his readership and providing them a consumable product. The consummate literary insider, in his biography Ireland offers up much about Emerson, little about himself. Ireland did not pander to a book-buying public hungry for intimacies, try though he might to generate sales and good reviews, but his work shows a careful awareness of the contemporary debates over biography as a genre and a shrewdness in avoiding extremes. On the one hand, Ireland's stated aim—to "gather and dispose of" information about Emerson and provide nothing more than a "sketch" of Emerson's life—would appeal to those who believed biography was necessarily an interpretive act and should be approached with care. Ireland was what Margaret Oliphant called in 1883 a "disciple-biographer," whose passion and devotion "give of themselves a certain greatness to the subject" and who fall between the fulsome puffery of family members and the gratuitous criticism of cynics.[84] Ireland chose sufficient personal detail to satisfy those who had by the 1880s begun to criticize biographies as bloodless and tediously inspirational but not enough to invoke the criticism of those who complained, with the *Spectator* of London, about biographers' "love of gossip."[85] As Holmes wrote Ireland approvingly in early 1885, "I think you have taken the right ground about the publication of circumstances not meant to go beyond the household walls and *obiter dicta*, not intended for publication. I think also that public opinion so far as I know anything of it is in entire accord with you."[86] By studiously claiming *not* to write a biography, Ireland managed to steer a middle course through the debates over the genre, though sometimes he came dangerously close to crossing the line. In a country weaning itself from what Edmund Gosse would later call the "big-biography habit" and turning away from commemorative "life and letters" volumes toward more limited treatments like Macmillan's "English Men of Letters" series, Ireland's expanded compendium managed to satisfy the demand for completeness without entombing Emerson in a "monstrous catafalque of two volumes (crown octavo)."[87]

On the other hand, Ireland's emphasis on the playing out of Emerson's philosophy in day-to-day acts of benevolence anticipates Leslie Stephen's influential statement a decade later that a biography "should be such a portrait as reveals the essence of character."[88] In itself, character as the focus of biography was not new, though in an age rapidly becoming fascinated with psychology, the shift was toward seeing character as the result of social, genetic, and familial influences. (Stephen talked of "the development of the human character" and said biographers should expose "what [the subject] was and how he came to be what he was."[89]) Ireland seems to have had little interest in how Emerson became Emerson. But as a philanthropist and humanitarian reformer, Ireland had great interest in how Emerson impacted the world around him. For Ireland, character revealed itself in individual action, not merely in ideas; therefore, Emerson's personal impact was what made episodes in his life "characteristic." At once retrograde and forward-looking, cautious and daring, flirting with readers' patience but gratifying their need for information, revealing character through actions yet judicious in recounting private details, Ireland the biographer—like Ireland the man—was far more complex than he appears at first glance.

— V —

As Ireland prepared the second edition of *In Memoriam* in the summer of 1882, Moncure Conway was shaping his experiences with Emerson into the book that would most directly compete with it in England, *Emerson at Home and Abroad*. Like Ireland, he drew on the unpublished Hotten introduction from a decade before, though to a much greater extent, since he had written the majority of it himself, 119 of the 139 printed pages.[90] Like Ireland, too, Conway would struggle to create a coherent portrait out of what, after all, was a relatively late friendship that began when Emerson was nearly 50 and lasted only a decade, until Conway left for England in 1863. Unlike Ireland's books, though, Conway's biography was a more comprehensive treatment of Emerson's milieu and contemporaries, as well as a relentlessly impressionistic study that placed Conway prominently at Emerson's side.

In the weeks and months immediately following Emerson's death, Conway busied himself with preparations for a book-length tribute. He turned first to the periodical press, publishing a longish memoir in the *Fortnightly Review* for June 1, 1882, which he sent to Ellen Emerson along with condolences on the death of his "spiritual father and intellectual teacher."[91] Conway's insinuation of himself into the grieving Emerson family, which may strike us today as presumptuous or crass, seems not to have bothered the family themselves, whose relationship with the Conways had always been warm. Moncure and Ellen Dana Conway had named their second son Emerson (1861–1864); in his letter of condolence to Lidian Emerson, Conway mourns the death of two Emersons, his son and now his "father," "the man I love most in the earth."[92] Conway's emotional connection to the Emersons would prove to be a blessing and a curse to him as biographer: if it established his bona fides as a family insider, it also threatened his credibility by making his prose maudlin and excessive.

Much as they liked him personally, the family themselves surely had reservations about this emotive Southerner who had been both the instigator and the whistle-blower on the embarrassing Hotten edition. As they knew, Emerson himself had "dreaded" Conway's getting hold of his literary papers,[93] and not without reason. Conway—the man one Cincinnati parishioner called in 1859 "a frivolous and reckless boy . . . whose judgment and logic are too feeble to command respect"[94]—had established a reputation for haste, inaccuracy, and imprudence that dogged him his entire life. Emerson himself was always clear-headed about the price of his friend's enthusiasm. "Good writing how rare!" he lamented in his journal in 1861. "Conway writes affectedly or secondarily with all his talent & heat of purpose."[95] A decade later, casting about for a suitable literary executor, Emerson wrote to Carlyle to find himself a good biographer, but not Conway, who, Emerson said, "cannot, in my experience, report a fact or speech as it fell. It suffers a strange distortion in his mind. But he is a good fellow, & bright, & I owe him only good will. So pray burn this note or blot it."[96]

Now, within weeks of Emerson's death and almost exactly coincident with Ireland's efforts, Conway dusted off "Emerson and His Friends" and began work on the book Emerson had feared he would write. In a letter of June 6, Conway told Ellen Emerson, "I am now engaged in writing out my reminiscences of the dear old days,—and of various people at Concord,—and shall call my book 'Concordia.'"[97] The Hotten introduction was more than a decade out of date, and while he had seen Emerson briefly in England in 1873 and had visited Emerson twice in the intervening years, during trips to the U.S. in 1875 and 1880 (Conway *EHA*, 379–380), to bring his knowledge up to date would require the family's cooperation—the same family who invited Cabot to write the authorized biography in order to keep men like Conway at bay.

Precisely when he needed it, in the summer of 1882, fate intervened to reestablish Conway's trustworthiness with the Emersons in a bit of literary intrigue involving stolen Emerson letters. As with the Hotten episode, it involved Ireland but primarily Conway. The story, often told, may be summarized thus. Soon after Thomas Carlyle's death in 1881, Edith Emerson Forbes had contacted Conway in England to ask him to search for some 30 missing letters her father had written to Carlyle—documents Carlyle had promised, in a letter Edith herself could no longer locate, to return to her. Now, in mid-summer of 1882, as Charles Eliot Norton was preparing an edition of the Emerson-Carlyle correspondence, Edward Emerson wrote another letter to Conway to ask him to track down the fugitive letters—four of which had appeared in the London *Athenaeum* and been reprinted in Ireland's *In Memoriam*.[98] What happened next, certainly in Conway's version of the events, is a Dickensian story of disguise and double cross. Conway learned that the thief was a former employee of Carlyle's, one Frederick Martin, who used the alias "Beckerwaise." In Conway's version, Martin was part of an underground network operating through a London manuscripts dealer named Anderson, who sent a mysterious woman one evening to the Conway home to offer the letters for sale. Conway and his wife asked to see several letters at a time, for verification, they claimed, and then secretly made copies. Little by little, in this way the Conways transcribed 27 of the letters and bought at least four original manuscripts, all of which they dutifully returned to the Emerson family.[99] Edith Emerson Forbes thanked Conway for returning the "precious" documents and inscribed a copy of Norton's edition of the Emerson-Carlyle correspondence to Moncure and Ellen Conway, "with grateful acknowledgement of their kind help in the recovery of these letters."[100]

In Conway's efforts on behalf of the Emersons there is no evidence of a quid pro quo; still, the effect was to shore up his standing with the family when he most needed their cooperation. He asked to dedicate his "Concordia" to them. Lidian and Ellen agreed, and Edith would have no objections, Edward assured him, since she and Conway were old friends.[101] Conway's dedication was a gesture of thanks, but it was more than that. Securing the family's imprimatur was crucial to establishing Conway's credibility, and in typical fashion he parlayed their approval into an endorsement of his own standing as an adopted Concordian: the dedication to *Emerson at Home and Abroad* would read, "To Mrs. Ralph Waldo Emerson, and her children, Ellen, Edith and Edward, who made kindly and beautiful my second birthplace." In fact, he had resided in his "second birthplace" for a mere seven months.[102]

The flow of letters and information across the Atlantic began almost immediately after Emerson's death: Conway gave Edward Emerson clippings and testimonials sent to him by his father's British friends and asked in return that Ellen and Edward write out for him the details of their father's final days,[103] which they did. A few old friends like Le Baron Russell of Plymouth provided reminiscences and family information.[104] But if Conway solicited further information from the family members themselves after their first flurry of letters in late spring, there is no evidence that he got much of it. It was a busy time for the Emersons: Edward and his family took an extended vacation in the Adirondacks, and he was closing up his medical practice for good by the end of July 1882.[105] Edith was recovering at Milton and the Forbes family compound on Naushon Island after giving birth to her eighth child, Alexander, on May 14. The dutiful Ellen remained in Concord, tending to the household, welcoming the seemingly endless stream of visitors, and looking after her grieving mother. Housekeeping and caring for Lidian occupied most of her waking hours. "If I attend to my work I omit her," Ellen told her sister, with a hint of weariness. "If I attend to her I do nothing else." Cabot was hounding Ellen for material, as was Norton; royalty arrangements for the Emerson-Carlyle correspondence awaited her decision; by August she faced a "huge pile" of unanswered letters.[106] In short, Emerson's children would have had little room in their busy lives to help Conway get his facts straight. And there is little in the correspondence to suggest that Conway asked them to.

Instead of researching, in the summer of 1882 he was already busy writing and arranging publication for his new book. He mined "Emerson and His Friends" for the material for "Concordia," pulling entire sections from the first to second,[107] and by early August he was ready to submit a draft to English publishers. What happened next would severely limit the sales, and the effect, of *Emerson at Home and Abroad*. The likely choice of publisher would have been the firm of Chatto & Windus, the successor to John Camden Hotten that had brought out most of Conway's work since the mid-1870s, including his biography of Carlyle just a year earlier. Chatto & Windus was an active and respected firm. But Conway's relationship with Andrew Chatto was strained, for he had begun to blame his publisher for the flagging sales of his books. Conway's *Carlyle* (1881) appeared too late to sell well, after Froude's edition of the *Reminiscences* had already captured all the attention, and Ireland told Conway heatedly that he should have taken the book to Kegan Paul or Macmillan instead.[108] A year later, in 1882, when Conway was shopping the manuscript of his Emerson biography, the situation with his publisher had gotten worse. Sales of Conway's books had flattened—an accounting in August 1882 showed that Conway *owed* his publisher £2—and while Conway's letters to Chatto & Windus do not survive, the firm's responses to him imply that he continually complained of their failure to promote his work.[109] Conway's complaints were not completely unfounded: when Conway's *Carlyle* appeared, the firm seemed uninterested in promoting it, doling out only eight review copies to the press.[110] In the mid-summer of 1882, his Emerson manuscript nearly ready, Conway bypassed his usual publisher and approached instead the powerful London firm of Macmillan and Company.

Conway's dealings with Macmillan, ultimately unsuccessful, are a case study in the frustrations and deceptions of the Victorian publishing world. He brought a partial manuscript to the firm on or about August 2, 1882, the day he received Chatto & Windus's disappointing royalty report; one can easily imagine Conway tossing the crumpled accounting on the carpet and snatching up his manuscript as he stamped out the door on his way to Macmillan. Perhaps he had been too upset to present the manuscript clearly, since later the same day he sent Macmillan a letter clarifying the state of the manuscript and calling attention to the book's eventual strengths. In his most sober business prose, Conway listed points for Macmillan's reviewer to keep in mind:

1. That the opening chapter, which I call "Vigil" is only blocked out, and that I have much work to do on it in order to give it finish, and do away with everything that might seem of doubtful taste.
2. That I have yet to use in the latter part of the book nine important letters of Emerson to myself & my friends.
3. That there will be an important chapter on "Emerson in England" made up of things not found in his "English Traits" or other volumes. Persons in the country here, at whose houses he visited—the Brays of Coventry, the Flowers of Stratford, etc.—have given me interesting accounts for my book. When Emerson was last here I saw much of him, and we visited Wales together, where I had conversations with him of great interest.
4. There are to be given my personal recollections of student days in Concord, and subsequent residence there, which will include personal reminiscences of Hawthorne, Thoreau, and others.[111]

Setting aside his frankness about the "doubtful taste" of his first chapter, Conway is clearly marketing his book's unique selling points: unpublished correspondence, new anecdotes about Emerson's English visits, and first-hand testimony about Emerson and his neighbors. Again, Conway highlights and exaggerates his authority as a Concord insider: he was never a student there, and his "subsequent residence" in the town was brief.

Hoping to seal the deal, on August 4, 1882, Conway and his friend William Dean Howells visited Macmillan personally "to talk about my 'Concordia' which Osgood wants to publish."[112] But little more than a week later Conway got disappointing news: Macmillan turned down the book, apparently because it was too short. "I think now I won't send it to any other publisher till it is nearer complete," he wrote his wife from Belgium. "There is as yet no sketch of Thoreau, or Hawthorne, or Margt Fuller in it."[113] And so he added material on Emerson's circle and resubmitted the manuscript to Macmillan just four days later. But a day afterward, for the second time in a week, Macmillan again rejected Conway's manuscript, this time because it was too long. "Macmillan says that my valuable information about Emerson is mixed up with too much that would not is not [sic] of equal importance &c but is very grateful for the offer &c," he told Ellen dryly on August 18. "I have decided to revise the whole thing when I get home."[114]

Conway's interest in Macmillan was eminently practical. It was rapidly becoming a leading literary house in England, and there was a natural and lucrative connection with Emerson: it had arranged to issue the forthcoming Riverside Edition of Emerson's *Collected Works* in England. Nearly a year before he approached Macmillan about his Emerson biography, in fact, Conway had inquired about the publication schedule for the *Works*. "If it is to be postponed until next year I should like to make a suggestion, and to see you for a few moments about the publication," he wrote Macmillan in October 1881.[115] There is no further record of their conversation, but it is intriguing to speculate that Conway may have offered "Concordia" or some version of it as the introduction to Macmillan's English edition. If so, he was refused in that as well. The introduction to the British edition, delayed until 1884, was written by the prolific editor and journalist John Morley, who was also general editor of Macmillan's English Men of Letters series. (Not until 1907, the year Conway died, did Macmillan include an Emerson volume in its English Men of Letters series, written by the American academic George Edward Woodberry.)

In the end, it was Howells who interested the Boston publisher James R. Osgood in the project—albeit well after Conway assured his wife that Osgood had already accepted it—by convincing the publisher that Conway's "book about Emerson and Concord" was not gossip but "seriously and valuably reminiscential of the place and the man" and included personal information supplied by the family. (Shrewdly playing all sides against each other, Howells also told Osgood that Macmillan and Holt both wanted the book, and that Conway hoped for $1,500 but would sell the rights for less).[116] Osgood thus became the American publisher of two early biographies of Emerson, Cooke's and Conway's, as well as of Norton's edition of the Emerson-Carlyle correspondence. But finding an English publisher for Conway's book was a much greater challenge. Turned away by Macmillan, and his bridges burned at Chatto & Windus, Conway contracted with the smaller and more general London publisher Trübner and Company, whose varied catalogue included expurgated editions of Whitman (which Conway himself helped to arrange), but also such diverse and arcane titles as *A Simplified Grammar of the Roumanian Language*; Sir Edwin Arnold's *Pearls of the Faith, or, Islam's Rosary, Being the Ninety-nine Beautiful Names of Allah*; and a series of editions for the Early English Text Society. Conway could not have been cheered by the prospect of publishing with Trübner. The company worked closely with Osgood on some projects—a plus—but Trübner cut close bargains with its authors, and the firm could be tepid in its promotion of literary works, as Conway well knew from the firm's dealings with his friend Howells.[117] Nonetheless, his Emerson biography appeared with the Trübner imprint in the fall of 1882 as part of a series with the unpromising title "The English and Foreign Philosophical Library," which Trübner issued jointly with Osgood.

Conway's "Concordia," now retitled *Emerson at Home and Abroad*, was published in Boston on November 18, 1882, with an initial American printing of 1,500 copies.[118] Trübner's English edition appeared almost concurrently with the American edition;[119] it was listed in the London *Times's* "New Books and New Editions" column on November 22, 1882, though the book bore an 1883 copyright date. The English edition was identical in content to the American but typeset separately from it, on somewhat larger pages that made the book appealingly shorter.

As numerous reviewers would point out, there was a miscellaneous, impressionistic, slapdash feel to the book, which no doubt reflected Conway's hasty behind-the-scenes revisions as he rewrote and shaped his decade-old "Emerson and His Friends" to suit Macmillan, to position his book in a competitive marketplace of Emersonian recollections, and to race against the imminent publication of the Emerson-Carlyle correspondence and the Riverside Edition of Emerson's *Works*—books that might have stimulated sales of his biography but might just as easily have depressed them. Tellingly, two American reviews both called *Emerson at Home and Abroad* "Conwayish," though for quite opposite reasons. To the Boston *Commonwealth* (Conway's old newspaper, which he had coedited with Frank Sanborn in the 1860s), the term was positive: the reviewer found the book charming and entertaining.[120] To the *Christian Register*, the by-now conservative weekly of American Unitarianism, the term was negative, referring not only to the mawkish chapter titles (Emerson's early liberalism was discussed in chapter 10, "The Wail of the Century," where Conway calls Unitarianism "Christianity made easy" [Conway *EHA*, 93]) but also to Conway's tendency toward emotionalism, unattributed borrowing, inaccuracy, digression, and block quotation. "Much that is not in quotation marks will not be new to many," said the *Register*, awkwardly but pointedly.[121]

Emerson at Home and Abroad supports both charges of "Conwayism," negative and positive. As the title suggests, Conway casts a wide net, though in fact his attention to Emerson "abroad" is minimal, much of it the result of Ireland's reminiscences. (The title was likely an attempt to generate sales in England.) Of its 30 chapters, the first 20 are largely given over to those who influenced Emerson or the contexts in which Emerson's thinking is best understood. In the chapter "Culture," for instance, Conway develops Emerson's debt to Milton, Carlyle, and Wordsworth; in other chapters, the formative contexts of Harvard, of liberal religion, and of his friendships in England. Among the most original are the chapters on Emerson's debt to women. Claiming that Emerson's heart and mind "drew to him the trust of women" (Conway *EHA*, 88), Conway outlines the sustaining influence not only of family members like Ruth Haskins Emerson, Mary Moody Emerson, and Sarah Bradford but also of later friends such as Margaret Fuller, Elizabeth Palmer Peabody, and Mary Rotch. He faithfully recounts the major literary achievements through the 1840s, positing Emerson always against empty convention. Still, the biographical chapters dealing with Emerson's first 50 years—his ministry, his early lecturing, his marriages and the death of young Waldo, and the publications of *Nature*, *Essays I*, *Essays II*, *Poems*, and *Representative Men*—these chapters add little to what was known already in 1882. Derivative or not, Conway's biographical chapters paid significant attention to the details of Emerson's personal life and professional career. But, thickened by pages of context, they are history at second hand, for Conway did not know Emerson personally until 1853.

In place of historical reliability, in these chapters Conway offers the sort of hero worship and bombast his critics hooted at, as well as the sometimes overpowering presence of Conway himself and a tendency toward digression that occasionally leaves Emerson out for pages at a time. Conway's preface, "A Vigil"—which William Sowder calls "one of the most embarrassing chapters in English literature"[122]—encapsulates not only Conway's intimate connection to the man who "changed my world and me" (Conway *EHA*, 4) but also the stylistic and emotional excesses that made reading Conway's book such a chore. For instance: Conway begins with a refusal to acknowledge Emerson's passing; he clutches a tiny evergreen bough plucked from a sprig meant for Emerson's casket and in a mawkish apostrophe wills it to bring Emerson back to life:

> Is this bit of evergreen, already dust, all the Amen Nature can give to the faith of its greatest heart? Ye pines and oaks of Sleepy Hollow, awake! Wrestle, as Herakles for Alcestis, grapple with Death for your poet and lover! Search with every rootlet for the seed of that brain, and lift it again to upper air! (Conway *EHA*, 2)

While Conway himself worried in his letter to Macmillan about the "doubtful taste" of "A Vigil," the chapters that follow are fraught with the same stylistic excesses and interpretive dead ends. Little concerned with Emerson's literary achievement, Conway proposes him as a religious and philosophical rebel both above the world and fully engaged in it. If on the one hand Emerson is the "born believer" temperamentally incapable of skepticism (Conway *EHA*, 128), on the other hand Conway depicts him as the rough-and-tumble iconoclast whose work brought down "the sanctities, sacraments, symbols, of an exhausted revelation" (Conway *EHA*, 174). Conway's interpretive generalizations tend toward the mercurial and honorific, such as this one about Emerson's early essays: "Emerson's theology changed to a spiritual positivism, and then to a poetical philosophy" (Conway *EHA*, 108). It was the sort of fuzziness that Victorian readers found least appealing about Emerson himself. Similarly, Conway's tropes run the gamut from the bombastic to the inept. Reflecting the Victorian vogue for Arthurian legend, for instance, he portrays the religious struggles of the Transcendental controversy as a modern quest for the Holy Grail, with Andrews Norton depicted as a fallen Arthur and Emerson himself as "our virginal Sir Galahad in America" (Conway *EHA*, 175). And finally, though its presence in the book is easy to exaggerate, there is Conway's own preoccupation with himself as the consummate insider, always at the elbow of Emerson, Carlyle, Theodore Parker, Elizabeth Peabody. After his synecdochical address to the pine bough, he turns abruptly to name-dropping: "Once, as I walked with John Stuart Mill alone, he questioned me concerning Emerson" (Conway *EHA*, 2).[123] The rest of "A Vigil" is devoted to

Conway's earliest relationship with Emerson, and much of *Emerson at Home and Abroad* reflects the closeness of that friendship. At its worst, the book is maudlin, imprecise, reverential, and larded with quotes.

But if the biography suffers from Conway's intimacy with his subject, that is also the source of its great strength—what Howells called its "reminiscential" quality. Its final chapter, "Lethe," recounts Emerson's decline to death from the perspective of Conway's last two visits to Concord in 1875 and 1880—the sadness of Emerson's mental failure barely compensated for by his cheerfulness, aphasia just another word for serenity. For all his excesses elsewhere in the book, no other of the early biographers wrote with such restraint and candor about Emerson's last years. Throughout the biography, Conway's deft personal touch illuminates Emerson as much as his self-indulgent excesses sometimes obscure him. "Lessons for the Day" (chapter 22), studded with Emersonian aphorisms, traces his progress from a "dreamy and visionary" poet to "the most helpful teacher of his generation" (Conway *EHA*, 213, 225). "Concordia" (chapter 23), likely the centerpiece of Conway's original study, develops Emerson's sympathetic relationship with his town and townsfolk. "The Python" (chapter 27) depicts the heroic Emerson and his abolitionism. Even the supposedly digressive chapters on Brook Farm, on the Hawthornes, on Thoreau—which Conway might have expanded in an attempt to please Macmillan—contextualize Emerson and define him by his opposites. And "The Diadem of Days" (chapter 29), apparently a catchall for anecdotes Conway could not fit elsewhere, is an impressionistic development of personality; here we see Emerson in his garden, swimming at Walden Pond, alternately grave and playful as he accompanies his townsfolk on a huckleberrying expedition. Through Conway we hear Emerson discoursing on health, advising a workman on a broken plough, offering practical advice for the spiritually lost—even offering the "little wayside surprises" of his sense of humor (Conway *EHA*, 369), which was so subtle that Emerson himself was often bewildered when people laughed at his jokes.

The net effect of Conway's personal approach to Emerson, once we get beyond the purple prose and self-serving posturing, is to humanize Emerson by placing him always in the company of others. Like Ireland, Conway offers up an anecdotal account of Emerson's personality—the manifestation of character in the world of affairs. Always the emphasis is on Emerson's influence: he is the intellectual leader of antislavery who "invariably spoke the right and serviceable word" and "gave leaders their texts and the rank and file their watchwords" (Conway *EHA*, 309), the good citizen of Concord who "sought no morose solitude" but "was by nature given to hospitality" (Conway *EHA*, 235). Unlike the noble loner of popular opinion, here is Emerson the social animal—sometimes driven into solitude because his idealism outstripped the ability of his fellows to understand it, but ever the man in the world, possessed of "as much practical sagacity as genius" (Conway *EHA*, 302). Conway may have abandoned the titles of his work-in-progress—"Emerson and His Friends" and "Concordia"—but he retained their essential emphasis on community, social relations, and progress.

Given his familiarity with Emerson and the exuberance with which he pressed his case, why did Conway's version of Emerson get such a lukewarm reception among readers and reviewers? It is tempting to see Conway's depiction of a vibrant, personable, and socially engaged Emerson as out of step with prevailing cultural views of him. Just as likely, though, *Emerson at Home and Abroad* was overlooked because of a complex of personal and business circumstances that had little to do with either taste or ideology. "Conwayish" had come to be a derisive adjective, a vestige of the ill will that followed the man whose political blunder during the Civil War delighted his enemies and embarrassed his friends. Nor was the reception of *Emerson at Home and Abroad* helped much even by some of its early supporters, who tended to balance praise for the book with apologies for Conway's well-known excesses as a writer. The reviewer for *Harper's New Monthly Magazine*, for example, thought *Emerson at Home and Abroad* a "very generous and genial sketch" but blasted Conway as "unduly fond of displaying his own egoisms [and] too intent upon parading his own cynical and arrogant skepticism."[124] Even Conway's friend and fellow abolitionist Thomas Wentworth Higginson, at work himself on a forthcoming biography of Margaret Fuller, recognized in Conway's book a host of problems: "a certain exuberance of material, some neglect of arrangement, and an occasional want of minute accuracy in details."[125] What Higginson excused so delicately, the religious periodicals seized on. The *Southern Presbyterian Review* for April 1883 sneered at Conway's "erratic genius" and his "multifarious intellectual and 'spiritual' vagaries"[126]; the *Academy's* reviewer thought him insulting to Christianity in his reverence for Emerson as a "new Messiah."[127]

If Conway was disheartened by such criticism, he might also have been wary of those who praised him. Likely the first review appeared in England's *National Reformer* (December 3, 1882, and January 14, 1883), the organ of radical "Secularism" whose founder, Charles Bradlaugh, had been famously denied a seat in Parliament in 1881 because he refused to swear an oath on the Bible. It was Bradlaugh who wrote the laudatory review in the *Reformer* that opens, "If we cannot make our readers eager to read this book it will not be for want of will; we have friendly feeling for the author and reverent admiration for his subject."[128] Conway did not profit by the endorsement of England's most notorious atheist; neither, likely, did Emerson.

The reaction of the Emerson family was, like the published reviews, mixed. Lidian and Ellen Emerson received a copy of the book in Concord just before Christmas 1882 and, according to Ellen, her mother pored over it for a month, enjoying the "loving spirit" of it. Ellen herself told Conway she found the book "easy and pleasant to read."[129] Edith Emerson Forbes read her copy "with much pleasure": "There is much in it that I am glad to have said and preserved, and it is always most pleasant to read what is written by one who regards Father with love for his character not merely with admiration for his intellect."[130] Edward and Annie Emerson read it in early May 1883 and were "increasingly pleased and are very glad that the work has been written."[131]

Their friendship with the Conways notwithstanding, however, the Emerson children were dismayed by the book's inaccuracies. Though the London *Athenaeum*'s sympathetic reviewer called it "a little hastily put together"[132] and Higginson excused Conway's errors as "mostly such as would naturally be made by one writing in England about American affairs,"[133] in fact the book is riddled with factual mistakes, including the embarrassing misstatement that Edward had been wounded in the Civil War (Conway *EHA*, 313). Edward's failure to see combat, he told Conway testily after the book came out, "though it was at my parents' desire, who distrusted my strength," was nevertheless "a sore point" to him.[134] Ellen wrote Conway with a litany of other errors: Ellen Tucker Emerson, Waldo's first wife, was entombed in Roxbury, not in Concord; Dr. Francis's first name was Convers, not Conners; Mary Rotch had no daughter; and so forth.[135] When friends asked her about the dependability of Conway's book, Ellen confessed to her sister, "I told them I saw much that was true, much of which I couldn't know whether true or not, and much that wasn't true."[136]

While Conway's expressionistic approach limited interest in his book, *Emerson at Home and Abroad* was finally a casualty less of censure than neglect. There seem to be at least two reasons why, both of them having to do with the economics of book publishing. Ireland, the consummate literary businessman, believed he had isolated one reason. "You bring us very near the Man, make us see his features, & listen to his voice, as those golden sentences of his fall from him like Grecian pearls to be stored up for ever," Ireland told Conway in late December 1882. But he despaired that such a subtle and substantial treatment could compete with the travel narratives, popular novels, and "'paste & scissors' biographies" crowding the review pages. "It is disgusting, degrading & damnable,—& my blood boils when I think of it," Ireland fumed. "Emerson, the Author of his age—must be brushed aside for *these*!! . . . These editors are conceited, ignorant jackasses who do not know the works & worth of men such as Emerson. They have heard of him, as a Yankee Essayist & that is all."[137]

A second reason involves not taste but timing: as much as Conway tried to rush his book into print, its publication late in 1882 quickly put it in competition with Norton's edition of *The Correspondence of Thomas Carlyle and Ralph Waldo Emerson*, which appeared in Boston and London in February 1883. Published by Conway's own American publisher, James R. Osgood, the *Correspondence* went through three American printings by May 1883.[138] From its first appearance, the Emerson-Carlyle letters monopolized the attention of reviewers and readers alike, perhaps owing to the still-fresh debate over Froude's editing of Carlyle. In fact, 1883 was a banner year generally for Emerson studies. Reviews of the *Correspondence* dominated the magazines through the summer, after which attention turned to the first volumes of Cabot's long-awaited Riverside Edition and then in late 1883 to Matthew Arnold's inflammatory lecture on Emerson. This intense attention to Emerson's work and reputation effectively crowded out Ireland's and Conway's biographies, which sputtered in the reviewers' columns after February 1883 and all but disappeared from them by summer. Ironically, the fault for Conway's neglect was partly his own. At the same time Conway was shepherding *Emerson at Home and Abroad* through the press, he was also at work on a heavily illustrated gift volume entitled *Travels in South Kensington, with Notes on Decorative Art and Architecture in England*, which appeared simultaneously in England with the Emerson biography, both published by Trübner. The firm may well have been more interested in promoting a gift book than a biography. In any event, Trübner was noticeably lax in advertising its new list. *Emerson at Home and Abroad* was announced in the "new books" column of the London *Times* only twice in November 1882 and once in December, a time when other publishers typically repeated their ads several times a week in anticipation of holiday sales. In the United States, James R. Osgood was somewhat more proactive. On an undated advertising card, Cooke's and Conway's biographies are announced together, with Conway's accompanied by an editorial blurb touting his long acquaintance with Emerson and other Concord luminaries such as Hawthorne and Thoreau.[139]

Osgood's advertising is telling in another way: physically, at least, it pits Cooke's intellectual biography against Conway's very personal one, for the books appear on opposite sides of the card. By the spring of 1883, a year after his death, Waldo Emerson was represented by three quite different biographers: Cooke, Ireland, and Conway—each useful in his own way. As one reviewer pointed out, "it is not easy to say which should be accorded the palm."[140] But none of them, despite their several merits, would exert much influence on Emerson's reputation. Partly, that can be explained by the notable faults of each book; partly, by the vagaries and accidents of their publication histories. Partly, too, these earliest of Emerson's biographers operated in a transitional period where the cultural signals were contradictory at best. When Ireland and Conway first began their biographical work, in 1870, the English critic Robert Goodbrand was suggesting "a new kind of biography"—"a biography with a passionate love and an enthusiastic admiration of the subject of it, in which, nevertheless, there should be an equally strong feeling not only of failure in the close, but of imperfection and dependence at every point."[141] Two decades later, in 1893, Leslie Stephen would call for the biographer to function as a mere narrator, the "connecting wire" who puts the subject at one end of the telephone and the reader at the other.[142] Passionate engagement or reportorial objectivity? Ireland and Conway stood firmly for the first at a time when the genre was shifting toward the second. Closeness to Emerson, on which they based their credibility as biographers, was more and more seen as a biographer's fault; reminiscence, on which they based their method, was becoming, in Stephen's words, "the last new terror of life."[143] Their discipleship earned them high marks for "interest" but low marks for accuracy, at a time when facts counted for more than impressions. Had Ireland and Conway published "Emerson and His Friends" in 1870, their work would have been in the mainstream of thinking about the genre. Barely a decade later, their assumptions about biography and biographers were already slipping out of public favor, and with them, their depiction of Emerson himself.

FOUR

Diagnosing the Gentle Iconoclast

Dr. Holmes on Emerson

⁓

OLIVER WENDELL HOLMES's *Ralph Waldo Emerson* appeared in December 1884, the fourth major biography of Emerson in three years and the seventh volume in Houghton, Mifflin's American Men of Letters series. It was a quick and documentable success, at least measured by its brisk sales, which catapulted it within its first month well past any competing biography of Emerson—indeed, well past any other volume in the AML series, before it or after.[1] Even so, Holmes himself readily admitted the book's shortcomings. In a letter to Franklin B. Sanborn just a month after its publication, Holmes acknowledged his factual mistakes, while shrugging them off with his typical affability: "they are just such scraps that critics live on when they have nothing else[,] like the bite of old shoes that starving shipwrecked folks live on, for want of beef-steaks." And it was true, Holmes also conceded, that he had downplayed Emerson's reformist activities—particularly abolitionism, as readers had already pointed out. "I have no reason to complain of my critics," Holmes told Sanborn. "I know very well my task was not a difficult, but an impossible one—that of satisfying readers each of whom had already formed his personal estimate of Emerson, from some of whom I must widely differ, with out one of whom I should be in perfect accord. But I meant to be fair and my book has been more generously received than I expected."[2]

One reason Holmes's expectations were so low was the widespread perception—even Holmes seemed to believe it—that his lifelong skepticism toward Transcendentalism rendered him unable to write a book about Emerson with sympathy and understanding. Holmes acknowledged being "a late comer as an admirer of the Concord Poet and Philosopher,"[3] a judgment echoed both by early reviewers of his book, who often expressed polite surprise at how well it turned out, and by cronies of Emerson like Rockwood Hoar, who privately thought Holmes's mind "not commensurate" with Emerson's.[4] The opposition of Emerson and Holmes is as persistent as it is wrong-headed. If Eleanor M. Tilton, Holmes's best modern biographer, burlesques the case when she says Emerson's admirers considered Holmes a "satanic materialist,"[5] a belief in the essential incompatibility of the two New England Brahmins was nevertheless commonplace by the end of the nineteenth century. Holmes's nephew by marriage, John Torrey Morse Jr., who wrote the standard life-and-letters biography of him, put the case typically in 1896: "Emerson wrote of religions, Holmes wrote of creeds; Emerson dealt with Man, Holmes concerned himself with men; Emerson found his topics in idealities, Holmes found his in things concrete."[6] As assiduously as Victorian America nudged the idea of Emerson ever closer to Holmesean respectability, historians a century later have driven the two men apart again, with Emerson lionized and Holmes kicked to the literary curb—a prolific but unimaginative poet-for-hire who saw the world with a wry skepticism but meekly knuckled under to the status quo.[7] In the words of one recent intellectual historian, Holmes "had all the equipment for debunking convention and, for the most part, no impulse to use it."[8]

In part the misperception derives from Holmes's own studied diffidence about his talents as a writer and thinker. A medical doctor and professor of anatomy, he cultivated a reputation for being "outside of the charmed circle drawn around the scholars and poets of Cambridge and Concord" and confessed to Emerson himself that he had "nothing to do with thoughts that roll beyond a certain width of orbit."[9] But there is something disingenuous about Holmes's claims to outsider status, for the record of his half-century friendship with Emerson paints another picture. Sons of ministers and Harvard, close in age and cultural geography, they enjoyed a longstanding acquaintance, their lives intertwined in pervasive if intermittent ways that remind us how small the neighborhood of Boston was. Holmes's brother John was Emerson's pupil in Cambridge in the early 1820s;[10] Emerson's son Edward was Holmes's pupil at Harvard's medical school a half-century later. Waldo's brother Charles attended Harvard in the class of 1828, just a year ahead of Holmes; upon Charles's death in 1836 Holmes mourned him in verse as "too fair to die!"[11] Holmes's undergraduate classmates included James Freeman Clarke and William Henry Channing, second-generation Transcendentalists and protégées of Emerson.[12] When fate placed Holmes and Emerson in France during the summer of 1833, one to study medicine, the other to escape the trauma of his wife's death, Emerson sought out Holmes and visited him in his Paris apartments.[13]

Increasingly, the dynamic new culture of literary celebrity brought the two authors together at literary events and anniversaries, beginning with the 1837 Phi Beta Kappa ceremonies at Harvard, where Holmes provided the after-dinner poem and Emerson delivered the "American Scholar" address that Holmes later recalled as "our intellectual Declaration of Independence" (Holmes *RWE*, 115).[14] Emerson routinely included Holmes on the list of those receiving complimentary copies of his books; and from 1857 on, for nearly two decades, the two met regularly in the dining room of Boston's Parker House at monthly gatherings of the Saturday Club.

No other fact so well illustrates the temperamental affinities between Emerson and Holmes than this celebrated gathering of some of Boston's leading civic and literary figures on the fourth Saturday of each month for conversation, cigars, and a good meal. According to Edward Waldo Emerson, still the best historian of the group, the Saturday Club was his father's brainchild, a corrective to his "too constant association with philosophers and reformers." In Edward's telling, his father longed for a place "where lonely scholars, poets, and naturalists . . . might find a welcome resting-place when they came to the city."[15] This sentimental account of Waldo Emerson's yearning for the society of like-minded men and women is perhaps too convenient; as in *Emerson in Concord*, Edward's agenda included portraying his father as down-to-earth and companionable. But to dismiss Emerson's relationship with Holmes as merely "social rather than spiritual"[16] is to underestimate the importance of camaraderie to Emerson—what Robert D. Richardson Jr. has convincingly argued was his "constant hunger for village society, for 'association' and friendship."[17] More than just cordial, the relationship between Holmes and Emerson seems to have led them to a genuine respect for each other's work. In the beginning, admittedly, their mutual admiration was guarded: in 1846, at the inauguration of Edward Everett as Harvard's president, Emerson found Holmes's commemorative poem "a bright sparkle" in an event he otherwise considered torturously dull.[18] Too, the genteel language of social intercourse strikes a modern ear as insincere or glib. But if Emerson's praise at Holmes's fiftieth birthday celebration sounds pro forma—"a Civilizer whom every man & woman secretly thanks"—there is yet something heartfelt in Emerson's private expressions of his admiration for Holmes.[19] Around 1868, for instance, he recorded in his journal a list of men whose conversation he found most inspiring; among them was Holmes, who "has some rare qualities."[20] Three years later, he included Holmes in a list headed

"My Men," alongside Thoreau, Alcott, and Carlyle.[21] Likewise, if Holmes often couched his esteem in the numbing bombast of the Victorian compliment (in 1869 he thanked Emerson for "reach[ing] the springs of thought and action and call[ing] out all the bravery and nobleness of the souls open to their influences"[22]), when he had no need to stand on ceremony Holmes confessed to finding Emerson a "remarkable being."[23] Latecomer though Holmes was, his admiration for Emerson had a long foreground.

This is not to deny some major intellectual disagreements that would eventually help to shape Holmes's biography. Like a number of other Northerners in Emerson's circle of friends (notably Hawthorne), Holmes was a Unionist, not an abolitionist, and in March 1850 he joined nearly a thousand other Bostonians in signing a letter supporting Daniel Webster's position in the Compromise of 1850. Infuriated, in his journal Emerson called the signers "ideots," a judgment he toned down to "aged & infirm people."[24] For his part, Holmes had little patience with the airy speculations of the Transcendental group or the peculiar argot of New England Idealism. At Harvard's Phi Beta Kappa anniversary gathering in 1843, soon after Emerson had taken over as the *Dial*'s editor, Holmes lampooned the magazine's contributors in "An After Dinner Poem":

> With uncouth words they tire their tender lungs,
> The same bald phrases on their hundred tongues:
> "Ever" "The Ages" in their page appear,
> "Alway" the bedlamite is called a "Seer";
> On every leaf the "earnest" sage may scan,
> Portentous bore! their "many-sided" man, —
> A weak eclectic, groping vague and dim,
> Whose every angle is a half-starved whim,
> Blind as a mole and curious as a lynx,
> Who rides a beetle, which he calls a "Sphinx."[25]

Clearly both Emerson and Holmes entertained doubts about the other's political and literary affiliations. Nonetheless, they managed to find a little to tolerate about each other, much to like, and a surprising amount to admire, not only personally but intellectually. In a remarkable comment preserved among his typed notes for the biography, under the expansive heading "Intuition, Mysticism, Obscurity, Mathematics," Holmes writes:

> Intuition is all very well, so far as Kant's conditions are concerned. But time and space and abstract right and wrong, me and not me, subjective

and objective do not go very far, "categorical imperative" and all that are convenient but they are new handles to old tools that we have used all our lives. . . . We may look inwardly to find an empty chamber or seven devils or divine illumination or the call to child murder.[26]

The passage captures Holmes's ambivalent reaction to Emerson's idealism: a profound fear that introspection might reveal emptiness or evil, balanced by a willingness to concede that the terminology of Transcendentalism was merely a semantic innovation, "new handles to old tools that we have used all our lives."[27] Despite his skepticism, Holmes was willing to contend with Emerson on his own terms (quite literally), not simply reject him. Over the years, Holmes recognized in Emerson a practical idealism that approached his own. In his late poem "At the Saturday Club," written the same year he published his biography of Emerson, Holmes memorializes Emerson as "a wingèd Franklin, sweetly wise, / Born to unlock the secrets of the skies" and praises his "soaring nature, ballasted with sense."[28] Clearly it was a recognition of Emerson's continuity with an enlightened American past, as well as a reminder of how Franklin's scientific inquiries were transformed in the spiritual "secrets" the Transcendentalists explored. In the biography, as we shall see, equating Franklin with Emerson would legitimize his "sagacity," reconfigure his intellectual lineage, and mitigate his idealism. But the equation also remade the Sage of Concord in Holmes's own pragmatic image—an Emerson who could build castles in the air and still put foundations underneath them.

— I —

Holmes's decision to undertake Emerson's biography in 1883, fifty years after the two men shared an expatriate visit in Paris, culminated a lifetime of negotiated understandings between two literary celebrities. In the end, though, it was not affection that motivated Holmes to memorialize Emerson, but a series of circumstances much more practical. As he entered his seventies, Holmes was vigorous, artistically productive, and in Tilton's words, "Boston's most accessible celebrity": the genial "Autocrat of the Breakfast-Table."[29] Though the federal census lists his occupation in 1880 as "retired physician," Holmes remained on the medical faculty at Harvard, lecturing in anatomy for seven months of the year. He, his wife Amelia, and three Irish servants lived comfortably at 296 Beacon Street in the fashionable new Back Bay neighborhood and summered north of the city in the seaside village of Beverly Farms, where he rented a house near the railway depot, across the street from the poet Lucy Larcom. In his advanced age Holmes retained both his energy and his cheerful outlook. As his nephew John Torrey Morse Jr. diplomatically put it, Holmes had always been "hard-working, but never really overworked."[30]

It was opportunity, not longevity or ill health, that enticed Holmes into retirement from Harvard in late 1882, the year of Emerson's death.[31] As Tilton makes clear, the timing was right. Weary of debates at the medical school over faculty governance and the admission of women,[32] he was eager to "spend whatever days are left me in literary pursuits," he wrote his friend S. Wier Mitchell in October. And there was another inducement: he had "very lately received a proposal from my publishers so tempting that I could not resist it."[33] As he told another friend, the new arrangements would free up his time to write and also be financially "very advantageous."[34]

In the century before Social Security, Medicare, pension plans, and IRAs, not even a celebrity retiree like Holmes could ignore the prospect of steady income. The proposal from his publisher, Houghton, Mifflin, that lured him from Harvard took several lucrative forms. One was the reissue of his best-loved (and best-selling) literary works, beginning barely a month after his retirement: *The Autocrat of the Breakfast-Table* with "illustrative notes" and a new preface by the author (November 1882), *The Poet at the Breakfast-Table* (January 1883), and *The Professor at the Breakfast-Table* (February 1883).[35] In addition, he agreed to increase his contributions to the *Atlantic*, whose new editor, Thomas Bailey Aldrich, had been begging him for material.[36] A publisher's announcement coinciding with his retirement promised that Holmes would write exclusively for the magazine in 1883—though as Tilton points out, he was too busy that year to provide Aldrich with much more than a few poems.[37]

In fact, Holmes's main project during his first years of retirement was his biography of Emerson,[38] the writing of which formed the third part of his new arrangement with Houghton, Mifflin.[39] The biography was part of the American Men of Letters series, inaugurated in late 1880 at the suggestion of Charles Dudley Warner. Intended to occupy a bibliographical middle ground between the thick, garishly bound "mug books" that fed the vanities of prosperous Americans and the ponderous editions of life-and-letters that entombed their subjects in what Edmund Gosse later called a "monstrous catafalque of two volumes (crown octavo),"[40] the AML joined a host of biographical series on both sides of the Atlantic that coalesced in 1882: not only Macmillan's English Men of Letters but similar ventures by the American publishers George P. Putnam's Sons, James R. Osgood,

Henry Holt and Company, and D. Appleton. The AML made no consistent claims about American authors, but like Macmillan's series it had clear nationalist aims. Houghton, Mifflin's 1899 catalogue, issued when the AML was nearly complete, claimed its volumes "not only treat of the career and attainments of the individual subjects, but give such account of the conditions of the literary life as to constitute, when taken together, a literary history of the United States."[41] There were more specifically literary agendas as well. As a series, the AML would champion the values of antebellum Romanticism against the corruptions of Realism, assert the development of American letters from their Colonial antecedents, and offer up a vision of "literary manliness" that disparaged sentimentality and valorized independence of thought.[42] Though some of the series' projected subjects were part of Houghton, Mifflin's stable of New England writers—Hawthorne, Thoreau, Longfellow, and of course Emerson—its editor Warner intended the AML "to represent the development of our literature in *all* its phases," geographically, historically, and generically.[43]

Along with these cultural goals, the AML of course also had commercial ones for the crowded and competitive market, and on this point, sometime in the late spring of 1881, corporate needs and Holmes's situation converged. By this time, as Casper puts it, Warner had already begun "[t]he double process of selection—picking the 'men of letters' who would be the series subjects and the 'men of letters' who would write their lives."[44] Emerson was not on the initial list of subjects in 1881, for the series would profile only deceased authors, but behind the scenes Warner was busy anticipating the inevitable and soliciting biographers whose names would sell books. The Holmes-Emerson match-up was a natural.[45] On June 19, 1881, Warner reported to H. O. Houghton that he had contacted Holmes, who was more than a year away from retirement. "Dr Holmes said neither yes nor no, but rather kindled to the idea of Emerson, and I regard the forecast as hopeful."[46] Three months later, though, Holmes was still dragging his feet, so Warner, about to leave for Europe, wrote him again:

> I need not say that I should go off in better spirits and probably be in
> less danger of sea-sickness if I knew you had made up your mind, at
> your leisure, to write the biographical study of Emerson for the Ameri-
> can Men of Letters Series. And yet I do not make it altogether a ques-
> tion of humanity to myself. I am more and more anxious to have the
> series a worthy study of American literature, one that no American will
> be ashamed of.[47]

Left unsaid in this rhetoric of the personal and the patriotic was the enormous financial payoff from a book written by one New England icon about the life of another. A letter Warner began playfully ended up all business: "If you can give me a line of encouragement I shall go my way in peace."[48] Before he sailed, he visited Holmes in Beverly Farms and may have gotten a tentative yes, but a month afterward the deal was off again, as Holmes began to feel "the warnings of breaking down from over work" and gave up the project.[49]

For the next year and a half, Warner, Frank Sanborn (who wrote the Thoreau volume for AML), and Henry Houghton badgered Holmes to accept the offer. Even abroad, Warner worried whether Holmes had yet decided to write the "biographical essay?" He wrote Houghton from Salzburg in the summer of 1882: "It would not interfere at all with the ponderous and full biography which is to come in due time."[50] Finally, in February 1883, following the reissue of the *Breakfast-Table* volumes and after consulting with Cabot and with Edward Emerson, Holmes said yes to the Emerson biography.[51] It had been a frustrating 18-month courtship for Warner and Houghton. But for Holmes, the delay was worth it. For years he had enjoyed an annuity arrangement with his publishers—first with James R. Osgood and Company, later with Houghton, Mifflin. Under this arrangement, which was not unusual at the time for established authors, Holmes received a retainer guaranteeing the publisher exclusive rights to his work and assuring Holmes a steady income regardless of sales. From 1877 through 1882, Holmes's annuity was $1,000. But on December 1, 1882, three days after he gave his final lecture at the medical school, Holmes's contract with Houghton, Mifflin was renegotiated and his annuity quadrupled, to $4,000, on the condition that for the next three years Holmes "write exclusively" for the firm.[52] In a classic case of win-win, Houghton, Mifflin got its big-name author for the Emerson biography—and Holmes got the money for a new summer house. He moved from the noisy location near the Beverly Farms railroad depot, where autograph-seekers made a beeline for his front door, to a grander, more secluded Victorian "cottage" on Hale Street, with a commanding view of the sea.[53] As it turned out, for the next two years the Emerson biography would keep him almost too busy to enjoy it.

— II —

Once he agreed to write Emerson's life, Holmes set to the task with workmanlike diligence. As he reported to his friend John O. Sargent, he spent the first half of 1883 "reading and studying to get at the true inwardness of this remarkable being and his world."[54] He seems to have turned first to Emerson's three earlier biographers, then to Emerson's writing. Among his five working notebooks at the Houghton Library—which appear to be preliminary to the writing, containing notes from other authors, reminders to consult certain printed sources, outlines of chapter titles—is one full of detailed columns collating the Cooke, Ireland, and Conway books.[55] In June he asked Houghton, Mifflin to send him copies of all of the Emerson works he lacked, almost half of the volumes in the new Riverside Edition. Significantly, by the time he began his Emerson biography Holmes did not own, and may not yet have read, the first and second series of *Essays*, *Representative Men*, and *English Traits*—nearly all of Emerson's most incisive early prose.[56] During the summer of 1883 he made at least two "pilgrimages" (his word) to Concord with Emerson's friend Rockwood Hoar as his guide. "What I want to do is to visit the 'Holy Places,'" he wrote Hoar on June 21, "—to get the hang of the localities—in a word to shade and color the mental outline I got during my last visit."[57] Visiting Concord gave Holmes a much-needed feel for Emerson's cultural landscape. For instance, he visited the "Bullet House" across Monument Street from the Old Manse, where a Revolutionary-era musket ball lay embedded in the siding, outlined in paint, and he wrote to Hoar, "Nothing left a more vivid impression on my mind than the white diamond with the dark spot in it. That made [the] Concord fight seem like yesterday's happenings."[58] He seems not to have stopped by the Emerson household while in Concord, at least not according to the otherwise attentive Ellen Emerson, who would certainly have recorded his visit in her letters. From the family he wanted not "shades and colors" of Concord but personal details, and those he would ask for later.

During the second half of the year, Holmes's research became more systematic and his attention even more focused. Mrs. Holmes was ailing by the summer of 1883 and required rest and quiet; her illness confined them both to Beverly Farms. (Holmes was asthmatic and disliked travel anyway.) Still, he admitted to Sargent, "If I tell the whole truth, I am pursued with the idea of the little book I am at work on and grudge even a single day away from my writing-desk"[59]; to James Russell Lowell he confessed, "I find the study of Emerson curiously interesting."[60] He had been reading Emerson's work and trying to make sense of it. The undated "Emerson Notes" at the Library of Congress start with Holmes's handwritten comments on and extracts from the eight volumes of prose in the Riverside Edition, organized by title in the order Emerson originally wrote them. Following these are typewritten notes on topics like "Birthplace" and

"Saturday Club," interspersed with Holmes's handwritten notations—some of them reminders ("See what E. says of clubs in Soc. and Solitude"), others personal observations ("E. likes Ossian. I saw a copy of it on his table"). By far the largest section are the notes labeled "Poetry," followed in size by "Preacher" and "Religion."[61] The book was shaping up. According to a penciled notation in his partial fair copy entitled "Emerson manuscript," also at the Library of Congress, Holmes completed a chapter called "Family History" (retitled "Introduction" in the finished book) by December 3, 1883. At intervals appear similar marks of his progress: on January 2 he wrote about the Dartmouth oration, on January 19 he wrote about *English Traits*, and so on, through March 4, 1884.[62] Though the fair copy lacks five of the final chapters, it contains drafts of eleven others, and its table of contents matches almost exactly the one in the finished book. Holmes clearly had the writing well in hand by the early spring of 1884.

Not until he had actually begun drafting did he correspond in earnest with Emerson's friends and family. Holmes had an aversion to letter writing. Besieged throughout his lifetime by correspondents asking for critiques, advice, and autographs, Holmes had developed a brevity that was famous among his friends, one of whom called him "not a man of letters, but a man of notes."[63] In his correspondence about Emerson, however, Holmes was garrulous, probing, and relentless. Judging by his surviving letters, his strategy was to ask for information only as the need arose in the particular chapter he was working on. Thus in December 1883, while Holmes was writing the chapter on Emerson's ancestry, Edward Emerson provided him family history.[64] In January 1884, when Holmes had moved on to Emerson's early career and acquaintances, Caroline Sturgis Tappan sent recollections of Emerson's wedding, his friendship with Fuller, and his opinions of Hawthorne and Thoreau.[65] The next month, Le Baron Russell of Plymouth reminisced about Emerson's marriage to Lidian and his supposed "spiritualism." (Russell insisted that "his mind was too well balanced to entertain that nonsense.")[66] And in March, Frank Sanborn gave Holmes part of his 1854 journal about walking to Walden with Emerson and promised to send him Whitman's account of his last meeting with him.[67] It was Cabot, though, now just beginning his own biography of Emerson, to whom Holmes sent the longest and most involved letters. For instance, on February 6, 1884, he wrote Cabot:

> There are many things I wish to ask you, but I hardly know how far I
> have any claim to tax your time and patience. I submit a few questions,
> hoping you may be able to answer them.

How far can Mr. Conway's list of Emerson's published works be depended on for the *date of writing*?

If the *publication* is an uncertain guide, is it possible to get a list of them all in the *true order of writing*?

Was Emerson acquainted at first hand with the great German Metaphysicians—with Kant, Fichte, Schelling, Hegel,—or did he go deeply into any one of them?

Did he ever get as far as Schopenhauer, and had he any opinion about his doctrines?

By what writers does it seem to you that he was most deeply influenced?

What books did he most affect in the later period of his life?

Do you recognize any distinct period or phases of intellectual life in his career?

To whom shall I go for particulars of his daily life—his visitors— his visits—his habits etc. Would Miss Ellen take questions kindly, or Dr Edward Emerson?

These are questions enough—I fear too many, but answer one or two of them if you can, and I shall be greatly obliged.

Very truly yours,

O. W. Holmes

Did Emerson ever take to mathematics or to logic, or would he follow long trains of thought in such books, say, as Edwards on the Will etc?[68]

Cabot answered every one of Holmes's questions—the next day.[69]

Letters like these reveal how tentatively Holmes approached Emerson's philosophical thinking and how unabashed he was about asking for help understanding it. What's more, the correspondence points out Holmes's practical problem, as Emerson's fourth biographer in three years, of saying something new about his celebrated subject. Even after a year of research, several chapters in draft, and two successful lectures on Emerson—a memorial address for the Massachusetts Historical Society in May 1882 and a talk on Emerson's poetry at the Century Club in April 1883—Holmes still felt as if he had "a blank page before him and a Publisher's demon behind him."[70] He asked his old Harvard classmate James Freeman Clarke, "Is it possible for you to write out for me any reminiscences of Emerson,—of the 'Transcendental' people and times, of E.'s relations with yourself—with Margaret Fuller?—anything not already before the public? . . . I find myself somewhat in the position of Carlyle's editor—threshing the thrice-beaten straw."[71] Later he wrote, "I am in want of something which has not already been used by Cooke, Conway and the rest," after Clarke sent along a few of Emerson's letters; "I should be thankful to be able to lard my lean page with these new documents."[72] To save time, he asked Houghton, Mifflin to recommend a good typist so he could dictate text.[73] But speed was not the problem: the problem was the abundance of existing published information about the Sage of Concord that made it difficult for him to come up with anything original and "fatally easy" simply to restate what had already been written.[74] For all his good humor, by the summer of 1884 Holmes was wearying of a book that seemed to be merely a recitation of common knowledge, with no end in sight.

What helped to bring the work to a close was a devastating family tragedy: the death of Edward Jackson (Ted) Holmes—always the witty, light-hearted younger son—who died on June 17, 1884, after a brief illness, at age 37.[75] By late June, Wendell and Amelia had retreated to their summer residence at Beverly Farms. Warner and Houghton were respectful of their grief, but deadlines were deadlines. "How far has Dr Holmes got on?" Warner asked Houghton, Mifflin barely two weeks after Edward's death. "He wrote me some time ago that he had sent the beginning to you."[76] The publisher answered by sending Warner proof of the first 152 pages of the book.[77]

In his grief Holmes sometimes found the Emerson biography a source of frustration. He complained to Warner in July, "Emerson's life and writings have been so *darned over* by biographers and critics that a new hand can hardly tell his own yarn from that of his predecessors, or one of theirs from another's."[78] Still, he immersed himself in routine, spending his summer reading and correcting copy, overtaking the printer by July, pushing Houghton, Mifflin to send him more proof, faster. By September he was hand-carrying copy from Beverly Farms to the Riverside Press in Cambridge and writing new material even as he proofread the old.[79] He worried that the speed would affect the quality of his work. "These Chapters have been written, or rewritten, at considerable intervals and are liable to have *repetitions*, if not carefully looked over in connection with each other," he warned Houghton, Mifflin—yet he appended to the top of his letter, "I send more copy today."[80] Sometime in the early fall, the entire book went to press, and by late fall Holmes had apparently seen it in boards. He wrote his publisher on December 4, 1884, "I am very much pleased with the *look* of the Emerson. I hope other people will like its insides."[81] A day later he received advance copies from the binder.[82] The book appeared for sale on December 10, in red cloth boards with gold lettering—the standard binding of the entire American Men of Letters series—and priced at $1.25.[83] Holmes's royalty was the standard 10 percent of the trade-list price, with a 50–50 split on the revenues from any selections or abridgements.[84] He greeted the book's publication with a mixture of relief and exhaustion. Now that the work was done, John Holmes offered his brother a humorous prescription: "[T]ake a turn at novel-reading and have a blow-out on tea, if you won't go anything stronger."[85]

— III —

Perhaps because he claimed to have little interest in theoretical issues and his experience with the genre was limited, Holmes's ideas about biography have been largely ignored or unappreciated.[86] But two years spent on the Emerson book had matured his thinking as well as his craft, and by the time he finished writing he was growing comfortable with the medium of biography and refining his own ideas about the genre. In yet another example of the biographers looking over their shoulders at each other, he had known all along that Elliot Cabot would be responsible for the authorized biography—the "ponderous and full" book to come later, as Warner put it—and seems to have tried to avoid overlap.[87] One of the distinctive features of Holmes's book is the almost total absence of Emerson's letters or journals, except for those few examples where friends provided material in their possession; as always, Emerson's manuscripts in the family's possession were reserved for Cabot's use. Holmes recognized the more modest aims of his study, compared with the authorized biography. He was writing, he told Alexander Ireland, for "that class of readers which dreads a surfeit, though it wants to be fed to a modest amount, and may be made hungry for more if we do not begin by cramming too hard."[88] But his middlebrow audience had spending power, Holmes knew—their tastes had made him financially comfortable—and he took his memoir writing seriously, with an eye not only to his readership but also to popular debates about life-writing. In September 1884, for instance, he asked Ellen Emerson about her father's personal habits, his eating and drinking preferences, whether he exercised daily and kept late hours, the color of his eyes and the shape of his head ("the circumference especially").[89] These were the details, Holmes insisted, that would humanize Emerson just as Boswell's attention to personal details had made Dr. Johnson "real to us."[90] He makes essentially the same point in the introduction to the Emerson biography: Emerson's true life is in his writings, but the "human accidents which individualize him in space and time" are crucial to understanding the development of the man himself, and readers are rightly curious about them (Holmes *RWE*, 1). Biography, in short, made a subject mortal, not immortal, by providing "those lesser peculiarities which are as necessary to a true biography as lights and shades to a portrait on canvas" (Holmes *RWE*, 268). Still, there were some peculiarities he considered off-limits. On the debate between revealing the *inner* subject or laying bare the *private* one, Holmes was predictably careful to avoid privacies—a position, he told Alexander Ireland, that the reading public approved of.[91]

For all his bristling about the constraints of the AML, the series' political conservatism was often agreeable with Holmes's own. He saw in Emerson's writings a therapy for an American culture growing more prosperous but less robust. Thus, Emerson's "plain and wholesome" calls for national autonomy in his lecture "The Young American" (1844) were a corrective to the pretensions of Gilded Age Americans "of suddenly acquired wealth" who squandered their national birthright by marrying into some impoverished European household (Holmes *RWE*, 180). Holmes's counter-canonical attacks on contemporary writers, well analyzed by both Len Gougeon and Randall Fuller, pit Emerson against indecorous upstarts like Whitman and Zola, realists who abused Emerson's attention to the "common aspects of life" and ventured into its "infected districts" for a "mere sensational effect" (Holmes *RWE*, 324–326). At the same time, he was unforgiving of those Romantic "idealists" who struck him as indolent and dreamy (Holmes *RWE*, 152–154).

If Holmes could sometimes be original where we expect him to be derivative, the reverse is also true: some of the book's reputed originalities are surprisingly uninventive. Take, for example, Holmes's attention to Emerson's poetry—a congenial subject, to be sure, and one that seemingly allowed the poet-biographer to avoid Emerson's troubling (to Holmes, at least) reformist agenda. Holmes adheres to the truism that Emerson was "essentially a poet," even in his prose—but not for the genteel reasons we have come to expect of Holmes. He argues that poetry was for Emerson a form of "self-revelation" (Holmes *RWE*, 314) or "semi-nudity" where his personal and emotional frailties, even his "bodily insufficiencies" (Holmes *RWE*, 363), could be expressed and transformed into art. "Though a born poet," Holmes pronounced, Emerson "was not a born singer" (Holmes *RWE*, 327); among his poetic deficiencies are limits of form ("I doubt if Emerson would have written a verse of poetry if he had been obliged to use the Spenserian stanza" [Holmes *RWE*, 335]), "incompleteness" (the "want of beginning, middle, and end"), and a "difficulty in the mechanical part of metrical composition" (Holmes *RWE*, 339). Yet, Holmes asserts, in their soaring inspiration Emerson's poems make up for their technical faults, "lift[ing] the reader into a higher region of thought and feeling"—for Holmes the truer test of poetic greatness. "This is the fascination of Emerson's poetry," Holmes insists; "it moves in a world of universal symbolism. The sense of the infinite fills it with its majestic presence" (Holmes *RWE*, 323). Holmes offers a bracing defense of Emerson's poetry. But in 1884 it was hardly an original one. Its clearest antecedent was Joel Benton's study *Emerson as a Poet* (1883), an expansion of the lecture Benton prepared for the Concord School of Philosophy's commemoration of Emerson in July 1882. Benton's essential position is that Emerson's technical skill is limited but the power of his poetry "springs largely from his loftiness of vision."[92] Holmes's argument, virtually identical to Benton's, gains gravity because Holmes made it, not because he made it first.[93]

A second truism about the Holmes biography, also complicated by a close reading of the book, is its essential antagonism toward New England Transcendentalism, which Holmes occasionally conflates with the equally loaded terms "mysticism" or "spiritualism." Holmes's position reflects a general trend in thinking about the movement by the 1880s, when—with almost all of its principal figures dead or inactive—Transcendentalism was widely dismissed as irrelevant and childlike, an immature "newness" that never grew up.[94] Stripped of its topical radicalism, Transcendentalism had become by the early 1880s an object of pity rather than derision. Given this context, Holmes could easily have repeated Le Baron Russell's glib dismissal of Emerson's spiritualism—that his mind "was too well balanced to entertain that nonsense." In fact, Holmes's treatment of Transcendentalism is both judicious and evenhanded. Sensitive to criticism about his own lack of sympathy, he places his criticism in Emerson's words—the words of "a friend and not a scoffer"—from the 1842 address "The Transcendentalist," by now more than forty years old: the transcendentalists were "not good citizens, not good members of society" (Holmes *RWE*, 152). In his early writings, of course, Emerson construed antisocialism fairly positively; Holmes, who saw most of the Transcendentalists as impractical and lazy, was inclined to take the criticism at face value. Yet Holmes moderates his own disdain for the movement in two ways. First, he personalizes Transcendentalism's excesses, making them behavioral, not philosophical; the great flaw of the movement was giving its adherents "reasons for doing nothing" (Holmes *RWE*, 153). Second, he recognizes that opinions of the Transcendentalists offered by observers "outside of their charmed circle" might admit of unfair "prejudice," and in fact closes his discussion by quoting Charles Dickens, who wrote in his 1842 *American Notes*, "If I were a Bostonian, I think I would be a Transcendentalist" (Holmes *RWE*, 155–156). Though he had throughout his life treated Transcendentalism with scepticism, in the biography Holmes comes across not as an antagonist but a mediator, doing his best to be evenhanded.

Holmes's moderation was more than a narrative strategy, however. It was rhetorically essential to his treatment of Emerson, who after all was Transcendentalism's chief inspiration (Holmes *RWE*, 147). Holmes cared little for Emerson's philosophical antecedents, and probably understood them even less. He left those subtleties to Cooke and Cabot. To compensate, Holmes paints Emerson as "a man who influenced others more than others influenced him" (Holmes *RWE*, 388). Beyond some obvious literary forebears like Shakespeare and Milton, Holmes focuses mainly on Emerson as an effecter of cultural change, not a product of it. Solving one problem, however, causes Holmes another one. Emerson becomes the intellectual progenitor of a profoundly dangerous anarchism, what the *Nation* called "an evil habit of thought for which transcendentalism is fairly responsible."[95] Thus Holmes's dilemma: how to claim for Emerson a role as an instigator of change without yoking him to the irresponsible antisocialism Holmes and many others thought of as Transcendental.

In this difficult negotiation to parcel out "the potential for antinomian and anarchic abuse embedded in [Emerson's] apparent devotion to self-reliance and nonconformity," as Charles E. Mitchell puts it, Holmes participates at least superficially in the Gilded Age's "genteel appropriation" of Emerson that Mitchell outlines: the creation of an iconic figure who deserved reverence rather than careful reading, and who in his elevation above the "sordid details of everyday life" both legitimized and embodied the expectation that society would be "well-mannered, polite, and politically united."[96] Other recent evaluations of Emerson's early biographers tend to confirm this view of Holmes's project, T. S. McMillin seeing in it an "early example of the detranscendentalization of Emerson"[97] and Randall Fuller seeing in it a culturally useful strategy to divert attention from "the hard conundrums of [Emerson's] prose."[98] Certainly Holmes's more extreme statements about Emerson's otherworldliness would suggest that for him, as for some others, what mattered most was who Emerson was, not what he wrote. But a closer examination of the development of Holmes's "sanctification of Emerson's personality"[99] complicates the view that Holmes was merely swept along by a general tide of adulation in order to avoid confronting the gritty truth of either Emerson or the world they both inhabited.

As part of his general motif, that Emerson influenced others but was not himself the product of influence, Holmes tries a number of strategies to distance Emerson from the "young enthusiasts" (Holmes *RWE*, 154) of Transcendentalism. Thus Thoreau, whom Holmes called a "nullifier of civilization, who insisted on nibbling his asparagus at the wrong end" (Holmes *RWE*, 86), taught Emerson nothing more than "wood-craft and a little botany" (Holmes *RWE*, 403). Of Hawthorne, Alcott, and others of Emerson's friends "who ran to extremes in their idiosyncrasies" (Holmes *RWE*, 86), none of them disturbed Emerson's balance or elicited more from him than a general sympathy leavened by "that exquisite sense of the ridiculous which was a part of his mental ballast" (Holmes *RWE*, 149). He could be among these social misfits but not of them, for he was rescued by an abiding sense of irony and a constitutional equilibrium that made him fundamentally dissimilar from them: "Nothing was farther from Emerson himself than whimsical eccentricity or churlish austerity" (Holmes *RWE*, 151).

It is easy to miss the subtlety in such broad statements as this, accustomed as we are to thinking of Emerson as distinctively individualistic and Holmes as a mouthpiece for conformity. Holmes is not denying Emerson "eccentricity" or "austerity," only whimsy or rudeness. Emerson's unconventionality is principled, Holmes implies; his austerity, based on law. His individualism is unalloyed, pure, almost perfect. In fact, Holmes describes Emerson in Christic terms, not just saintly ones: humble in his celebrity, an "unpretending fellow-citizen who put on no airs," yet in his personal relations exuding a "majesty" that made it seem "irreverent" to be familiar with him. Emerson resembled a spirit lost on its way to "some brighter and better sphere of being." "What was the errand on which he visited our earth,—the message with which he came commissioned from the Infinite source of all life?" Holmes asks with a flourish (Holmes *RWE*, 368–369).

These deifications of Emerson, the staple evidence of those who see Holmes's project as hagiographical, are so literal, bombastic, even blasphemous, that we might pause to wonder whether Holmes in fact meant them—whether Holmes with his legendary sense of irony and his suspicion of extremism might not be parodying his age's elevation of Emerson by phrasing it in such expansive overstatements. If anyone knew Emerson's essential human-ness, it was the literary peer who spoke with him on the same dais, the clubman who smoked cigars with him at the Parker House, the physician who knew the difference between a saintly expression and the blank stare of aphasia. It is difficult to miss Holmes's mock-sadness over the brevity of Emerson's "earthly existence": "[H]e had to be born, to take in his share of the atmosphere in which we are all immersed, to have dealings with the world of phenomena, and at length to let them all 'soar and sing' as he left his earthly half-way house" (Holmes *RWE*, 357). The image of a messianic, ascendant Emerson whose "white shield was so spotless that the least scrupulous combatants did not like to leave their defacing marks upon it" (Holmes *RWE*, 409) is so outlandish as to seem wholly inappropriate for a culturally cautious thinker like Holmes—unless we are meant to see it as outlandish. Holmes's tongue-in-cheek view of Emerson's deification shows up elsewhere as well: in 1883 he referred to Emerson's Concord haunts as "Holy Places," and in the preface to *A Mortal Antipathy* (1885), we recall, he identified Emerson as "a man . . . whom very many regard as an unpredicted Messiah."[100] In short, the vigor with which Holmes equates Emerson with Christ ought to caution us against taking the deification seriously. The Christic Emerson in Holmes's biography is more parody than paradigm.

If Emerson has any divine dimensions, in Holmes's estimation they are more behavioral than spiritual. What he shares with Christ, Holmes writes, is a devotion to the Good at all costs. In a passage self-consciously Biblical in language and allusion, Holmes returns to his earlier reference to Emerson's mission on earth at the point he resigned from the Second Church and parallels Emerson's vocational enlightenment to the beginning of Christ's ministry:

> In the year 1832 this young priest, then a settled minister, 'began,' as was said of another,—'to be about thirty years of age.' He had opened his sealed orders and had read therein:
>
> Thou shalt not profess that which thou dost not believe.
> Thou shalt not heed the voice of man when it agrees not with the voice of God in thine own soul.
> Thou shalt study and obey the laws of the Universe and they will be thy fellow-servants. (Holmes *RWE*, 370)

All humans bring with them "sealed orders" that determine the course of their lives, Holmes argues, and Emerson "was true to the orders he had received" despite "doubts, troubles, privations, [and] opposition" (Holmes *RWE*, 371), sacrificing his "comparatively easy life for a toilsome and trying one" and sacrificing the adulation that might have come with conformity: "He might have been an idol, and he broke his own pedestal to attack the idolatry which he saw all about him" (Holmes *RWE*, 372). A martyr for truth, an iconoclastic icon, Emerson comes "very near our best ideal of humanity" (Holmes *RWE*, 419–420).

In his focus on Emerson's behavior and character, Holmes effectively manages the troubling problem of Emerson's philosophical anarchism by moderating it with socially responsible actions. Emerson becomes for Holmes a tamer of his own radicalism, an "intellectual rather than an emotional mystic, and withal a cautious one" whose "ballast of common sense" saved him from floating too high in the ether of idealism (Holmes *RWE*, 396). In the language of the clinician, not the biographer, Holmes defines Emerson's sanity as balance, judgment, and moderation. Though Emerson could toy with dangerous ideas "as he would have played with a bundle of jackstraws," his sanity immunized him against harm; his "natural sagacity,—a good scent for truth and beauty"—enabled him to control the "sudden and searching flashes of imaginative double vision" that without balance lead to "extravagance, whimsicality, eccentricity, or insanity, according to its degree of aberration" (Holmes *RWE*, 366). In Holmes's diagnosis Emerson is both childlike (in his fascination with the intellectually and emotionally dangerous) and saintly (in his resistance to temptation and worldly excess). It is not Jesus to whom Emerson is best compared, but Franklin, whose "plain practical intelligence" in earthly affairs Emerson duplicates in the realm of the ideal (Holmes *RWE*, 235–236). By aligning Emerson and Franklin, Holmes not only refashions Emerson as an exemplary American—hinting at the self-made man Emerson would become in the appropriation of New Thought advocates in the early twentieth century—he also refashions Emerson's words as a national elixir, "tonic, bracing, strengthening to the American, who requires to be reminded of his privileges that he may know and find himself equal to his duties" (Holmes *RWE*, 181).[101]

If Emerson's example and words both function therapeutically, their particular medicinal purpose is not always clear. Sometimes, Holmes admits, Emersonianism stimulates our enthusiasms; at other times, it reins them in. Self-control is central to Holmes's depiction of Emerson, but the balance is hard-won. Throughout Holmes's biography Emerson emerges not as a placid Sage but as a bundle of intellectual and emotional oppositions tenuously held in check by his strength of character—he is at once neighborly and aloof, emotional yet calm, drawn to the ideal but anchored by the practical. Holmes associated idealism with danger, impracticality, insanity; but Emerson was "eminently sane *for an idealist*" (Holmes *RWE*, 366, emphasis mine). Holmes's paradoxical descriptions always reveal a tension in Emerson, a personality at war with itself: the "cautious mystic" who "never let go the string of his balloon" (Holmes *RWE*, 396); the poet navigating that "charmed region" between philosophy and poetry where the sublime and the ridiculous wage delicate war (Holmes *RWE*, 395); the "profoundly devout religious free-thinker" who rescued intellectual independence from lawlessness (Holmes *RWE*, 398); the "gentle iconoclast" holding in delicate balance the reverential and the revolutionary (Holmes *RWE*, 117–118).

After more than a century, conditioned as we are to expect of Holmes a safe ideological conformity, this depiction of a gentle and genteel Emerson seems a convenient evasion—in T. S. McMillin's words, a dilution of Emerson's challenges, a compromise to make "seemingly disparate elements coalesce," a "living synthesis of oppositions" created to explain away the troubling contradictions of Emerson's writings.[102] But Holmes does *not* diminish Emerson's radicalism; rather, he accentuates it by making it an inextricable function of Emerson's dynamic character. Politically, he is "as loyal an American . . . as ever lived" (Holmes *RWE*, 406–407) as well as the "citizen of the universe" (Holmes *RWE*, 322). Intellectually, the "oriental side of [his] nature" that indulged in "narcotic dreams" (Holmes *RWE*, 397) struggles with an intellectual discipline born of "concentration and drill" (Holmes *RWE*, 231). As a writer, Emerson elucidated dangerous doctrines yet cautioned readers against them (Holmes *RWE*, 230); as a reformer, he yet preferred his solitude and endured the "petty tortures" of those who dragged him into the limelight (Holmes *RWE*, 408); as a poet he was "full of poetical feeling" yet tongue-tied by a broken muse and always poised on the edge of parody and self-effacing laughter (Holmes *RWE*, 327).

Holmes's emphasis on Emerson's balance and control quite naturally seems to lead us to a Santayanan deprecation of his gentility: balance as the avoidance of extremism, a cultural middle-of-the-roadism confirmed elsewhere in the fastidiousness of the Gilded Age. Yet there is another explanation—one that allows for the intelligence we know Holmes possessed and the rich humanity without which Emerson becomes a sanctified bore, and also explains the curious insistence by Holmes and others that Emerson was "sane."[103] It is almost a truism that Holmes's medical training made him less adept as a biographer; Morse contends that Holmes "found it easier to get at the cranial bones and the brain-cells than at thoughts and mental processes."[104] What Morse ignores is the close relationship between mental processes and brain cells in the developing science of psychiatry in the nineteenth century, as sanity came increasingly to be defined in neurological and pathological terms. In broad brushstrokes, we can trace conceptions of sanity and madness from eighteenth-century notions of irrationality—a disease of the mind that manifested itself in the body— to the prevailing view of the later nineteenth century, that madness was a disease of the body that manifested itself in the mind—a physiological problem, and therefore treatable. Beginning with the clinical observations of Philippe Pinel, translated in 1806 as *A Treatise on Insanity*, Western psychiatry gradually turned away from incarceration and punishment of the insane and toward therapy and medication, in the belief that sanity was defined by emotional balance.[105] By the mid nineteenth century Pinel's new categorizations of insanity, particularly *manie sans délire* (loosely, "insanity without confusion of mind"), increasingly characterized Western psychiatric theory, allowing for the possibility of partial madness—monomania—and associating insanity with imbalance, lack of control, and emotional extremism.

The possibility for responding to insanity clinically rather than punitively—what was called the "moral management" technique—resulted in a medical optimism that naturally appealed to Holmes. Holmes was no psychiatrist. Indeed, the academic discipline of psychiatry was in its infancy when he was closing out his medical career. But he was a skilled diagnostician; his interest in the unconscious, the free association of ideas, and the effects of childhood trauma anticipated Freud and provided a congenial atmosphere at Harvard's medical school for young neuropsychologists like James Jackson Putnam, one of the founders of the American Neurological Association in 1875 and Holmes's colleague on the faculty.[106] And as a doctor, Tilton notes, Holmes thought "in terms of individual cases. . . . His attention is focused on the emotional-physical problems of individuals."[107]

Thus Holmes's attention to Emerson's sanity more likely reflects his diagnostic training and the observational habits of a lifetime in medicine than it reflects a confirmation of genteel values of order and normalcy. Holmes the physician-biographer, immersed in a medical culture whose most progressive members defined sanity in terms of individual self-governance, presents us with an image of Emerson congruent with the often conflicted figure who emerges from the private letters and journals—a rich resource that Holmes may have intuited but never actually saw. If Emerson's life indeed "corresponded to the ideal we form of him from his writings" (Holmes *RWE*, 409), it was due not to a flattening of his writings but to Holmes's ability to define in clinical ways an expansive emotional and intellectual life whose contradictions shaped and informed the philosophical condition Holmes calls "amiable radicalism" (Holmes *RWE*, 188). In that characteristic paradox resides Emerson's enduring psychological complexity. For Holmes, Emerson's "amiability"—his ability to dampen the fires within him, walk unscathed through a world of dangerous eccentricity, and bend his radicalism to practical power—"implied a self-command worthy of admiration" (Holmes *RWE*, 408). And in the parlance of nineteenth-century psychiatry, self-command meant sanity. The force of will struggling always to achieve self-control creates a distinctly modern Emerson in Holmes's reputedly antiquated account of his life. No cardboard icon fashioned by Gilded Age ideology, in Holmes's hands Emerson is an enormously complex and dynamic personality whose condition was informed by the medical terminology—and the psychiatric assumptions—of nineteenth-century debates over insanity and its treatment. It was a diagnosis far more clinical than cultural.

— IV —

After Holmes's *Emerson* appeared, in late 1884, the mail brought a spate of congratulations. Holmes received obligatory thank-yous from Bronson Alcott (incapacitated since 1882 by a paralytic stroke, Alcott scrawled his signature on a letter likely written by his daughter Louisa May),[108] Matthew Arnold (who confessed to reading only Holmes's Introduction),[109] the Social Darwinist Herbert Spencer (who wrote stiffly, "That the interest of the life will be heightened by the interest of the manner in which its facts are presented, I feel quite sure"),[110] and Henry James Sr. (who admitted he found Holmes's "most agreeable book" particularly fascinating because of its mention of him).[111] James Russell Lowell commended the chapter on Emerson's poetry, which "made me slap my thigh with emphatic enjoyment."[112] Another of Emerson's old friends and disciples, Christopher Pearse Cranch, wrote, "You have treated your subject with great skill, brilliancy, and justice."[113] Octavius B. Frothingham, whose book *Transcendentalism in New England* Holmes had borrowed from James Freeman Clarke, wrote, "My congratulations on your success in painting a great portrait on a small canvas. . . . His genius was elusive, and requires insight to come at. This you possess."[114] Rockwood Hoar, Holmes's erstwhile guide to Concord, pronounced the biography "admirably done."[115] President Rutherford B. Hayes, an admirer of Emerson, told Holmes almost a year after the fact that he found the book "so capital and satisfactory" that he immediately wrote Holmes three pages of thanks—but "I cancelled part of my obligation to you by wisely not troubling you with the letter."[116]

If Holmes was warmed by these compliments, he was likely not fooled by them, knowing so intimately the niceties of literary quid pro quo. (When he sent Ireland a presentation copy of the Emerson biography, he asked for nothing in return except Ireland's pledge to look it over sometime: "This

I say in all sincerity. A volume like this carries dismay with it when the recipient supposes he is expected to read it from title to finis, and it is only as a friendly token that I send it. I do not pretend really to read the stories and poems sent me."[117]) In one of several reflective statements, Holmes wrote Frank Sanborn a tepid self-review: "I have contributed a certain amount of ground in the neutral tint of fact—a few pieces of light and shade and some patches of color. I have succeeded at least in not exasperating the most devout Emersonians so far as I know."[118] Holmes was of course not among these Emerson devotees—and the intention of the American Men of Letters series was not to write for them. For Holmes's middlebrow audience, sales figures were the true barometer of a book's success, and the royalties told a very positive story. The book sold 3,822 copies in 1884—it went into a second printing within one week—and 4,103 the following year.[119] On August 20, 1885, Holmes happily acknowledged receipt of $1,092.25 in royalties on the Emerson book.[120] At the time of his death in 1894, Holmes's *Emerson* had sold 12,620 copies, nearly three times the series' average.[121] By 1925 the biography had gone through 35 impressions with total sales of about 21,800 copies.[122]

Financially, Holmes's *Emerson* rescued the American Men of Letters series, which had been operating at a loss.[123] But sales were more favorable than the reviews, which were mixed. As Holmes feared, it was impossible to please everybody, especially given Emerson's celebrity and the stiff competition from other biographers. Published commentary on the book ran the gamut from genuine praise to disappointment. On the positive side were those who found the book delightfully written and valuable for its record of both Emerson's and Holmes's thinking. Other reviewers complained that the book was derivative and offered only Holmes's fresh perspective on well-known events. For still others, the biography confirmed the commonplace perception that Holmes's lack of sympathy blinded him to Emerson's true genius or his full range of reformist accomplishments.[124]

Ironically, perhaps, it was two of Emerson's prior biographers whose criticism captured the poles of response to Holmes's book. As we have seen, objectivity was a contested value for biographers in the 1880s, as they negotiated the dictates between disclosure and reverence. In an odd twist, Moncure D. Conway turned Holmes's lack of sympathy to advantage by casting it as objectivity—proof that a biographer with no personal stake in the matter would find Emerson as admirable as his disciples did.[125] On the other hand, modern criticism of the book was in some ways anticipated by George Willis Cooke, who like Conway had a competitive ax to grind. The Holmes biography, Cooke wrote in the *Unitarian* for March 1885, "is by no means a piece of hack-work, and yet it is more than once apparent that the book was not written out of a spontaneous purpose" (as Cooke claimed to have done) but written to order, like Holmes's poetry itself, for a series "so perfunctory . . . that it is not conducive to the best work." Even worse, Cooke charged, the portrait is defective because it is incomplete: Emerson emerges only as a man of letters and not as a religious mystic, philosopher, and reformer, "as he is looked at by his admirers and disciples." Though brightly written, the book illuminates Emerson's "social and personal side" but ignores his reformist activities and misperceives his mysticism. Emerson, Cooke insists, was "an intellectual and not an emotional mystic,"—a criticism that must have especially stung Holmes, who in fact made the very same point, in identical words, at the end of his book (Holmes *RWE*, 396). In all, the problem for Cooke was not merely Holmes's lack of sympathy; it was his ignorance. Cooke was painfully blunt: Holmes "simply shows that he has failed to understand what Emerson was as a thinker."[126]

Despite his breezy confidence early in 1885 that he had "not exasperate[d] the most devout Emersonians," Holmes harbored some deep-seated anxieties about his biography of Emerson. He knew he could write for the masses, "that class of readers which dreads a surfeit," as he described them to Ireland; and to Sanborn, who became his primary correspondent about things Emersonian as the book drew to a close, Holmes expressed modest aspirations for himself and his audience: "I hope to induce a few of my readers to go to Emerson's books, of which I have given them such a fore-taste as will be like to make them ask for more."[127] But what about the experts, "the most devout Emersonians" whose worship for Emerson he did not share? To James Freeman Clarke he confided, "I could not help fearing I should not improbably disappoint those whom I was most anxious to satisfy."[128] Cooke's belligerent review must have confirmed his worst fears. Though he acknowledged the mosaic of approaches to Emerson, Holmes found it comforting when his own views were confirmed by others. Thus, for instance, he tells Sanborn, "I was glad to see that in some things at least I was in agreement with you, especially in the points of resemblance between Emerson and Milton."[129] Always, though, there lurked the accusations of superficiality, the suspicions about his qualifications. Frederic Henry Hedge, a founder of the Transcendental Club in 1836 and one of Emerson's oldest surviving friends, wrote to thank Holmes for his presentation copy of the Emerson biography, which "far surpasses my expectation although I expected of course a good thing from your pen." But Hedge found the book riddled with factual errors and lacking much personal authority. As Hedge remarked pointedly, he had himself been encouraged to write his reminiscences but had kept no written notes. "I have however imparted some things to E. Cabot wh. will appear in his book." The real reminiscences, he implied, would go to the real biographer.[130]

If the affable Wendell Holmes felt a lasting hurt from such remarks, there is no evidence of it. Thoughtful but not particularly introspective, Holmes tended to shrug off criticism, however he might have been concerned about it initially. Biography was not his forte, after all; he had attempted only one before this, a hastily thrown-together memorial for his friend John Lathrop Motley (1878), and would never attempt another. Indeed, like Ireland and Conway, at the same time he was writing his Emerson biography he was at work on another book—a medical novel, *A Mortal Antipathy*, which appeared serially in the *Atlantic Monthly* beginning in January 1885.

As the commercial success of Holmes's *Emerson* indicated, he had written the book his publisher—and many readers—wanted. But Holmes's *Emerson* was distinguished not just for its sales, which after all were partially a consequence of vigorous marketing by America's leading literary house. In terms of the debates over biography, Holmes successfully negotiated the Froudean challenge. Concentrating on the "inner" not the "private" man—it was, after all, a literary biography—might have been perfunctory (as Cooke charged) but it was certainly not scandalous. Holmes seems to have been playing it safe. Still, the implications of Holmes's clinical portrait of Emerson's complex emotional life were fraught with danger. Despite his modest aspirations for the book, he admitted privately to George Bancroft that the work on Emerson had affected him in a primal, visceral way: "I got from it some of those 'vibrations' that Milton speaks of which were impulses, I hope, in the upward direction."[131] Surely Holmes might have anticipated a similar vibration on the part of his readers. In any event, as a diagnosis of Emerson's psychological complexity Holmes's *Emerson* was unmatched for more than a century. Evenhanded and gracefully written, personal in its appreciation but objective in its treatment, informed by the published documents rather than the manuscripts, the book Tilton calls "useless for the modern student of Emerson"[132] in fact confirms a very modern view of Emerson, which we easily overlook in our willingness to dismiss Holmes as merely a spokesman for his genteel age. Like its subject, Holmes's *Emerson* was also gently iconoclastic, painting a portrait of Emerson's delicate sanity that was unexpectedly but fundamentally subversive of the bland icon he would soon become.

FIVE

Authorizing Emerson's Biography

Cabot and/or Edward Emerson

FROM 1875 THROUGH 1882, James Elliot Cabot (1821–1903) served as literary executor to a writer still living—very much like the relationship James Anthony Froude had with Thomas Carlyle. That Cabot was able to escape Froude's notorious fate as Emerson's fifth biographer is due in part to what Edward Emerson would years later call a "perfectly upright" rectitude that made Cabot constitutionally resistant even to appear to violate a private trust.[1] In part, too, Cabot subscribed to views of biography that were by the 1880s retrograde and relatively safe. But to a large degree, his work on the biography was shaped and limited by the complicated personal circumstances he found himself in, especially, it turns out, in his troubled collaboration with Edward Waldo Emerson.

— I —

It was Edward Emerson, we recall, acting for the family, who asked Cabot in 1877 to write Emerson's biography, in addition to the duties of literary executor that he had already agreed to two years before.[2] Cabot said yes, but not without reservations. Real biography, he believed, required the historical perspective of a half-century or more; he planned only to gather material for some better Emerson biographer in the future and "to put in shape what information is at hand & can be got from his journals & mss."[3] Cabot was probably right about the need for historical perspective. But he might also have thought himself an unsuitable biographer for more personal reasons.

Emerson's will officially named Cabot literary executor in 1876, more than three decades after the two men first met. What seemed like a long acquaintance, however, was (as in the case of all the biographers save Edward) a pretty sporadic one. A Harvard graduate in the class of 1840—by his own admission he was a lackluster and unfocused student[4]—Cabot followed his graduation with a three-year European tour that he called in his autobiography "mental sauntering and the picking up of scraps, very unfavourable to my *education*."[5] Actually, the trip was seminal to his intellectual development, for in Europe he discovered the German metaphysics that led him to a lifetime interest in "a harmonious reality that transcended the finite."[6] While there, he also discovered Emerson's writings, and upon his return to the United States in 1843 he began an acquaintance, first by mail, later (in 1845) in person, that would last until Emerson's death. Emerson found the young Cabot "a rare scholar, though a better metaphysician than poet" and cultivated the fledgling writer as he did so many other young men of promise[7]; throughout the 1840s and 1850s Cabot appears in Emerson's journals on membership lists for projected clubs and contributors' lists for proposed magazines. For his part, Cabot the son of privilege took a casual career path: completing a law degree but practicing only two years; studying natural history at Harvard with Louis Agassiz; trying his hand at architecture, translation, criticism, and editing. Not until Cabot was admitted to the Saturday Club in 1861 did he and Emerson have the opportunity for regular contact with each other at its monthly meetings. In short, Cabot's steadfastness, organization, and intelligence, rather than their personal relationship, may have recommended him for the task of managing Emerson's literary legacy. As Simmons aptly puts it, when Cabot was named Emerson's literary executor "he was neither family, disciple, a literary man in his own right, nor even a close friend."[8]

At least one other person close to the Emerson family shared Cabot's doubts about his suitability—William Henry Channing, one of the family friends who encouraged Edward to find a suitable biographer for his father in 1877 and offered frequent, albeit unsolicited, advice to Lidian about her husband's legacy.[9] During the summer of 1882, just months after Emerson's death, Cabot's wife Elizabeth visited England, where Channing had been living since the 1860s. On July 22 she wrote to her husband to say that Channing offered to have lunch with her and share information about Emerson. "I think all he really wants is to talk himself," Elizabeth noted wryly,

"& I shall try hard to get some facts out of him tho I doubt his accuracy."[10] Still, she reported later, the luncheon went well. Channing offered his help with the *Memoir* and told her he considered Elliot Cabot "the person of all others to write the Biography."[11]

Two days afterward, however, Channing gave Elizabeth a letter for her to pass along to her husband, and it was blistering. Channing conceded that Cabot ought to write his version of Emerson's life, "as full, rich & free as your literary conscience & your love of R.W.E. allow." But the qualification was crucial. As suited as Cabot might be for the scholarly task of writing Emerson's biography (he had the "disposition, intimate acquaintance with R.W.E., the confidence of his family, mental affinity, and intellectual power &c, &c, &c"), Channing thought Cabot lacked "enthusiastic admiration" for Emerson; he was too cold and dispassionate, was hampered by a "distrust of the 'effusive' & disgust at 'gush.'" Emerson, Channing insisted, was more than merely the thinker that Cabot had him. He was a feeler, a poet, and a visionary, and the patrician Cabot was incapable of appreciating his essence. When Channing once told him that Emerson's poetry would outlive his essays, Cabot "actually started in *surprise*—and courteously expressed *dissent*."[12] Emerson revealed his true nature to very few people. Channing considered himself one of them; Cabot, he thought, was not.

We might well chalk up Channing's criticism to petty, even professional, competitiveness. Apparently, Channing himself was planning a biography of Emerson, joining a number of others in his unfulfilled plans to do so.[13] One of the most earnest gadflies of the Transcendental circle, Channing valued insight, sympathy, and spiritual affinity over scholarship, rationality, and objectivity. That dichotomy defined disagreements not only about Transcendental friendship but also about biography, and in the early 1880s it both reflected and complicated the continuing discussion of the genre. Thanks to the Froude controversy, objectivity had come to be associated with disrespect and failure of judgment. For Channing, all of Cabot's virtues—his diligence, organization, cool rationality—were in fact drawbacks in the paradoxical biographical climate of the 1880s, when to render a subject with "impartial justice" was to risk the Froudean sins of slander, misunderstanding, and one-sidedness. Channing thought that Cabot, who lacked passion himself, would not recognize it in Emerson. Nor was Channing alone in that concern. As Thomas Wentworth Higginson recalled two decades later, Cabot's *Memoir* was "justly criticised by others for a certain restricted tone which made it seem to be, as it really was, the work of one shy and reticent man telling the story of another."[14]

Doubts notwithstanding, Cabot pressed on with the biography as he promised the family he would. There were frequent interruptions. He deferred writing the *Memoir* until after the Riverside Edition was completed in 1883, Edward reported,[15] and after that he was preoccupied with family issues: his son Ted's illness was diagnosed as diabetes,[16] and his aging mother required increasing care. Simmons speculates, plausibly, that he did not begin writing the draft until the spring of 1885, after his mother's death in March.[17] But, like Holmes, once he started he worked with almost single-minded devotion. He hounded surviving friends and relatives for reminiscences and anecdotes: Rockwood Hoar, Elizabeth Peabody, Frederic Henry Hedge, and Channing all sent material. Nearly ten years' work on Emerson's papers paid off. In Cabot's surviving notebooks for the edition and the *Memoir*, seven boxes full at the Houghton Library, we can see the dutiful executor culling, indexing, and abstracting both Emerson's papers and material sent by friends. Box One, for instance, contains some 20 neat blue-bound notebooks: indexes to letters by Emerson and other family members; extracts in Cabot's hand from some of Emerson's letters to his brother William; indexes and notes for Emerson's lectures (by year); topical indexes for Emerson's journals. In Box Three is a thick notebook in which Cabot pasted clippings and handwritten notes, a miscellany organized by subject headings (for example, "Dial pieces, marked by Miss Ellen and EWE"). Seven boxes of material, almost all of it reflecting a public record—Emerson's writings and lectures, newspaper clippings, reviews, reminiscences solicited from friends; even the one notebook marked "Personal" contains abstracts of Emerson's ideas and opinions. One is struck with the thoroughness of Cabot's research—and the almost total absence of Cabot.[18]

Considering the enormity of his task, the work moved quickly. He wrote at his home in Brookline, at the Emerson house in Concord, at his summer retreat in Beverly Farms. By late April 1885, Cabot gave the family the first 61 pages in draft for review; toward the end of July, he told his wife he had completed 550 pages. By early September 1885, Ellen and Lidian Emerson had read about 200 pages of the manuscript and were "delighted" with it.[19] By April 1886 Cabot had brought Emerson's life through 1872 and was nearly finished with the draft.[20] Ellen told her sister, "We read it aloud together and criticize and enjoy it at leisure."[21] Sometime in early 1887, *A Memoir of Ralph Waldo Emerson* went to press.[22] Family and friends received "confidential copies" of it on May 25, 1887, Emerson's birthday.[23] The book was published by Houghton, Mifflin the following September, a weighty 803 pages in two volumes.[24]

Cabot's selection as literary executor in the summer of 1875 came at the expense of Edward Emerson, although the implications of that choice would become apparent only years later. As Ellen Emerson reported to her sister, soon after the fire at Bush in 1872 her father became obsessed with the custody of his manuscripts. "'What to do with them?' he keeps saying. 'They are invaluable to anyone like me. If Edward were a scholar by profession, they would be a mine of riches to him. Otherwise they are worthless'" (*ETE*, 1:690). Waldo Emerson's dismissal of his son from consideration may seem cold, especially when we consider that Cabot seems no better credentialed than Edward as a professional scholar. But when we know the younger Emerson's personal situation in the early to mid-1870s, his father's decision seems charitable.

In 1871, Edward was in his third year of medical training at Harvard. Always suffering from delicate health (of medium height, he claimed to weigh 140 pounds at the peak of his strength), he had recently survived two bouts of varioloid, a mild form of smallpox that developed into abscesses on his lungs. In health Edward was his father's son: lung problems plagued him for years to come, as would the poor vision he had complained of since his undergraduate days. In August 1871 he left for Berlin for a year of medical study; before he sailed he became engaged to Annie Shepard Keyes of Concord.[25] After he completed his M.D. in 1874, Edward set up practice in Concord with Dr. Josiah Bartlett, and he and Annie married in September, when he was 30. Thus, just as Cabot began work in earnest on Waldo Emerson's papers, Edward Waldo Emerson was embarking on marriage, starting a long-deferred career, becoming a parent (he and Annie suffered the loss of their first-born child, William, in July 1875, the first of three sons to die in childhood by 1880), and struggling with chronic illness induced by exhaustion.[26] Under the circumstances, Waldo Emerson's decision to spare his son the additional burdens of literary executorship was both practical and humane. Yet we may speculate that Edward saw it differently, another in a series of disappointments in a life spent, as Bliss Perry characterized it, "making the best of second choices."[27] He had entered Harvard in 1861 but claimed to be "delighted" when a bout with typhoid fever prevented his return to classes; instead, during the summer of 1862 he traveled west from Omaha to California with a wagon train of "gold-seekers & emigrants" on a Parkmanesque rite of passage that, he recalled, had him taming wild horses and braving the threats of Indian attacks.[28] But the trip designed to strengthen him broke his health instead, and he returned in disappointment to Harvard. A skilled horseman, he desperately wanted to serve in the Civil War, preferably in the cavalry, but his parents objected—Waldo because of the danger, Lidian because she thought Lincoln insufficiently committed to abolition.[29] Twice Edward tried to enlist anyway, only to be dissuaded by his sister Edith (or her future father-in-law John Murray Forbes—the stories vary), who convinced him not to risk his *father's* peace of mind for whatever small contribution his military service would make.[30] He returned to Harvard, was graduated in 1866, a year behind his class, and hoped to study painting. Under pressure once again to be practical, he set that dream aside and entered medical school.[31]

It is painful to see Edward always struggling in the shadow of others—his famous father; his brother Waldo, who died in 1842 but remained an emotional presence in the family; his brother-in-law Will Forbes, a Civil War hero.[32] Clearly his father's death freed Edward to pursue old interests. Within three months, he closed his medical practice to assist Cabot with the Emerson papers and return to his first love, painting, which he began to study under his old Harvard classmate Frederic Crowninshield.[33] Edward's correspondence over the next few years shows him to be intimately involved with the preparation of the Riverside Edition, from restoring manuscript readings to negotiating publication schedules to choosing colors for the books' covers. In other words, he began acting like a literary executor, which was really Cabot's job.

During the long process of assembling the Riverside Edition—beginning in 1875, when Cabot was called in to help Ellen assemble the material for *Letters and Social Aims*—Cabot's friendship with Waldo Emerson deepened and matured, as did his relationship with the family.[34] With the help of Ellen and Edward Emerson, he organized Emerson's papers, patched together the lectures and fugitive pieces, and created three volumes that so bore his imprint that Emerson routinely referred to *Letters and Social Aims* as Cabot's book. Because their efforts were so successful, it is easy to assume that the family's collaboration with Cabot was uniformly cordial. Certainly, the two families got along famously: the Cabots visited Concord often from their home in Brookline, Lidian Emerson "adopted Mrs Cabot as a daughter and agreed to call her Lizzy," and Ellen fixed up an upstairs room for Elliot Cabot to work in. ("The present method of four in the study at once is bad," she recognized.)[35] Family members, distantly related by marriage, addressed each other as cousins. After receiving his presentation copy of the *Memoir* in 1887, Edward wrote Cabot on behalf of the family, "We can never be grateful enough to you for what you have done for us and others in having consented to assume this work."[36] There is no reason to doubt Edward's gratitude, nor his sincerity when he recalled of Cabot in 1917, "It was a cause of active joy to see him whether at my father's house, in his own study, or surrounded by his wife and children in his charming home. It was good to know that such a man existed."[37] But the contemporary record, privately revealed in letters, tells a more troubled story. By 1883, strains between Elliot Cabot and the Emerson children had begun to show. In part it was a disagreement over the direction of Emerson's legacy; Simmons reports that family members were much more committed to a new, uniform edition of Emerson's writings than Cabot was.[38] In part it was simply a clash of personalities. Cabot's "devotion is entire and his judgment admirable," Edward reported in May 1883 to Moncure D. Conway, "although we, the family, sometimes warp it a little from the Grecian severity that recommended it to Father."[39] Gratitude was not affection. The best Edward could muster for Cabot as a person was to praise him in somewhat cool terms as "perfectly upright morally, and almost of the ascetic type."[40]

The strain of working together on crabbed and often inchoate masses of text inevitably resulted in disagreements between what the family wanted and what Cabot the executor thought best. Emerson's revised will specified that Cabot was to act "in cooperation with my children" on all editorial matters, phrasing that left plenty of room for misinterpretation.[41] The confusion worsened when the family entered into negotiations with Houghton, Mifflin for the publication of the Riverside Edition. The contract, dated March 15, 1883, reveals a complicated set of overlapping responsibilities and prerogatives. Cabot as executor, "acting in cooperation with said children," had the authority to publish or withhold any of Emerson's unpublished papers; but by the terms of Emerson's will Edward held "the copyright, plates, and ownership of all his published writings and also all his contracts for the publications of said writings." The Emerson heirs could publish any previously unpublished writings and letters—"subject to the advice of said Cabot"—*except* for the Carlyle correspondence (already being prepared by Charles Eliot Norton) and "such new matter as the said Cabot may desire to use exclusively in his life of Emerson." On literary matters, in short, Cabot trumped the Emersons; in affairs of business, the Emersons overruled Cabot, with Edward (as the heirs' representative) given the "power to exercise all options, make all selections, and give all directions, permissions and notices."[42] The contract that might have untangled the knotted relationship between Cabot and the family merely tightened it.

Despite their occasional discomfort with this fragile working arrangement, the Emerson daughters tended to be conciliatory, though Edith could be forthright in her criticism: in a very modern statement of taste, she told Mrs. Cabot that she wished there were "more of [her father] personally" in Cabot's book, "and I do not care so much for the resume of his lectures. In reading a biography I always skip that part & read the personal letters & stories &c—."[43] Still, both Ellen and Edith conceded that in matters textual and biographical, Cabot was the boss. To her brother, Edith wrote, "Whatever our wish was—it was [Mr. Cabot's] judgment Father trusted to & I did not think we ought to reverse his decisions."[44] But by the summer of 1886, with the final years of Emerson's life left to write, Cabot was running out of material, and his patience with the family was wearing thin. He began badgering the Emerson daughters for reminiscences, even threatening Ellen that if the ending of the book were weak, she had only herself to blame.[45] Edith shrewdly recognized in Cabot's desperation the opportunity to personalize his very public narrative. Send Mr. Cabot all those things he has refused before, she urged Edward: "As he forgets & does not remember things he has once seen I advise you to offer again anything you wish him to use—he is in the mood to accept now & feels the need. He was so thankful for the reminiscences I wrote & said he should use almost all—I think he would take more—than he used to think he should."[46] To Ellen she wrote a few days later, "I hope you will pay attention to Mr Cabot's request and remind him strenuously of all the things to put in." Edith scribbled in the margin, "I write for Mr Cabot at every spare minute."[47] Ellen and Edith in their behind-the-scenes maneuverings struggled to rescue their father from an iconic whitewash and quietly asserted the family's prerogatives against Cabot's "Grecian" resolve.

There were financial tensions, too. Independently wealthy—his occupation was listed in the 1880 federal census as "gentleman"—Cabot had accepted the literary executorship out of loyalty to Emerson, with no interest in being compensated for it by the family. But in a codicil to his will in 1881, Emerson provided $1,000 for each of Cabot's seven sons. Cabot knew nothing about this bequest until July 1882, when Edward, Ellen, Edith, and even Will Forbes began pressuring him to take it.[48] Cabot, who neither needed the money nor wanted it, resented what he saw as an under-the-table payment for his labor. The issue lingered uncomfortably in the air while Cabot and Edward did their separate biographical work, and it may never have been resolved, even years later. Of all the possible biographers, Cabot would complain to Edward in 1887, "you preferred me, & now you feel like paying for your fancy."[49]

For all of these reasons, as they worked together on the Riverside Edition there developed a rivalry between Edward and Cabot that often erupted unexpectedly, in petty ways. Ellen wrote about a day in May 1883 when she and Cabot were trying to piece together Emerson's manuscript lecture "Education" and Edward entered the room:

> I sat by Mr Cabot and read the manuscript with him word by word. His patience in following me through the labyrinths of my proposed changes was wonderful. He accepted most of them. In one case he refused, but when Edward came in he requested Mr Cabot to yield. I said, no, Mr Cabot was chosen by Father because he knew what should be published and what not, and he ought to have the say in the end. Edward said "Father added 'acting with my children' so that we might have our way too." So it goes in our way.[50]

Clearly, there was some friction between the two men—and it only got worse. When Cabot prevailed in a dispute over a projected title for one of the volumes—Edward favored "Essays 3d Series"—Edward wrote his sister with a bitter metonymy, "Boston has been deferred to another time."[51] The completed volume appeared instead as *Lectures and Biographical Sketches*. When a printed announcement for an "Edition de Luxe" of the *Works* noted that it would be prepared by both Cabot and Edward Emerson, in Cabot's copy the reference to Edward was struck through in ink.[52] By late summer 1883 Ellen was writing confidentially to Mrs. Cabot about the growing rift:

> I became convinced, I hope mistakenly, that Mr Cabot is regarding the work as Edward's work and himself as second partner in the firm. This note is not to be read to Mr Cabot, but I thought I would write to you about it before Edward's arrival for Edward isn't sufficiently bold in talking with Mr Cabot for me to be sure that if I asked him to find out he would really find out. I think the only proper way on Father's account, the only comfortable way for Edward, is that Mr Cabot should mount the throne and stay there, treating us like babes as we are.

Could Elizabeth *please* intercede between her husband and Edward, Ellen asked, and convince Elliot Cabot to "take the ruling place once for all"?[53] This solution, if it worked at all, worked imperfectly; that entire summer Cabot and the Emersons suffered through what Simmons calls "an uneasy peace."[54] Usually willing to grant Cabot the last word, Edward continued to dig in his heels over relatively minor textual matters, even when it pitted him against his sisters. For instance, in a letter to Cabot about a disagreement over the ordering of some stanzas in the poem "May-Day," Edward suggests a tangled set of allegiances: "[I]f Father allowed one of his children to make a different arrangement it might not be going too far if another of them, who perhaps knew more than the first of [these?] events, should revise it."[55]

One is tempted to use the term "sibling rivalry" here, despite the generational difference in their ages. Certainly, the more they worked together, Cabot came to resent Edward's meddling, Edward occasionally treated Cabot like a hired hand, and each became increasingly sensitive about his own prerogatives. However it affected their day-to-day personal relationship, the conflict between Elliot Cabot and Edward Emerson had a serious effect on the course of Emerson's biography, for it turned the two collaborators into competitors.

Because Edward Emerson's *Emerson in Concord* appeared in book form in 1889, it is easy to conclude that his work on the book postdates Cabot's 1887 *Memoir*. In fact, it did not. The book—or initially, a much shorter memorial statement—was commissioned soon after Emerson's death by the Social Circle in Concord, 25 influential men who met each Tuesday evening from October through March. Membership in the Social Circle was by invitation to residents only (Waldo Emerson had become a member in 1839, Edward in 1875; Cabot, who lived in Brookline, was ineligible) and continued until a member moved from Concord or died, after which it was customary for some other member of the Circle to write a brief memorial. On October 10, 1882, at its second meeting since Emerson's death, the Social Circle voted that Edward Emerson and Rockwood Hoar should undertake the sketch of Ralph Waldo Emerson.[56]

Hoar's role in the project is unknown. He and Edward Emerson were part of the four-man "Committee to Edit Memoirs" that also included William T. Harris and John Shepard Keyes, Edward's father-in-law. The Social Circle's minutes record nothing further about the memorial for the next four years, and the surviving epistolary record is curiously silent: neither Edith, Ellen, Edward, nor Cabot mentions Edward's work on a biography of his father. But Edward must have substantially finished his writing very early in 1887—precisely when Cabot finished his—for at the Social Circle meeting of February 22, 1887, Edward "read part of the life of his father"—as he did again at the meetings of March 1 and March 8, 1887, according to the minutes, where the reading preceded supper and (by special vote) continued after the meal.[57]

The timing of these readings is significant for what it reveals about the competitive situation in which Cabot and Edward Emerson wrote. Cabot's

Memoir was published first, we recall, and presented to family members on May 25, 1887, and for general sale the following September.[58] But Edward's biography was *made public* first, in readings at the Social Circle three months before Cabot's book came out and possibly at Edith and Will Forbes's home a week before Cabot presented his book to the family. Given what else we know about their relationship, Edward's preempting of Cabot seems a gesture of victory in a rivalry that flared up in small but frequent ways. Ten years after Edward had asked Cabot to write the authorized biography, Edward wrote one of his own and beat Cabot to the punch. Included with the sketches of 62 other members of the Social Circle, most of whose memorials ran to five or ten pages, Edward's "sketch" of his father was entitled "Memoir of Ralph Waldo Emerson"—coincidentally, the title of Cabot's book. Separately paginated and indexed for ease of republication, it occupied the last 266 pages of *Memoirs of Members of the Social Circle in Concord, Second Series, from 1795 to 1840*. The book was completed in October 1888 and privately printed in a run of 261 copies on January 1, 1889, for Social Circle members and friends. The Social Circle agreed to postpone the book's private distribution until Houghton, Mifflin formally released Edward's biography separately in early May 1889 under its new title, *Emerson in Concord*.[59]

— III —

The rivalry between Cabot and Edward Emerson resulted in some significant differences between their two books, as each man struggled, perhaps not always consciously, to differentiate his narrative from the other's and from the four that had preceded them. Yet the *Memoir* had much in common with the earlier biographies. Cabot's book, as Simmons points out, develops an Emerson whose life held in suspension the "finite and infinite, fate and free will, nature and spirit."[60] Thus, like other biographers before him, Cabot emphasized Emersonian balance; as Conway attributed it to personality and Holmes to character, Cabot attributed it to intellect. Cabot placed Emerson in a tradition that ran from Puritanism through late-eighteenth-century Unitarian liberalism through the new views of Emerson's age (*Memoir*, 1:307–310). Both Puritanism and its liberal descendents had succumbed to a reliance on sectarian dogma, according to Cabot, replacing religion with scholastic theology on the one hand and sterile rationalism on the other. Emerson reclaimed the vitality of both; he becomes for Cabot no unsettler of Christian belief but a restorer of it, replacing Christ's "official authority" as a religious icon with the "real and living authority" to transform human lives (*Memoir*, 1:318–319). Like the other biographers, too, Cabot mitigates Emerson's philosophical extremism by imaging him as a calm center in a storm of Transcendental excess.[61] (Significantly, Cabot separates the chapter on "Religion" from the one on Transcendentalism.) While granting that Emerson was in the center of the Transcendental circle, Cabot refigures the metaphor to make Emerson's centrality a position of distance and objectivity. For Emerson, Transcendentalism was the "vision of the absolute, the look to the ideal as our reinforcement against the tyranny of mere use and wont tending to shut us up in petty cares and enjoyment." As the movement's central figure, "[h]e was as much alive to the extravagances as anybody, having frequent occasion to observe them," but his "restraint" shielded him from the "extreme manifestations" of the movement (*Memoir*, 2:412–413). Thus Cabot does not deny Emerson's centrality, but sees it as a vantage point from which he can remain observant and neutral. Personally and intellectually, Emerson's centrality to Transcendentalism in fact put him far from its extremes.

For Cabot, again like the other biographers, Emerson's avoidance of extremism derives partly from principle, partly from character. He embraced the ideals of abolition but resisted its manifestations (said Cabot, at least); he kept his distance from Fruitlands and cast a jaundiced eye on the economic experiment at Brook Farm. What others perceived as coldness or lack of commitment derived from Emerson's distrust of dogmatism but also what Cabot called "a necessity of his nature, which inclined him always to look for a relative justification of the offending party or institution" (*Memoir*, 2:428). Again, it was a deft and ironic redefinition: Emerson's apparent standoffishness was actually a sign of his deep compassion.

In sum, Cabot participates in the ur-project of the 1880s biographers—not to make Emerson safe but to reveal his essential safety, which Cabot, like the others, defined in terms of balance. His insistence on fidelity to Emerson's wishes led Cabot "to put the final stamp on the self-image Emerson had been creating for many years," as Simmons puts it—reassuring those who knew him that he had "neither abandoned his youthful vision nor attempted to smash idols."[62] What distinguishes Cabot's biography—and it is as much a matter of access as of viewpoint—is his grounding of the *Memoir* in Emerson's own words, both published and (at the time) unpublished. Not only does Cabot capitalize on Emerson's manuscripts in ways that only an authorized executor could, but also by quoting extensively from the lectures and journals he allows Emerson to speak for himself. Cabot's judgments appear, as a result, to be merely summaries or reiterations of Emerson's own words, not interpretations of them. There are at least two reasons for this strategy. First, there is Cabot's personal preference for "transparency" as a biographer, his intention (as he told Charles Eliot Norton in 1882) of "doing what Emerson would like."[63] He outlined his strategy for the *Memoir* to Ellen Emerson, who told her sister, "He means it to be a sort of *auto*-biography of Father made up in great measure of self-description in characteristic phrases collected from all writings, printed & manuscript, and that it shall give one clear sharp impression of the man himself."[64] As Cabot put it in the preface to the *Memoir*, he would "furnish materials for an estimate of [Emerson], without undertaking any estimate or interposing any comments beyond what seemed necessary for the better understanding of the facts presented. Where I may seem to have transgressed this rule, I am in truth for the most part only summing up impressions gathered from his journals and correspondence, or from the recollections of his contemporaries" (*Memoir*, 1:iii–iv). Higginson exaggerated, but only slightly, by calling the *Memoir* a tale of shyness told with reserve.

The second reason for the *Memoir*'s apparent objectivity reflects Cabot's views of the genre of biography, however muted their expression. He was scrupulously attentive to facts, a task made easier of course by his ready availability to the human and textual sources. More than any of the other biographies, Cabot's book balanced reverence with accuracy; Ellen, who had found dozens of mistakes in Conway's and Cooke's studies of her father, commended Cabot's for its "absolute exactness."[65] In addition, he intended to break no new ground. Aware of how Emerson's celebrity had already begun to create an image in the public mind, he had no plans to violate it. As Simmons points out, his prepublication distribution of the book reminds us that Cabot saw his primary allegiance to Emerson's family and acquaintances.[66] In the preface to the *Memoir* he reiterated a promise made some years earlier to Ellen, not to reveal a new Emerson but to "supplement the accounts . . . the public already have."[67] Instead of "attempt[ing] a picture which should make [Emerson] known to strangers," Cabot pledged to reinforce for "readers and friends" the Emerson they knew already while offering little "of first-rate importance to add to our knowledge of Emerson" (*Memoir*, 1:iii–v).

It seems an eminently safe strategy, especially in the post-Froudean climate where biographical manipulation could be as dangerous as wholesale, undigested quotation of primary documents. But Cabot almost immediately compromises his role as mere conduit for Emerson's words with a curious (and apparently unnecessary) self-defense: "I have been entirely free . . . from the gravest embarrassment that can meet the biographer of a man of letters who aspired to be a public teacher,—I mean the traces of a discrepancy between the teachings and the character" (*Memoir*, 1:v). The language is revealing in its ambiguity: Is it Emerson who is "free of embarrassment" or Cabot as his biographer, or both? And what could be the cause of that potential embarrassment for Cabot—finding those "traces of a discrepancy" in Emerson's life or revealing them in the *Memoir*? Citing a passage in Emerson's journal that is oddly self-aggrandizing, Cabot reminds his readers that Emerson himself would not have concealed his innermost being from "a witness more intellectual and virtuous than I," only from "a witness worse than myself" (*Memoir*, 1:v). Taking his cue from Emerson, Cabot reiterates that, with the proper audience—those close to Emerson, who already knew him—Emerson's inner being could not be sullied by revelation. Indeed, Cabot says, "he could only have gained by it" (*Memoir*, 1:v). However, Cabot knew the vagaries of the reading public, especially those fed by the celebrity of the "Sage of Concord," and he believed that most readers would be Emerson's inferiors in intelligence or virtue and hence be likely to misapprehend him. For a readership of insiders, revelations of the heart were safe but unnecessary; for a wider readership of outsiders, for whom Emerson was the "public teacher" (*Memoir*, 1:v), those revelations would likely be misunderstood, a source of embarrassment both to Emerson and to the biographer who offered them up.

And so Cabot undertook to reconcile, minimize, or simply ignore those very human moments when Emerson did not confirm his own high expectations. His shaping of Emerson's life to show the consistency of word and deed reflected not so much ideology as the politics of genre. To Cabot, the biographer's task was to reconcile the inner and outer man, not to expose discrepancies. His book would be no Froudean exposé, would include no revelations that might cause the admiring masses to misinterpret their teacher. In any case, Cabot argued, Emerson's private documents "do not often bring us closer to him than we are by his published writings" (*Memoir*, 1:iii–v). Modern studies of Emerson amply reveal that they do—that in his journals and letters Emerson revealed the anxieties, fears, inconsistencies, and nobilities that characterize a normal human emotional life. Cabot simply could not have failed to see them. But if Emerson himself were unwilling to lay bare his soul for fear of being misunderstood, then certainly Cabot would not do it for him. Instead, for ideological, temperamental, and generic reasons shaped by his conception of biography, Cabot declared Emerson a fully integrated personality. Simmons makes the point forcefully, though not quite in the language of the 1880s debate: the *Memoir* depicts an Emerson whose "perfect correspondence between the public and the private" exemplified Cabot's own conception of the complete man.[68] It was "Emerson passed through a prism named Cabot—Emerson translated into intellectual terms."[69] Though the contemporary debate was more accurately over the inner and outer self—privacy still being sacrosanct for biographers like Cabot—the essential point still stands. Notwithstanding Cabot's intention "of simply allowing [Emerson] to tell his own story" (*Memoir*, 1:iv), the argument of the *Memoir* is a narrative construct shaped by the personal and commercial forces around it.

— IV —

In March 1887, when her husband was busy reading the draft of his *Emerson in Concord* to family and neighbors, Annie Keyes Emerson remarked, "It is wonderful to see the different effects produced by Mr Cabot and Edward with the same material."[70] On the contrary, Edward seems to have studiously *avoided* duplicating the material Cabot used, preferring instead family stories, juvenilia, and childhood anecdotes, as well as the journal entries that Cabot's "Grecian severity" probably caused him to ignore. In his book Edward staked out a very different territory from Cabot's, promising to "pass lightly over" his father's public activities (*E in C*, 2) and to do instead what the "symmetry" of Cabot's book (*E in C*, 1) could not: to reveal Emerson as "the citizen and villager and householder, the friend and neighbor" (*E in C*, 189). As its title suggests, *Emerson in Concord* also offered a much more localized take on what was by now standard fare for Emerson biographies. Where Cabot and Holmes had emphasized genealogy, for example, and Cooke an intellectual line of descent, Edward emphasized family life as the formative context for his father's rigorous principles. The anecdotes of Emerson's early years are Algeresque, almost fabulous in their sentimentality: the fatherless Emersons cold, destitute, and hungry until Ezra Ripley brings them to his Concord house and feeds them; the brothers together at Harvard, waiting tables and living "frugally among the frugal" but devoted to their studies and each other; Mrs. Emerson accepting charity but always as merely a loan; young Waldo sending his Boylston prize money to his mother so she could buy a shawl, but brother William using it to pay the baker instead (*E in C*, 16–27). We see young Ralph's schoolboy silliness and adolescent struggles to fit in gradually give way to a realization that "neither in horse-play nor social gatherings did he find his natural recreation" (*E in C*, 25). Emerson emerges from his youth and early manhood (now calling himself "Waldo") as a noble but still flawed character, frail in health, undistinguished as a teacher, struggling with his vocation in the ministry and devastated by his first wife's death.

In Edward's telling, not until his father settled in Concord did he experience the therapeutic joys of "householding," the love of gardening, and the sustaining interest in his town's affairs that stabilized his life and set him on his true path. His house on the Cambridge Pike situated him advantageously between the bustle of the village and the calming solitude of the woods (*E in C*, 55), a symbolic balance between the civic and the spiritual that runs as a motif throughout the book. Emerson moved to Concord frail and emotionally battered, and the town "sheltered" him (*E in C*, 66), a trope that images him as lost and needing protection. Throughout his life "the people of the village felt his friendly and modest attitude towards them and were always kind," especially in his old age, when "he found helpers and protectors start from the ground, as it were, at his need" (*E in C*, 149–150). For his part, Emerson repaid their kindness not only in his public capacity as the town's commemorative poet but in the more pedestrian roles as curator of the Lyceum, a member of the Social Circle, a committeeman for the public school and the town library.

A thorough egalitarian with his "respect for humble people and for labor," enjoying the "racy vernacular and picturesque brag" of "horsemen and stage-drivers" (*E in C*, 151, 98), Emerson emerges in his son's estimation as conventional in his dress, his habits, his taste in food—in short, in those appearances and behaviors that would otherwise have set him apart from his neighbors. Eventually Emerson would become Concord's world citizen, but his first civic honor was the traditional election of a newly married man to the post of hog-reeve—and he accepted it in good humor (*E in C*, 66–67). He was cerebral and worldly, but "in speaking to his townsfolk in the Lyceum he never wrote down to them" (*E in C*, 147). To reinforce the image of Emerson as workingman, *Emerson in Concord* emphasizes his early lessons in hard labor, his long years of travel on the lecture circuit, and especially his interest in gardening and animal husbandry. "Work with hoe and spade for an hour or two of the day was part of his plan of country life," Edward notes (*E in C*, 125), and he never lost his fascination with the transparent divinity of the natural world; but as the practical Emerson found that fieldwork robbed him of time for his proper vocation, he gradually confined himself to caring only for his orchard, which became his passion (*E in C*, 129).[71] In his personal habits he was neither intemperate nor prudish, enjoying wine with dinner and a cigar afterwards, skeptical of fads like cold-water baths, "neat and inconspicuous" in his clothing (*E in C*, 155). He was enamored of nature but indifferent toward flowers and house pets (*E in C*, 157–159), fun-loving and witty but never guilty of loud laughter (*E in C*, 163), a strong swimmer but an unskilled horseman (*E in C*, 157), tender toward little children (*E in C*, 166) but ill suited to "romping" with them (*E in C*, 168). If Holmes showed Emerson's balance to be a victory over his extremes, Edward Emerson argued instead for a man who found extremes unnatural and preferred the middle road. What emerges in *Emerson in Concord* is a personality reserved in its actions, in many ways the picture of Victorian restraint and domesticity.

The final chapters of *Emerson in Concord* are devoted to an examination of Emerson's ideas and writing. Edward's strategy here is to defend his father against popular misconceptions and myths. (It was a strategy Edward would employ again years later in his 1917 reminiscence, *Henry Thoreau as Remembered by a Young Friend*.) Predictably, these misconceptions involved Emerson's extremism. Unlike other champions who explicated Emerson's writings, Edward defended his father with a wealth of family anecdotes that showed him to be less dangerous and more decorous than was popularly believed. He was no "dupe of the Reformers"—Edward calls them "men-of-one-idea," recalling the medical designation "monomania" (*E in C*, 201, 207)—though he tolerated their idiosyncrasies and felt tender toward them in their oddness. (In an echo of Emerson's brash challenge in "Self-Reliance," Edward claims that "these were his poor" [*E in C*, 201]). Yet he had his limits, and in matters of politeness he adhered to conventional rules. Edward tells the story of his father's rebuking a radical reformer, "short, thick, hairy, dirty, and wild-eyed," who refused to remove his hat indoors (*E in C*, 209–210). In religion Emerson "believed in Spirit, not in forms" (*E in C*, 248), a position he held consistently since his days at the Second Church in Boston; his "pantheism" was no different from the currently held belief in an "omnipresent God" (*E in C*, 40, 248–251). Finally, dismissing the "idle" charges leveled late in his life that Emerson "found his beliefs barren" and retreated to conventional Christianity, Edward offers some previously unpublished letters to show his father's membership in "the Church Universal" (*E in C*, 253–254) and his continuing reverence. Opposed to dogma and empty ceremony, Emerson still kept the Sabbath, "not with the old severity, but with due regard for a custom which he valued for itself as well as for association, and also for the feelings of others" (*E in C*, 169).

What, then, of Transcendentalism, clearly Emerson's most extreme "ism"? Remarkably—or perhaps not, given Edward's mission as a chronicler of his father's domestic life—the term is mentioned only once in *Emerson in Concord*, and then as an excuse for the "fantastic and startling imagery and rude expression" of his early poetry (*E in C*, 227). Transcendental excess, as Cabot and Holmes would have seen it, becomes an intellectual corollary to the behavioral extremism Edward saw as the truly manic movement of his father's day—"the epoch when philosophers and reformers sought him constantly and sat as guests at his table shuddering at flesh or stimulants, or products of slave-labor, or foreign luxuries, or even at roots because they grew downwards" (*E in C*, 153). Not a single member of the Transcendental circle appears in Edward Emerson's book, save the village neighbors Alcott and Thoreau, and (once) Margaret Fuller. There is no mention of the Divinity School address, the defense of Theodore Parker, or the "heresies" of Jones Very, of the Transcendental Club or the miracles debate or the mocking reception of the *Dial*. Had he felt it appropriate to discuss it, we can only assume that Edward's position would have resembled Cabot's or Holmes's: that Transcendental idealism was essential to Emerson, while Transcendental extremism was not.

Like Cabot's *Memoir*, *Emerson in Concord* reveals a congruence between Emerson's life and work. For Cabot, the congruence is between character and ideas; for Edward, between ideas and behavior. Edward Emerson had pledged to "pass lightly over" Emerson's public life and works and focus instead on how his father's "daily life was in accord with his teachings" (*E in C*, 1–2). By the end of *Emerson in Concord*, Edward could rightly claim to have met his goal, to prove for his father "the agreement of his acts with his words . . . the symmetry and harmony of his life" (*E in C*, 247). It was by now a familiar theme in Emerson biography. Though the book aimed at a somewhat more partisan readership ("those whom his writings have helped or moved" [*E in C*, 2]), it was not significantly more partisan than Cabot's focus on readers who already knew Emerson well.

The clearest explanation for the domestic and community focus of *Emerson in Concord* is, of course, the reason Edward Emerson wrote it in the first place: the Social Circle in Concord expected sketches that showed their members operating on the local scene. But Edward may have had additional reasons. He always harbored dreams of becoming a successful and widely known writer and lecturer, using his inside knowledge of the Concord writers. Certainly, claiming a separate focus would serve to differentiate his book commercially from Cabot's, while at the same time defusing the competition and allowing Cabot's *Memoir* pride of place as the "story for the world" (*E in C*, 1). That praise notwithstanding, *Emerson in Concord* hints at Edward's continuing ambivalence toward Cabot, the official biographer. Admitting on the one hand, for instance, that his father "felt towards Mr. Cabot as to a younger brother" (*E in C*, 189), Edward emphasizes on the other hand that Cabot did not know Emerson well until his election to the Saturday Club in 1861 and that Cabot was "early known, but then seldom met" and "a friend, whom he had never seen so much of as he desired" (*E in C*, 123). What's more, *Emerson in Concord* seems to have been not only a defense of family's importance to their patriarch but also an act of individuation that justified the Emerson siblings' importance in their own right, not just as Emerson's children. It was a lifelong issue for the children. Years later, when age began robbing Edward of his memory, Annie discussed the burden her husband bore even in his dotage. "Here [in Concord] his weakness is no matter, for every one knows him, but away from home he is considered only as his father's son and much would be expected of him."[72] Even while he was writing *Emerson in Concord*, Edward struggled with fears of his own insignificance, and he hinted to Edith in a frank and painful letter that the book might be a means to memorialize more than just their father:

> [I]t is well not to be too scary about our individual privacies in unim-
> portant matters when it would help the picture of Father to bring us in.
> Who are we? I wish that it might happen that we should be remembered
> long for good on our own account, but surely believe that it will prove
> to be as Emerson's children. Now as father said, Plato had no wife and
> children as far as anecdote or tradition could give them life; he was
> Plato, the thinker, and "ground them all into paint." Father has ground
> us into paint but if it could be shown that he had a happy and interest-
> ing domestic side to his life instead of being mere essayist, "seer" or
> poet, all the better for him, and incidentally, for small us.[73]

To establish Waldo Emerson as father and husband would confirm the importance of the "small" family who were at once ennobled and eclipsed by his formidable public reputation.

As an alternative to Cabot's book, *Emerson in Concord* domesticates its subject, painting an affectionate portrait of Emerson's rise from genteel poverty to decorous celebrity, and it does so in a way that Cabot would have found difficult if not impossible. Full of personal reminiscence about Emerson's moderation, tolerance, civic pride, and paternal virtues, it is a book only a family member could write, not a "scholar by profession" (*ETE*, 1:690). As Emerson's iconic stature as the Sage of Concord was solidifying, *Emerson in Concord* offered instead an alternative glimpse of Citizen

Waldo, who enjoyed an active emotional, domestic, and social life, albeit a fairly conventional one. If Cabot showed a man for whom greatness was ordinary, Edward revealed the ordinariness of a great man.

— V —

Almost inevitably, Cabot's and Edward Emerson's biographies were compared to the earlier ones, and to each other. Although Cabot's intent was to exclude "correspondence *en masse*" and let Emerson speak for himself,[74] in its size and execution the *Memoir* resembles the thick "life and letters" volumes being challenged in the 1880s by shorter "sketches" like those in the American Men of Letters series. Cabot's *Memoir* sold well—3,654 copies in 1887, falling off to 559 the following year—far better than Cooke, Ireland, or Conway, though not quite as well as Holmes. *Emerson in Concord* also sold briskly in its first two years, a testimony to readers' continuing fascination with Emerson. Houghton, Mifflin recorded sales of 2,471 in 1889 and 430 the following year, fewer than Cabot's *Memoir* but respectable nonetheless.[75]

Public and private responses to Cabot's biography recalled his own first reactions to the project—cautious, polite, and aware of his shortcomings as a biographer. Among his papers at the Radcliffe Institute's Schlesinger Library is a bound volume of thank-you letters that were predictably positive in acknowledging gift copies of the book. The self-effacing Cabot must have been gratified by the comments of Sarah S. Storer, Rockwood Hoar's sister, who noted, "The other Memoirs have been '*about*' Mr. Emerson[;] this is Emerson himself."[76] Joining others who found the *Memoir* organized and dignified, George William Curtis, the former Brook Farmer later famous for editing the "Easy Chair" column at *Harper's Monthly Magazine*, cited it for a "thoroughness of comprehension, a fullness of sympathy, a felicity of form, and a grace of modesty."[77] Rockwood Hoar called Cabot's biography "complete, adequate, and governed by a good taste which has never failed."[78] James Freeman Clarke, at 77 one of Emerson's oldest surviving friends, thought it "a treasure" and marveled, "How much remains to say about him, after all that has been said!"[79] Surely Cabot must have been pleased to hear his work confirmed by correspondents like these, many of whom had known Emerson far longer than he had.

If the published reviews sometimes repeated these sentiments, at other times their praise was much more muted. The reviewer for the London *Athenaeum*, who saw Emerson in the same terms as Cabot did (a teacher, rather than a prophet), praised the *Memoir* for its measured presentation of Emerson's "tranquil life": "The tale is told with simplicity and good taste, with full appreciation of its subject, but without extravagant eulogy."[80] Perhaps predictably, Horace E. Scudder—one of the editors at Houghton, Mifflin—reviewed the book for the *Atlantic* and found it "admirable" for its "wise selection of material and careful arrangement" of facts.[81] The crusty Henry Hedge, who had also criticized Holmes, was less charitable. Privately, he took Cabot to task for not making more use of Hedge's extensive memories of Emerson's early years. Publicly, while he commended Cabot in the *Unitarian Review* for his "sympathetic appreciation" of Emerson's life, he grumbled over small details and acknowledged that, after all, Cabot had advantages others did not. If Holmes could produce a book "so brilliant and charming" with so little material to work with, Hedge maintained, then "Mr. Cabot's must be judged by his superior opportunity" as the privileged insider. By those standards, the *Memoir* is deficient: "Mr. Cabot has given us the phenomenal, historical Emerson,—the scholar, the sage, as he wrought and taught in the days and scenes of his intellectual activity,—but not the interior, spiritual, fate-determined Emerson, whom no biography can report, whom we can only appreciate as inferred from his outward manifestation in history."[82] Channing's early doubts about Cabot's temperamental suitability were rehearsed in an 1889 review by William Henry Thorne of the Philadelphia *Globe*, a self-professed "convert" to Emersonianism who called Cabot "neither prophet, poet nor philosopher" but "simply a commonplace, practical New England writer," good on the facts but deficient in the spirit of Emerson's life and work.[83]

These nagging doubts about Cabot's rigorously cerebral approach to Emerson continued to surface after the publication of *Emerson in Concord*, whose obvious contrasts with the *Memoir* inevitably raised comparisons in the press. Scudder, who praised Cabot for the personal details that made Emerson seem friendly and familiar, was almost alone in doing so. Cabot himself admitted with critics of the *Memoir* that "it would have benefited by a freer tone."[84] *Emerson in Concord*, by contrast, struck most reviewers as charming and intimate. A long and positive review in the *Atlantic* by George Edward Woodberry, a scholar who would later write the Emerson volume for Macmillan's English Men of Letters series (1907), commended Edward Emerson for a "mosaic of reminiscences" that "puts the whole story upon the common footing of life." *Emerson in Concord* remedied the deficiency in the *Memoir*, an "admirable" book but an impersonal one that presented Emerson "in a most abstract form, almost a spirituality [sic]." Edward Emerson's book, on the other hand, retained Emerson's essential character as a writer and thinker but did not allow those accomplishments to usurp Emerson "the citizen, neighbor, and friend, the son, husband, and father."[85] The *Christian Union* offered even more enthusiastic praise. Calling Edward Emerson "a natural artist" whose portrait of his father's "inward life and outward habits" made up for the deficiencies in Cabot's study, the unnamed reviewer attributed the beauty of the book to its avoidance of "rhetorical effect" and Edward's straightforward attention to the "simple truth" of his father's life that "only one who had full sympathy with him could have given." The reviewer said with heated exaggeration, "The book answers the thousand questions about Emerson which everybody has been asking, and which Mr. Cabot failed to answer."[86] Frank Sanborn was more negative toward *Emerson in Concord*, claiming that Edward Emerson "stands too near the mountain to command the best view" and his book lacked "boldness in comment and delineation." Even so, Sanborn conceded, Edward's biography included valuable biographical details not to be found elsewhere.[87] With rare exceptions, *Emerson in Concord* came out favorably in comparison to Cabot's *Memoir*. Readers found it relaxed, unpretentious, and anecdotal.[88]

And yet the attention was short-lived. Commentary about *Emerson in Concord* dried up by September 1889, barely five months after the book appeared. After six original biographies in eight years, and the countless reviews, newspaper accounts, and appreciations that accompanied them, there was still no unanimity over the status of Emerson's lives. Though Sanborn complained that Emerson's "real biography . . . has yet to be composed,"[89] the *Christian Union* declared that *Emerson in Concord* was "doubtless the final word" on the subject.[90] The reviewer for the London *Athenaeum* hoped it was true. *Emerson in Concord*, he or she said with a sniff, was nothing more than a gathering of biographical "crumbs" of interest only to the "village club" that commissioned it. The *Memoir* and *Emerson in Concord* were later bound into special sets of the Riverside Edition, which made Cabot and Edward Emerson appear to share the official biographical mantle, and both biographies appeared in small British editions, with Edward Emerson's later translated into German (1904). But as the decade of Emerson's death drew to a close, so too did the first wave of biographies. The *Athenaeum* reviewer sounded the death knell: "There is in reality nothing more to be said of Emerson's life and habits."[91] For critics and defenders alike, it was time to call it quits.

SIX

Shelf Life

The Legacy of Emerson's First Biographies

⌒⌒

THE EXHAUSTION OF INTEREST in Emerson's biography by the close of the
1880s did not signal flagging attention to Emerson himself. By the end of
the nineteenth century, as numerous critics have shown, his cultural use-
fulness was being vigorously asserted and debated. Yet the early biographies seem to have had little effect on Emerson's developing iconization.
We would think they should have, both for the claims of their authors
to special knowledge of their subject and also for the sheer durability of
books themselves: collected, passed along, reread, and relatively expensive,
books last, with a life on bookshelves far more enduring than other print
media, especially before libraries routinely collected and preserved newspapers and magazines. But Emerson emerges from the nineteenth century
as neither an activist nor a philosopher, an approachable neighbor and parent nor inspiring friend, a Christian mystic nor an insightful poet. None of
these versions of Emerson—the versions promoted by each of the six early
biographers—took hold in either the popular or academic constructions
of him for nearly a century. To understand why, we must look to the later
stories of the books and those who wrote them, and balance claims for
their importance against the other, extra-literary factors that combined to
crowd out Emerson's complicated biographical interpretations in favor of a
"one dimensional ideal" as the Sage of Concord.[1]

Though their interpretations of Emerson still vied with each other for legitimacy, as commercial products the first biographies no longer competed by the end of the 1880s. By then, all of the early Emerson biographies save Ireland's (long out of print) were owned by Houghton, Mifflin and Company, whose acquisition of failing competitors, conscious pursuit of the literary market, and corralling of the most illustrious names in New England letters constitute a textbook case of the growth of literary commerce in Victorian America.[2] George Willis Cooke's contracts with James R. Osgood and Company were transferred to Houghton, Mifflin on May 1, 1889, and he continued to publish there from time to time, bringing out an *Anthology of Transcendentalism* in 1902 and an Emerson bibliography in 1908. By the time of Cooke's death on April 30, 1923, however, Houghton Mifflin had begun making room for new projects, and in 1926 the firm wrote Cooke's surviving daughter to close out accounts. There were no copies of her father's *Emerson* left in stock, they reported, and only one copy of his *George Eliot*, and as the "sales of these books recently have been too slight to warrant us in reprinting," would she like to buy the plates at half price— for the *Emerson*, $211?[3]

Alexander Ireland's expanded biography fared no better. When he and Conway were at work on "Emerson and His Friends" in 1870, Ireland had mused about a plan to "some day print at my own expense, or to be sold at a very cheap price, a little volume of thoughts from Emerson, which might help to make him better known in England." He hoped that whatever revenue that might accrue to him from his part in Hotten's project would help finance such a labor of love.[4] But Ireland's first Emerson book was also his last. Increasingly impoverished as the 1880s wore on, Ireland lost his income from the failing Manchester *Examiner* and was forced to put his Inglewood home on the market and sell off 10,000 volumes of his beloved library; one of his daughters hired out as a governess, and his wife, Anne, helped support the household by giving lectures and writing a popular biography of Jane Carlyle.[5] In 1893, citing his literary accomplishments and "his unwearied efforts to enhance the happiness of all sections of Society," several friends petitioned for Ireland to be granted a pension from the Queen's Civil List.[6] Ireland died in Manchester the following year, on December 7, 1894.

Moncure Daniel Conway's biography met a similar end. In 1882 he negotiated (perhaps fittingly, for Conway) wildly optimistic terms for *Emerson at Home and Abroad*: 10¢ apiece for the first 5,000 sold, 10 percent royalty on each copy in excess of 5,000, and (the only part of the contract that actually bore fruit) a $500 advance against sales.[7] After selling out its initial printing of 1,500 copies, however, *Emerson at Home and Abroad* languished. Houghton, Mifflin bought Conway's contract in 1889 as part of the firm's acquisition of Osgood. Perhaps hoping to capitalize on Conway's growing fame as an author, the publisher reissued the biography in 1889 and again in 1896; Trübner—by then Kegan Paul, Trench, Trübner & Co.—offered an English reprint in 1890. None of these reissues generated any interest, though an early review reprinted in London in 1896 that dismissed Conway's biography as "transcendental gush" would suggest that the book's reputation had not improved in the decade or so since its first appearance.[8]

Conway never wrote much of significance about Emerson after 1882. The next decade saw productive writing years for Conway, crowned by his 1892 biography of Thomas Paine, still considered authoritative. Yet with his literary success came an increasingly deep disillusionment over the state of American politics that tested and eventually destroyed the optimism that first drew Conway to Emerson. Family tragedies only deepened his pessimism. The Conways lost their son Dana to typhoid in 1886, and Ellen Dana Conway died of cancer on Christmas Day, 1897. Conway was ravaged emotionally and spiritually: no longer, he wrote bitterly in a memorial tribute to his wife, could he delude himself by ascribing "any providential purpose to the diseases and griefs that desolate mankind."[9] Emerson's compensatory optimism now seemed to him a cruel joke. Like many deluded philosophers, Conway wrote of him around the turn of the century, "Emerson had not dealt with evil in nature, avoiding the difficulty in the spirit of that Chinese philosopher of whom Confucius said his eyes 'would not look on a bad color.'"[10] Conway, who was dividing his time between New York and Paris by 1903, did not attend the Emerson centennial events in Boston or Concord, though he contributed an emotionally muted recollection, extracted from the biography, to a commemorative issue of the *Critic*.[11] More revealing than that essay are his remarks at a dinner meeting of the Society of American Authors in New York in May 1903. There, in the opulence of the Waldorf-Astoria hotel, Conway remembered his old mentor in patronizing terms as "a man of peculiar charm in his playfulness, simplicity, and childlikeness . . . [who] drew our attention away from the sorrows of life by making us forget them in the joys of existence."[12] Thus the man who once adored Emerson as a spiritual father joined the chorus of skeptics who dismissed Emersonian Transcendentalism as juvenile escapism. Conway died in Paris on November 15, 1907.

Oliver Wendell Holmes in his final years saw no waning of his celebrity, only his energies, and his work continued to sell well in reprint. When Holmes died on October 7, 1894, at the age of 85, the self-described "last leaf" of the Fireside Poets had already buried his son Ted in 1884, his wife Amelia in 1888, and his daughter Amelia in 1889.[13] Like Cooke, Ireland, and Conway, Holmes never wrote again about Emerson after his 1885 biography of him. But his *Emerson* outlived him, easily becoming the best selling of the early lives. By 1925 it had gone through 35 impressions with total sales of about 21,800 copies.[14]

Edward Waldo Emerson's *Emerson in Concord* was published in 1889 as a commission book, a handshake arrangement[15] he continued with an edition of *A Correspondence Between John Sterling and Ralph Waldo Emerson* (1897) and *Henry Thoreau, as Remembered by a Young Friend* (1917). Edward Emerson died on January 27, 1930. Two years later, Houghton Mifflin approached Edward and Annie's youngest son, Raymond, about the disposition of the remaining 152 copies of *Emerson in Concord*, which they eventually offered to give him for the cost of shipping "so that we may drop the book from our list" and free up warehouse space.[16] In 1939 Raymond finally agreed to take some of the remaining stock, with the rest consigned to his cousin Edward W. Forbes. Across an in-house memorandum okaying the shipment, someone at Houghton Mifflin scrawled in pencil, "Please ship Friday if possible to get it out of my paper tray!"[17]

The ignoble fate of *Emerson in Concord* as a separate volume ignores its reach into the twentieth century in two other forms. For one, beginning in 1893 Edward's biography was included, along with Cabot's *Memoir* and Charles Eliot Norton's edition of the Emerson-Carlyle correspondence, as part of an expanded, specially bound edition of the Riverside *Complete Works* that remained in print until 1913.[18] A second, more important incarnation of Edward's biography came in his 40-page introduction and detailed notes to the 1903–1904 Centenary Edition of Emerson's works. Edward retained the familial, anecdotal emphasis of *Emerson in Concord* in his brief introductory sketch, where he yokes his father's personal and intellectual lives in explicit if tenuous ways: "As he was a good citizen of his village and a patriotic American, so he was a happy and trusting soul in the Universe, seeing everywhere, in Protean forms, the inseparable Trinity of Truth, Goodness, and Beauty." But the more valuable biographical work exists in Edward's comprehensive notes to his father's texts, devoted to showing "the correspondence between the passages and his own traits and experiences."[19] Capitalizing on the family's private papers and on Emerson's as yet unpublished journals and letters, Edward skillfully blends personal circumstance, cross-textual comparisons, source study, and publication history to create a writer's biography of his father that contextualized his work in the conditions of its production. Whether the interrupted narrative contained in Edward's endnotes could ever approach the coherence of a seriatim biography is doubtful. But the Centenary Edition extended the reach of Edward Emerson's personal portrait forward in time and outward in readership. As Joel Myerson points out, in its various formats the edition was a great success, selling more than 75,000 volumes by 1908.[20] The Centenary Edition at last earned Edward the recognition denied him as he worked in Cabot's shadow. At his death the *New York Times* hailed him, in the telegraphic prose of the newspaper headline, as the "Literary Executor of His Famous Father, the 'Sage of Concord' / ONCE PRACTICED MEDICINE / Had Devoted Much Time to Writing on Own Account and Was Also a Painter."[21]

Having completed an authorized biography he had undertaken reluctantly and supervised an edition he thought was unnecessary, after the Riverside Edition added its final volume in 1893 the loyal James Elliot Cabot called it quits and never again wrote about his friend Ralph Waldo Emerson. The continuing success of his 1887 *Memoir*, however, justified the family's faith in him. Not only did it appear alongside Edward Emerson's biography as part of the expanded Riverside Edition, it was also included as the final two volumes of the 1894 Standard Library Edition of Emerson's Works, printed from the Riverside Edition plates and sold only by subscription. The Standard Library Edition enjoyed some commercial success. By March 1906, when it went out of print, it had sold approximately 4,800 sets, making Cabot's *Memoir* the second-best selling of the early biographies, after Holmes's.[22] Cabot died on January 16, 1903, just months before the celebrations of Emerson's centennial but long after Cabot's health and interests had ceased to make him a force in Emerson studies. Thirty years later his biography met the same fate as the others, as Houghton Mifflin decided in 1933 to clear out "those books which are no longer active" and melted down the plates of Cabot's *Memoir* for scrap.[23]

The demise of each of the original six biographies, perhaps a consequence of their incongruence with the increasingly iconic view of Emerson, finds other explanation in Houghton Mifflin's corporate history. By the early twentieth century, Emerson had lost his early champions there—authors and business people alike—to death, disillusion, or old age. Absent those who would defend his complexity, his reputation was increasingly left in the hands of those who had never known him and were more likely as a result to parrot the oversimplifications that characterized his reputation by the turn of the century. The company, too, was changing. Incorporated in 1908, and thereafter more subject to the wishes of its shareholders and directors, Houghton Mifflin gradually moved away from its focus on New England authors, as those in the company with a personal commitment to them died: the venerable Henry O. Houghton in 1895; Horace Scudder, tireless editor of the *Atlantic*, in 1902; George H. Mifflin, who had encouraged the publication of both Emerson's and Thoreau's journals, in 1921.[24] With the passing of the old guard came new priorities, particularly a focus on realists whose work the company had earlier rejected.[25] Add to this the ascension in the 1920s of Houghton Mifflin's textbook and trade departments, and it seems clear that the flagging interest in Emerson's first biographies for their publisher was as much a result of commerce as of culture.

— II —

As attention to the first biographies waned, so heteroglossic conversations about Emerson's cultural significance gradually flattened into an iconic monotone that imaged Emerson as praiseworthy, exemplary, forward-thinking, high-minded—and to some readers and critics in the twentieth century, crushingly dull.[26] By the centennial year 1903, Emerson's apotheosis was firmly under way. But the chronology is crucial. As Todd H. Richardson shows in great detail, in the 1880s and 1890s Emerson's various selves were still being sorted out in contemporary magazines, and the debate waged over Emerson's cultural heroism was by no means quickly or easily settled. If ideological needs contributed to this debate, so too, recalling Louis Althusser's distinctions, did the materiality of ideology, particularly its manifestations in the worlds of publishing, genre, and authorship. The fact that we are slow to recognize the influence of biblio-commerce, the circumstances of his biographers, and the demands of the genre on Emerson's reputation shows how powerfully that reputation held sway: because Emerson as Sage has always seemed so otherworldly, we have not before now fully considered the ways in which "real world" circumstances influenced and shaped his construction.

As I have argued in the preceding chapters, some potentially subversive biographical views never got the attention they deserved because of the conditions of their publication and distribution. In the 1880s Cooke, Ireland, and Conway had little standing as biographers—the first two largely unknown, the third notoriously inaccurate—and their books all suffered from small press runs, limited distribution, half-hearted promotion, stiff competition, and bad timing in a market suddenly glutted with competing Emersoniana. Had they been more available and better promoted, who knows how Emerson's reputation might have changed? Speculating about what did *not* happen may be a fool's errand, but conjecture is hard to avoid when the questions pile up. Might Hotten's edition of Emerson's unrevised topical pieces have preempted the worked-over selection that appeared in 1876 as *Letters and Social Aims*? What if Conway's and Ireland's warm and socially engaged Emerson had been the first version presented to the public in 1870, long before his iconic reputation had crystallized? How carefully would Cooke's *Emerson* have been read had he written it with the authority of a New Englander, not as a newcomer from Indianapolis? Might Conway's biography have succeeded had Macmillan said yes to it in 1882 and then promoted the book with all the resources and prestige of a major publishing house? At the least, since Cooke, Ireland, and Conway stressed Emerson's engagement with the world of affairs, they would have challenged the growing construction of him as effete and distant. But given the circumstances of their publication, they didn't stand a chance.

And what of Holmes, Cabot, and Edward Emerson, whose biographies far outsold the others and whose work remained more or less active well into the twentieth century? Their complex representations of Emerson, different from each other and certainly different from the icon he would become, seem to have had no more impact on his eventual reputation than those of the early biographies that sold far less. Why not? And if the biographies with their rich and diverse interpretations of Emerson made so little difference in his developing iconization, what did? Two less studied contexts had a direct impact on the effectiveness of the early biographies: the growth of a celebrity culture and the rise of mass media.

— III —

The formative power of celebrity exerted an enormous influence on Emerson's reputation in ways that are only recently becoming clear to us, thanks to recent studies of the complex interactions between fame, public need, and media construction.[27] Emerson wore his fame uncomfortably, straddling definitions and defying categorization. In an often cited "calculus of celebrityhood," for instance, James Monaco distinguishes *heroes*, who are celebrated for what they do, from *stars*, who are celebrated for who they are.[28] By the time of his death Emerson fit both of these classifications, his life and his work inseparable. But Emerson's apotheosis might in some ways have resulted from the particular *type* of celebrity that accrued to writers. According to Leo Braudy in *The Frenzy of Renown* (1986), literary celebrities are presented special problems, for they must try to remain "unspoiled by the public gaze," at once rising above commercialism while enjoying its rewards.[29] What's more, Braudy argues, literary celebrity in nineteenth-century America—in the absence of a usable past and with a skeptical, if not reproachful, view of the present—encouraged "the belief that absolute fame is a turning away from time itself."

> Writers like Emerson, Thoreau, Dickinson, and Whitman (and for that matter Washington and Jefferson and Paine) helped evolve a democratic spirituality that would equally combat commercialism, technology, and the flatness of constant change. They wrote directly and often explicitly *for* the future and so paid their present readers the compliment of standing with them outside the accidents of time and place.[30]

Braudy's analysis gets at a salient fact for Emerson's reputation, for if Braudy is correct—if there is in American literary celebrity an expectation that authors must transcend crass circumstances and live outside of time and space—then everything from the aphorisms slapped on best-selling calendars and Concord souvenirs to the widely reprinted photographs taken in his later years, when the formalities of portraiture and the ruin of aphasia made him look dreamy, fragile, and angelic,[31] reinforced an expectation of wisdom, piety, and elevation against which the engaged and complicated Emerson of the six biographies stood little chance.

Emerson's celebrity was of a different, if not unique sort. Even in life he became, in Mutlu Konuk Blasing's phrase, "the paradoxical private-person-as-public-hero."[32] The closer Americans got to Emerson, the more distant he seemed; the more his illness robbed him of control of his environment and expression, the easier it was to infer that he was above everyday realities, thinking more rarified thoughts. In life, he was at once distant and accessible, the venerable Sage of Concord whom visitors could (and did) regularly hallo in the street and greet in the post office. Bonnie Carr O'Neill, in an analysis of his lecture career, has called this phenomenon Emerson's "democratic availability": the "highly subjective and widely available" interpretability that encouraged and empowered Emerson's listeners constantly to reimagine and redefine him. Only later, O'Neill contends, after Emerson's death, did his critics and supporters try to "wrest authority from the masses" by creating "an authoritative interpretation" of him.[33]

Approaching Emerson's apotheosis as a phenomenon in the history of celebrity recontextualizes the work of the early biographers by placing them amidst all those interpreters who struggled to navigate his multiple possibilities and eventually landed on the comforting shore of just one. Emerson's "democratic availability" rendered him a cultural Rorschach test that equated the opinions of those with the authority of firsthand knowledge—the early biographers—and those who knew him casually or not at all. Endlessly interpretable, Emerson as celebrity both encouraged the process of biographical diversification and hastened its end.

— IV —

The growth of celebrity in the late nineteenth century points to a second, closely related influence on Emerson's biographical creation: the expansion of mass media that nurtured fame. As Monaco and others point out, new technologies played a pivotal role in the creation of celebrity, a truism today that makes it easy to ignore their phenomenal novelty *precisely* at the time the hagiographic Emerson was beginning to crowd out alternative versions of him. Prior to the late nineteenth century, Monaco observes, celebrity was limited, local, and visual. Most people knew only their fellow villagers by name and by sight, and other figures, ones only heard about but never seen, had no "immediate presence." But the rise of mass communication technologies and new media like the reproducible photograph changed all that. The development in the 1880s of the halftone process for reproducing photographs in newspapers "provided the striking visual image to go with the narrative story," and new rotary printing presses allowed for the cheap dissemination of printed material, particularly magazines and newspapers.[34] By the last decades of the nineteenth century, the shaping effect of periodicals and photography on Emerson's reputation was profound, as the periodical press increasingly challenged the power of books to shape the public's immediate understanding of people and events.

As John Tebbel points out in his comprehensive history of book publishing in the United States, the future of books versus periodicals was a topic of some debate in the 1880s, some of it alarmist and self-interested. (The publisher Henry Holt, for example, speaking at Yale in 1887 on "Some Practical Aspects of the Literary Life in the United States," foretold the imminent death of the book, sales of which had fallen 33 percent in the previous decade.) Serious but busy readers were turning increasingly to quality periodicals for their understanding of a rapidly changing world. Cheaper, more timely, and certainly more responsive to public opinion than published books, newspapers and magazines were nimble registers of the competing claims for Emerson, adept at conveying news and information that, as Holt conceded, "would stale long before it could get between the covers of a book."[35] Todd H. Richardson notes that, while Americans debated and later fine-tuned their "hagiographic critical judgments of Emerson," it was magazines, not books, which provided "the open-ended forum for this sort of makeshift debate on Emerson's place in culture."[36] Still, the effects of periodicals on Emerson's constructed reputation may not have been as monolithic or as fast as we have hitherto thought. As Todd H. Richardson has shown in his deep reading of the *Literary World*, the *Woman's Journal*, and the *Free Religious Index* from 1872 to the centennial year of 1903, while Emerson's reputation was negotiated publically in magazines as they strove to coordinate him with their particular political agendas, there was in these influential periodicals little attempt to make his reputation uniform or his significance permanent. Through the process of debate, however, Emerson's canonization went forward nonetheless, as possibilities were winnowed and the "personal reports and memories" published in magazines gradually gelled into "his imagined reconstruction as a cultural hero."[37] Similarly, Len Gougeon's careful examination of 70 American newspapers during Emerson's centennial year shows that while Emerson's "apotheosis was virtually complete" by 1903, there remained some considerable debate in the press about what sort of saint he had become, with newspaper writers claiming him variously as a "spiritual idealist," "transcendental prophet and seer," and "an orthodox Christian." Thus, Gougeon shows, the cultural judgment of Emerson as a "vaguely conceived and decidedly conservative Brahmin" would have been premature in the 1880s, when the six biographers wrote, and to some extent even at the turn of the century, when his cultural significance was still up for grabs.[38] If Emerson's reputation was in a sense on trial in the last decades of the nineteenth century, the competing arguments and evidence were presented in periodicals. Readers of biographical books got only the verdict. What appears with the advantage of a century's hindsight as a spectrum of biographical possibilities must have seemed to fin-de-siècle readers merely a half-dozen more idiosyncratic and somewhat long-winded answers to questions they were still asking about their celebrated but indeterminate Sage of Concord. Emerson's early biographies need to be read not as confirming his iconic reputation but as part of a process in which that reputation developed.

The value of Emerson's first biographers is thus qualified by what seems to be their failure to influence what the public knew of him, as their books were supplanted by bland narratives of Saint Waldo, outsold by magazines, mothballed by their publisher, and too slow to register the active conversations that appeared in newspapers and magazines. What then do the first biographies offer us today?

First of all, whether violating, confirming, or ignoring the generic debates of the 1880s, the early biographers reveal the sweeping changes that complicated the act of Victorian life-writing. As writers, they left behind a remarkably detailed record of their attempts to negotiate the major issues of the genre. Emerson was certainly no typical subject, but his biographers faced typical issues that were magnified by Emerson's celebrity and by the biographers' almost total inexperience with their craft, which caused them to struggle openly and repeatedly with generic issues and debates. (Only two, Holmes and Conway, had written a book before.) In the battle over biography in the 1880s, Emerson's first biographers seemed always on the losing side. They were respectfully circumspect as the reading public hungered for privacies. Their books were longer when the trend was for brevity. They focused on character and documents as biographies increasingly emphasized privacies and personal testimony. They were protective of their subject despite a trend toward biographical objectivity and revelation. On the question of whether life-writing was essentially documentary or interpretive, all but Cabot (whose book most closely approached a life-and-letters biography) leaned toward interpretation, from Ireland's relatively transparent claims for Emerson's activism to Holmes's sophisticated diagnosis of Emerson's psychological health and Edward Emerson's relentless emphasis on his father's amiability and civic presence. On the issue of privacy, the biographers were uniformly conservative, either for self-serving reasons—the fear of stepping into a Froudean minefield—or principled ones. Only Conway hinted at Emerson's emotional volatility in ways that skirted indiscretion. The rest were unwilling to reveal "circumstances not meant to go beyond the household walls," as Holmes put it.[39] By defining flaws in character as the discrepancy between public utterance and personal conduct, all agreed that Emerson was, in this sense, not flawed. But consistency of word and deed was a far cry from the hagiographic claims of moral perfection that would characterize later appraisals of him.

Second, writing Emerson's life raised the issue of biographical authority, which was for Transcendentalists bound up with the thorny concepts of friendship and sympathy. A central concern of Transcendentalism, authority was a delicate issue for the early biographers, whose insistence on their own credentials was sometimes expressed obliquely in criticism of the others'—as, for instance, Cooke's negative review of Holmes, and Holmes's doubts about Conway. Of the six biographers, only Conway would have been comfortable being called a Transcendentalist. For members of the Transcendental group who survived Emerson, however, who knew him best was a sensitive and crucial issue. Frederic Henry Hedge wrote petulantly to Holmes after the publication of his book: "I wonder a little that knowing my intimacy with [Emerson] you did not consult with me. . . . Alcott touched him only on one side & Thoreau on another, but I on many. At the risk of seeming conceited, I think I may say I had more of his confidence than most of those who came near him."[40] In his early letters to Cabot, William Henry Channing considered himself one of the few "to whom this wonderful Soul opened, at least by glimpses, his *Inmost Centre* of Life."[41] Bronson Alcott, who thought Cooke's biography would add little to an understanding of Emerson, changed his mind when he discovered how much of Cooke's book "was taken from my lips."[42] When asked his opinion of Cabot's *Memoir*, William Henry Furness called it "a model biography"; but when pushed to say whether he *liked* the book, he confessed, "It is a little conceit in me, [but] I felt that I knew [Emerson] better than Mr Cabot did."[43] Transcendentalism as a movement, we recall, was being roundly criticized by the 1880s. But the issue of biographical authority, raised in non-Transcendental contexts such as the furor over Froude and Carlyle, took on a distinct resonance for biographers of Emerson. Authority was *a*, maybe *the*, central idea of Transcendentalism in New England. Epistemological authority came through right seeing. Moral authority resided in the self. But biographical authority resided in the sympathetic relationship to one's subject that the Transcendentalists called friendship. Over and over, we hear biographers, friends, and family members addressing the same question: Who knew Emerson well enough to reconstruct his life accurately? To us, this issue of biographical ownership sounds petty and competitive, and perhaps on some levels it was. Yet to them, the question of personal authority was anything but insignificant. For his first biographers, writing Emerson's life with the authority of true friendship raised again the ultimate Transcendental challenge, which in turn testified to the continuing resilience of Transcendental ideas even as the movement was being publicly dismissed as irrelevant.

In short, their sympathy and understanding of Emerson both complicated and credentialed the early biographers—and brings us to the final significance of their work. While Emerson's public image was being transformed by the culture of celebrity into a palatable but distant icon, all of the early biographers (even Cooke, whose firsthand knowledge of Emerson was severely limited) aimed to create an Emersonian person-ality that would complement and enrich the image created for the public. Committed as biographers to elucidating Emerson's character, they sought as well to capture the ways his character manifested itself in distinctive personal behavior. Holmes, in many ways the most self-conscious of the biographers, cautioned Ellen Emerson about the importance of individuation. "In a generation or two, your father will be an ideal, tending to become as mystical as Buddha but for these human circumstances, which remind us that he was a man."[44] Taken together, the early biographers gathered a wealth of personal information about Emerson available nowhere else, preserving his "human circumstances" until Emerson's readers were ready to hear them.

In this hermetic function they were joined by Emerson's adult children, whose rearguard efforts against the distillation of their father into an embodiment of moral platitudes reveal a very modern sense of the biographical genre. Edward Emerson of course wrote the most familial and personal biography, but the involvement of Edith Emerson Forbes and Ellen Emerson reveals a larger pattern of influence and stewardship implicating all three of the Emerson siblings in the construction of their father's posthumous reputation. As we have seen, Ellen dutifully fact-checked Cooke's biography, bemoaned the inaccuracies of Conway's, and praised the precision of Cabot's. Edith, we are reminded, insinuated herself into Cabot's memoir by capitalizing on his desperate need for family reminiscence. Behind the family's involvement were at least two motives, one personal, the other generic. Edward's painful question for his sisters, "Who are we?"[45] is echoed in an 1886 letter from Edith, probably written to Elizabeth Cabot, about her husband's book. After pages of miscellaneous anecdotes of her father, Edith writes: "I have been thinking that almost all record of his personal life in the book ends with his marriage to Mother or rather with the deaths of my uncles and Waldo—leaving him a sad and blighted man and by no means giving an impression of the long happy domestic life—which he adorned [sic], and the love and friendliness of the whole town to him." This may be the understandable defensiveness of children who are all but absent in the biographies; as Edith told her cousin Lizzy Storer, judging only by the existing biographies of Emerson "it was but by chance that it would be learned that he had any children." But Edith recognized in the effacement of her father's domestic life something more than just a personal slight. It raised a larger issue that gets at the heart of Emerson's problematic iconization and the challenge of writing a "whole-souled" biography of him:

> Father is so often represented so cold and thin-blooded, reserved and living in far heights of philosophy without human interests—so I do not like to have all trace of family life disappear from the book as soon as his marriage is announced, and I am quite sure that only a quarter part of the man is shown unless it is known what an *enchanting* father he was[,] what a sweet playful loveable house-mate he was, how full of human sympathy for everyone—what respect he had for every class of people.[46]

Edith's passionate rephrasing of the generic debate between public and private narratives reminds us that members of the Emerson family were in an especially tough spot. Much as they wished a more intimate view of their father, they were not willing to mete out unpublished material that would compromise interest in the Riverside Edition and limit its sales. Emerson's domesticity, a subject yet unexplored by scholars and biographers, was for his children a significant component of his biography that they were both eager and reluctant to exploit.

The complicated presence of the Emerson siblings as both the stewards and the beneficiaries of their father's reputation is an indication of how intricately the personal, familial, commercial, and generic intermingled in the story of Emerson's biographical construction and points to the enduring importance of the early biographers and their stories to considerations of literary history and cultural values. In the face of a massive cultural appropriation and biographical oversimplification, the first biographers recorded a diverse, complicated, deeply human Emerson whose complexity lurked hidden behind the iconic image of him for a century or more until revisionist studies such as Len Gougeon's *Virtue's Hero: Emerson, Antislavery, and Reform* (1990) and Robert D. Richardson Jr.'s *Emerson: The Mind on Fire* (1995) reclaimed for Emerson both a place in the history of American activism and a life of emotional fullness and integration. Their work constitutes an extraordinary episode in American biography and a case study of the pressures, practicalities, and rewards of life-writing during a most formative period of its history as a genre. But their value is much more than antiquarian. Long relegated to the critical dustbin of Victorian gentility, Emerson's first biographers, like the rich and "whole-souled" Emerson they created, emerge from the contexts of publication history, authorial needs, generic redefinition, and family interests as startlingly alive and surprisingly modern.

NOTES

INTRODUCTION

1. OWH to George Bancroft, 16 January 1885, George Bancroft Papers, Massachusetts Historical Society.

2. Holmes, *A Mortal Antipathy* (Boston: Houghton, Mifflin, 1892), 7:17.

3. "Reminiscences," *New-York Times*, 2 May 1882.

4. H. L. Kleinfield, "The Structure of Emerson's Death," *Bulletin of the New York Public Library* 65 (1961): 58.

5. Kleinfield, 64.

6. William Henry Channing, "R. W. Emerson," *Modern Review* 3 (October 1882): 852.

7. Conway to Ellen Tucker Emerson, 6 June 1882, bMS Am 1280.226 (3302). Ralph Waldo Emerson Memorial Association deposit, Houghton Library, Harvard University. Not to be reproduced in whole or in part without permission.

8. The six major biographies of Emerson in the 1880s are as follows: George Willis Cooke, *Ralph Waldo Emerson: His Life, Writings, and Philosophy* (Boston: James R. Osgood, 1881); Alexander Ireland, *In Memoriam. Ralph Waldo Emerson: Recollections of His Visits to England in 1833, 1847–8, 1872–3, and Extracts from Unpublished Letters* (London: Simpkin, Marshall, 1882), later expanded as *Ralph Waldo Emerson: His Life, Genius, and Writings. A Biographical Sketch* (London: Simpkin, Marshall, 1882); Moncure Daniel Conway, *Emerson at Home and Abroad* (Boston: James R. Osgood, 1882; London: Trübner, 1883); Oliver Wendell Holmes, *Ralph Waldo Emerson* (Boston: Houghton, Mifflin, 1885 [c. 1884]); James Elliot Cabot, *A Memoir of Ralph Waldo Emerson*, 2 volumes (Boston: Houghton, Mifflin, 1887); and Edward Waldo Emerson, *Emerson in Concord: A Memoir* (Boston: Houghton, Mifflin, 1889 [c. 1888]).

9. By concentrating on biographies by writers who actually knew Emerson, I am very consciously making a value judgment about the importance of biographical authority, which shall be pursued in chapter six. But it is worth noting several

full-length studies in the 1880s by writers who never met Emerson and whose work was largely derivative. Alfred Hudson Guernsey's *Ralph Waldo Emerson: Philosopher and Poet* (New York: D. Appleton and Company, 1881), mostly excerpts of published writing, was advertised on a tipped-in sheet as "published by arrangement with Messrs. Houghton, Mifflin & Co." I can find no other record of that arrangement, but since Appleton's line was often pitched at schoolroom use, likely Houghton, Mifflin saw the prospect of a financial return without serious competition with Cabot's promised volumes. Guernsey (1818–1902) was a popular historian and the editor of *Alden's Cyclopedia of Universal Literature* (1884–1891), writing most of its 20 volumes himself. Richard Garnett's *Life of Ralph Waldo Emerson* (London: Walter Scott, 1888) is a popular account based solely on secondary sources. Garnett (1835–1906), a prolific English historian and bibliophile, also wrote biographies of Milton, Blake, Carlyle, and Coleridge, most of them for Scott's "Great Writers" series. Bronson Alcott's *Ralph Waldo Emerson: An Estimate of His Character and Genius, in Prose and Verse* (Boston: A. Williams, 1882), written by one of Emerson's oldest friends and most consistent admirers, is actually a slightly modified reprint of Alcott's earlier lecture *Emerson* (Cambridge: privately printed, 1865) that was rushed back into print after Emerson's death and is not, despite its title, biographical.

10. Paul Ricoeur, "Objectivity and Subjectivity in History," in *History and Truth*, trans. Charles A. Kelbley (Evanston: Northwestern University Press, 1965), 27–28.

11. Susan Tridgell, *Understanding Our Selves: The Dangerous Art of Biography* (Oxford and Bern: Peter Lang, 2004), 165, 166, 27, 168.

12. Robert D. Richardson Jr., "The Perils of Writing Biography," in *Lives Out of Letters: Essays on American Literary Biography and Documentation*, ed. Robert D. Habich (Madison, NJ: Fairleigh Dickinson University Press, 2004), 254.

13. Stanley Fish, "Just Published: Minutiae without Meaning," *New York Times*, 7 September 1999. See also John Worthen, who calls biographical coherence a "confidence trick" ("The Necessary Ignorance of a Biographer," in *The Art of Literary Biography*, ed. John Batchelor [Oxford: Clarendon Press, 1995], 240).

14. Margaret O. W. Oliphant, "The Ethics of Biography," *Contemporary Review* [London] 44 (1883): 76–93. For other uses of the desecration metaphor see John Stallworthy, "A Life for a Life," in *The Art of Literary Biography*, ed. John Batchelor, 27–42.

15. George Eliot, *The George Eliot Letters*, ed. Gordon S. Haight, 9 vols. (New Haven, CT: Yale University Press, 1954–1978), 6:26.

16. Scott E. Casper, *Constructing American Lives: Biography and Culture in Nineteenth-Century America* (Chapel Hill: University of North Carolina Press, 1999), 245, 7–9.

17. Ronald A. Bosco, "We Find What We Seek: Emerson and His Biographers," in *A Historical Guide to Ralph Waldo Emerson*, ed. Joel Myerson (New York and Oxford: Oxford University Press, 2000), 269–290.

18. Randall Fuller, *Emerson's Ghosts: Literature, Politics, and the Making of Americanists* (New York: Oxford University Press, 2007), 30, 27–28, 40.

19. Charles E. Mitchell, *Individualism and Its Discontents: Appropriations of Emerson, 1880–1950* (Amherst: University of Massachusetts Press, 1997), 21, 35.

20. T. S. McMillin, *Our Preposterous Use of Literature: Emerson and the Nature of Reading* (Urbana: University of Illinois Press, 2000), 89, 58.

21. Fuller, 29.

22. Louis Althusser, "Ideology and Ideological State Apparatuses," in *Lenin and Philosophy and Other Essays*, Part 2, trans. Ben Brewster (New York and London: Monthly Review Press, 1971), 133, 162, 168.

23. John Tomsich, *A Genteel Endeavor: American Culture and Politics in the Gilded Age* (Stanford, CA: Stanford University Press, 1971), 24, 2–3.

24. David Hackett Fischer, *Paul Revere's Ride* (New York: Oxford University Press, 1994), xv.

25. Brodhead maintains that writing comes to be "in interaction with the network of relations that surround it." In Brodhead's formulation, "Writing always takes place within some completely concrete cultural situation, a situation that surrounds it with some particular landscape of institutional structures, affiliates it with some particular group from among the array of contemporary groupings, and installs it [in] some group-based world of understandings, practices, and values" (*Cultures of Letters: Scenes of Reading and Writing in Nineteenth-Century America* [Chicago and London: University of Chicago Press, 1993], 8).

26. Fuller argues, for example, that Conway's "claims for Emerson as an agent of social, political, and aesthetic change were largely overlooked" in favor of the book's "authorization of New England moral superiority concerning slavery" (*Emerson's Ghosts*, 39). Mitchell, who does not discuss Conway specifically, suggests a larger fear of Emerson's "potential for antinomian and anarchic abuse" (*Individualism*, 26) that would have limited the influence of *Emerson at Home and Abroad*. Conway himself all but ignores the finished book in his *Autobiography, Memories and Experiences* (Boston: Houghton, Mifflin, 1904).

27. Virginia Woolf, "The Art of Biography," in *The Death of the Moth and Other Essays* (San Diego: Harcourt Brace Jovanovich, 1942), 197.

28. Jerome J. McGann, *The Textual Condition* (Princeton, NJ: Princeton University Press, 1991), 16.

29. McGann, 62.

1. A GENRE IN TRANSITION

1. EWE to JEC, 10 November 1877, bMS Am 1280.226 (260). Ralph Waldo Emerson Memorial Association deposit, Houghton Library, Harvard University. Not to be reproduced in whole or in part without permission.

2. *ETE*, 1:690.

3. *The Correspondence of Emerson and Carlyle*, ed. Joseph Slater (New York: Columbia University Press, 1964), 586.

4. Edward Waldo Emerson, *The Early Years of the Saturday Club* (Boston: Houghton Mifflin, 1918), 266.

5. JEC to EWE, 13 November 1877, bMS Am 1280.226 (260). Ralph Waldo Emerson Memorial Association deposit, Houghton Library, Harvard University. Not to be reproduced in whole or in part without permission.

6. JEC to Ellen Tucker Emerson, 18 February 1881, bMS Am 1280.226 (3224). Ralph Waldo Emerson Memorial Association deposit, Houghton Library, Harvard University. Not to be reproduced in whole or in part without permission.

7. *ETE*, 2:414–415.

8. Cooke *RWE*, p. v.

9. AI to MDC, 8 October 1882, Alexander Ireland Papers, Special Collections Library, University of Michigan.

10. Holmes *RWE*, 1.

11. *E in C*, 1.

12. Sir Leslie Stephen, "National Biography," in *Studies of a Biographer*, 4 vols. (London: Duckworth, 1902–1907), 1:2.

13. Paul Murray Kendall, *The Art of Biography* (New York: Norton, 1965), 109. For a discussion of Macmillan's biographical project that posits traditional views of biography against the reportorial methods of new journalism from the 1880s onward, see Laurel Brake, "The Serialisation of Books: Macmillan's English Men of Letters Series and the New Biography," in *Print in Transition 1850–1910: Studies in Media and Book History* (Basingstoke, UK, and New York: Palgrave, 2001), 52–66.

14. A. O. J. Cockshut, *Truth to Life: The Art of Biography in the Nineteenth Century* (London: Collins, 1974), 16.

15. Elizabeth Porter Gould, "The Biography of the Future," *Literary World* 16, 16 May 1885, 171.

16. Gould, 171.

17. Gould, 171.

18. "The Biographical Mania," *Tait's Edinburgh Magazine*, n.s. 21 (January 1854): 16.

19. *Tait's*, 16.

20. "The Craze for Biographies," *Spectator*, 14 April 1888, 507.

21. For a similar indictment of the degeneration of biography in the United States, see M. A. Dodge, "The New School of Biography," *Atlantic Monthly* 14 (November 1864): 579–589.

22. Kendall, *The Art of Biography*, 104–109.

23. Henry David Thoreau, *Walden*, ed. J. Lyndon Shanley (Princeton: Princeton University Press, 1971), 153–154.

24. Richard D. Altick, *Lives and Letters: A History of Literary Biography in England and America* (New York: Knopf, 1965), 163.

25. James Anthony Froude, *My Relations with Carlyle* (London: Longmans, Green, 1903), 16, 4. Altick calls Froude "a rebel against the prevailing biographical policy of concealing warts and smoothing facial furrows" (*Lives and Letters*, 237). Trev Lynn Broughton, in *Men of Letters, Writing Lives: Masculinity and Literary Auto/Biography in the Late Victorian Period* (London: Routledge, 1999), argues that Froude's work initiated "a full-scale debate about lives, writing and the relationship between them" (89). A recent biography is Julia Markus, *J. Anthony Froude: The Last Undiscovered Great Victorian* (New York: Scribners, 2005).

26. Froude, *My Relations*, 34.

27. Frederic Harrison, "Froude's Life of Carlyle," *North American Review* 140 (January 1885): 18, 17.

28. Charles Eliot Norton to Mrs. Alexander Carlyle, 5 July 1882, *Letters of Charles Eliot Norton*, ed. Sara Norton and M. A. DeWolfe Howe, 2 vols. (Boston: Houghton Mifflin, 1913), 2:135–136.

29. Waldo Hillary Dunn, *James Anthony Froude: A Biography*, vol. 1 (Oxford: Clarendon Press, 1961), 1:vii.

30. Lytton Strachey, *Portraits in Miniature and Other Essays* (New York: Harcourt, 1931), 191.

31. See, for instance, Cockshut, *Truth to Life,* passim; Kendall, *Art of Biography,* 104; and Broughton, *Men of Letters,* 89 and passim.

32. Kendall, *Art of Biography,* 105.

33. Altick, *Lives and Letters,* 277.

34. Nigel Hamilton, *Biography: A Brief History* (Cambridge: Harvard University Press, 2007), 112–123.

35. Ed Folsom, *Walt Whitman's Native Representations* (New York: Cambridge University Press, 1994), 8. Folsom's analysis is developed in his chapter "Walt Whitman and Photography" (99–126), to which I am indebted. Useful recent histories of early photography are William Welling, *Photography in America: The Formative Years, 1839–1900* (New York: Thomas Y. Crowell, 1978) and Martin W. Sandler, *Photography: An Illustrated History* (New York: Oxford University Press, 2002).

36. Oliver Wendell Holmes, "Doings of the Sunbeam," *Atlantic Monthly* 7 (July 1863): 10.

37. Driven by advances in technology that replaced unwieldy dry and wet plates with the celluloid film roll, photography was by the 1880s within reach of almost everybody. The "detective camera," cheap and easy to use, was supplanted in 1888 by George Eastman's Kodak, which came complete with a roll of 100 exposures and sold for about 25 dollars. Photographic portraitists, always hampered by movement and darkness, benefited from the advance of electric lighting, which made it possible to pose subjects indoors, and light-sensitive film removed from the photography studio the cumbersome braces and head clamps designed to immobilize sitters while the daguerreotypist fiddled with the camera and waited for plates to be exposed (Sandler, *Photography,* 21, 25; Welling, *Photography in America,* 279).

38. "The Camera Epidemic," *New York Times,* 20 August 1884.

39. Welling, *Photography in America,* 185.

40. "Faces of Noted People: The Popular Craze for Photographs of Celebrities," *New York Times,* 25 February 1883.

41. "Actresses for the Album: Popular Artists Whose Pictures Sell Readily," *New York Times,* 5 November 1882.

42. Frank Luther Mott, *American Journalism: A History, 1690–1960,* 3d ed. (New York: Macmillan, 1962), 501–502, 588; Welling, *Photography in America,* 263.

43. As Holmes said as early as 1859, "The very things which an artist would leave out, or render imperfectly, the photograph takes infinite care with, and so makes its illusions perfect" ("The Stereoscope and the Stereograph," *Atlantic Monthly* 3 [June 1859]: 746).

44. Sir Leslie Stephen, "Biography," *National Review* 22 (1893): 180.

45. Edmund Gosse, "The Custom of Biography," *Anglo-Saxon Review* 8 (1901): 195.

46. William Torrey Harris, Concord School of Philosophy Scrapbook, 1879–1887. Folder 6 (1885), Vault A35, W. T. Harris Unit 2. Concord Free Public Library.

47. Henry James, *Hawthorne* (London: Macmillan, 1879), 84.

48. [H. W. Holland], "Mr. Emerson's Philosophy," *Nation,* 17 November 1881, 397.

49. Thomas Wentworth Higginson, *Margaret Fuller Ossoli* (Boston: Houghton, Mifflin, 1885), 5.

50. Fritz Oehlschlaeger and George Hendrick, eds., *Toward the Making of Thoreau's Modern Reputation: Selected Correspondence of S. A. Jones, A. W. Hosmer, H. S. Salt, H. G. O. Blake, and D. Ricketson* (Urbana: University of Illinois Press, 1979), 12, 15, 20.

51. Gary Scharnhorst, *Henry David Thoreau: A Case Study in Canonization* (Columbia, SC: Camden House, 1993), 24.

52. Henry Stephens Salt, *Life of Henry David Thoreau,* 1890. Enl. ed. (London: Scott, 1896). For a more complete discussion, see my chapter "Biography, Memoir, and Reminiscence" in *Oxford Handbook of Transcendentalism,* ed. Joel Myerson, Sandra Harbert Petrulionis, and Laura Dassow Walls (New York and Oxford: Oxford University Press, 2010), 426–437.

53. Robert D. Richardson Jr., *Emerson: The Mind on Fire* (Berkeley: University of California Press, 1995), xi.

54. Nathan Haskell Dole, "Life of Ralph Waldo Emerson," in *The Early Poems of Ralph Waldo Emerson* (New York: Thomas Y. Crowell, 1899), xli. See H. L. Kleinfield, "The Structure of Emerson's Death," *Bulletin of the New York Public Library* 65 (1961): 47–64 for a summary of Emerson's reputation in the two decades after his death.

2. AN ACT OF WHOLESOME AND PURE-HEARTED ADMIRATION

1. The most reliable brief biographies are J. T. Sunderland, "George Willis Cooke: An Appreciation," *Unity,* 14 June 1923, 249–254, and Robert E. Burkholder, "George Willis Cooke," in *American Literary Critics and Scholars, 1880–1900,* ed. John W. Rathbun and Monica M. Grecu (Detroit: Gale, 1988), 50–57.

2. Cooke estimated the attendance at 60 (GWC to Jabez T. Sunderland, 27 April 1918, Jabez T. Sunderland Papers, Box 5, Folder: Correspondence, 1918–1919, Bentley Historical Library, University of Michigan, hereafter abbreviated JTS Papers). *Unity* reported that "some 25 ministers and many other friends, old and new, were present either in person or by letter" (headnote to George Willis Cooke, "After Seventy Years—an Optimist," *Unity,* 9 May 1918, 163).

3. N. S. Hoagland, "Correspondence: Seventieth Birthday Reception of George Willis Cooke," *Unity,* 23 May 1918, 200.

4. Sunderland, "George Willis Cooke," 252–253.

5. See for instance Charles Harold Lyttle, *Freedom Moves West: A History of the Western Unitarian Conference, 1852–1952* (Boston: Beacon, 1952), or Robert D. Habich, *Transcendentalism and the "Western Messenger": A History of the Magazine and Its Contributors, 1835–1841* (Rutherford, NJ: Fairleigh Dickinson University Press, 1985), 25–48.

6. Olivet College records.

7. *History of Jefferson County, Wisconsin* (Chicago: Western Historical Co., 1879), 496–497.

8. *General Catalogue of the Meadville Theological School, Meadville, Pennsylvania, 1844–1910,* Rev. Walter Cox Green, comp. (Meadville: Privately printed, 1910), 41.

9. GWC to Sunderland, 30 November 1876, Box 1, Folder: Correspondence October–December 1876, JTS Papers.

10. GWC to Sunderland, 15 December [1877], Box 1, Folder: Correspondence November–December 1877, JTS Papers.

11. GWC to Sunderland, 6 August 1878, Box 1, Folder: Correspondence July–August 1878, JTS Papers.

12. GWC to Sunderland, 11 April 1878, Box 1, Folder: March–April 1878, JTS Papers.

13. GWC to Sunderland, 11 April 1878, Box 1, Folder: March–April 1878, JTS Papers.

14. GWC to Sunderland, September 1878, Box 1, Folder: Correspondence September–October 1878, JTS Papers.

15. *General Catalogue of the Meadville Theological School*, 41.

16. David Robinson, "Jenkin Lloyd Jones," *Unitarianism in America*, http://www.harvardsquarelibrary.org/UIA%20Online/47jones.html.

17. For instance, in a handbill announcing his proposed lectures on the "Origin and Growth of Religious Beliefs" in the autumn of 1879, Cooke claimed that "the first four in the course will have constant reference to Huxley, Tyndall, Spencer, Fiske, Carpenter"—all scientists associated with evolutionary thought. O. C. McCulloch Papers, Mss L363, Box 1, Indiana State Library, hereafter abbreviated McCulloch Papers.

18. GWC, "Open Letter," pasted into 1879 Diary page for 23 September, Mss L363, Box 1, McCulloch Papers.

19. McCulloch Diary for 1879, entries for 29 January, 3 November, 4 December, and 20 December, McCulloch Papers. An avid reader of the Transcendentalists, intellectually and temperamentally McCulloch had much in common with Cooke. Yet there is no mention in McCulloch's diaries of any real friendship with the forward-thinking Unitarian pastor, and despite McCulloch's interest in Emerson, he appears not to have read Cooke's biography of him.

20. GWC to Sunderland, 27 January 1879, Box 2, Folder: Correspondence January–February 1879, JTS Papers.

21. GWC to Sunderland, 26 June 1879, Box 2, Folder: Correspondence May–June 1879, JTS Papers.

22. GWC to Sunderland, 13 May 1879, Box 2, Folder: Correspondence May–June 1879, JTS Papers.

23. William F. Abbot, Secretary of Unity Church, to Sunderland, 30 March 1879, Box 2, Folder: Correspondence March–April 1879, JTS Papers.

24. GWC to Sunderland, 16 July 1880, Box 2, Folder: Correspondence July–September 1880, JTS Papers.

25. GWC to Sunderland, 27 August 1880, Box 2, Folder: Correspondence July–September 1880, JTS Papers.

26. A. Bronson Alcott, "Diary for 1880–1881," entry for 6 February 1881, MS Am 1130.12 (52), by permission of the Houghton Library, Harvard University.

27. Sunderland, "George Willis Cooke," 251.

28. *Indianapolis Directory for 1880* (Indianapolis: R. L. Polk, 1880).

29. GWC, "Open Letter."

30. *Indianapolis Woman's Club, 1875–1940* (Greenfield, IN: Wm. Mitchell Printing Co., Old Swimmin' Hole Press, 1944), 17.

31. *Indianapolis Directory for 1881* (Indianapolis: R. L. Polk, 1881).

32. Berry R. Sulgrove, *History of Indianapolis and Marion County, Indiana* (Philadelphia: L. H. Everts & Co., 1884), 18.

33. On Dempster Ostrander, see the *National Cyclopaedia of American Biography*, 63 vols. (New York: J. T. White, 1898–1984), 11:397.

34. *History of Jefferson County*, 479, 496–497, 646.

35. Evergreen Cemetery records, Fort Atkinson, Wisconsin.

36. Cooke *RWE,* [iii].

37. GWC to Ralph Waldo Emerson, 17 October 1879, bMS Am 1280 (700). Ralph Waldo Emerson Memorial Association deposit, Houghton Library, Harvard University. Not to be reproduced in whole or in part without permission.

38. GWC, "Emerson's Attitude Toward Religion," *Saturday Herald* (Indianapolis), 14 February 1880.

39. GWC to RWE, 17 October 1879.

40. GWC to RWE, 17 October 1879.

41. GWC to RWE, 17 October 1879.

42. Lecture announcement, L363, 1879 Papers, Box 1, McCulloch Papers.

43. GWC, "Unity Church," *Saturday Herald* (Indianapolis), 14 February 1880.

44. *Quinquennial Catalogue of the Officers and Graduates of Harvard University, 1636–1910* (Cambridge: Published by the University, 1910).

45. Ralph L. Rusk, *The Life of Ralph Waldo Emerson* (New York: Scribners, 1949), 500.

46. Ellen Emerson identifies Edward's Indianapolis correspondent as Alfred Ferguson, about whom nothing more is known (*ETE,* 2:373).

47. Edward Waldo Emerson, "Emerson vs. Cook," *Saturday Herald* (Indianapolis), 6 March 1880.

48. It is tempting to think that George Willis Cooke smoothed the way for the publication of Edward's letter in the *Herald,* but there is no evidence to suggest the family knew of Cooke prior to this time.

49. GWC, "Emerson's Attitude Toward Religion."

50. "A Study of Emerson," *Saturday Herald,* 14 February 1880.

51. "Local Summary," *Saturday Herald,* 21 February 1880.

52. GWC to Sunderland, 27 August 1880.

53. "George Willis Cooke," *General Catalogue of the Meadville Theological School,* 41.

54. GWC, "Society Small Talk," *Saturday Herald,* 10 July 1880.

55. Austin Warren, "The Concord School of Philosophy," *New England Quarterly* 2 (April 1929): 205–208.

56. Kenneth Walter Cameron, ed., *Concord Harvest: Publications of the Concord School of Philosophy and Literature with Notes on Its Successors and Other Resources for Research in Emerson, Thoreau, Alcott and the Later Transcendentalists,* 2 vols. (Hartford, CT: Transcendental Books, 1970), 1:248–252. Bruce Ronda convincingly argues for the conservatism of the Concord School in its presentation of Transcendentalism. See Ronda, "The Concord School of Philosophy and the Legacy of Transcendentalism," *New England Quarterly* 82 (December 2009): 575–607.

57. GWC to Sunderland, 27 August 1880.

58. Kenneth Walter Cameron, ed., *Response to Transcendental Concord: The Last Decades of the Era of Emerson, Thoreau, and the Concord School as Recorded in Newspapers* (Hartford, CT: Transcendental Books, 1974), 81.

59. Ireland *RWE,* 289–290.

60. GWC to Sunderland, 16 July 1880, Box 2, Folder: Correspondence July–September 1880, JTS Papers.

61. For Cooke's comments and Peabody's rejoinder, see Cameron, *Response to Transcendental Concord,* 81–83. Cooke specifically had in mind Dr. Hiram K. Jones

of Illinois, "a loose, uncouth thinker" who lectured on Platonism, and Denton J. Snider of St. Louis, whose lecture series on Shakespeare and Hegelianism Cooke called "an ingenious piece of work, too ingenious" (Cooke, "The Concord School of Philosophy," *Christian Register,* 28 August 1880). Alcott himself also worried about the "undue ascendancy" of Hegelianism at the school (*Journals of Bronson Alcott,* ed. Odell Shepard [Boston: Little, Brown, 1938], 518).

62. Alcott, "Diary for 1882," entry for 25 June 1882, MS Am 1130.12 (54). By permission of the Houghton Library, Harvard University.

63. GWC to Sunderland, 16 July 1880.

64. GWC to Sunderland, 3 August 1880, Box 2, Folder: Correspondence July–September 1880, JTS Papers.

65. GWC to Sunderland, 15 September 1880, Box 2, Folder: Correspondence July–September 1880, JTS Papers.

66. George Willis Cooke, *A History of the Clapboard Trees or Third Parish, Dedham, Mass. Now the Unitarian Parish, West Dedham 1736–1886* (Boston: Geo. H. Ellis, 1887), 137.

67. EWE to GWC, 5 April [1881], George Willis Cooke Manuscript Collection, Fruitlands Museum, Harvard, Massachusetts, hereafter abbreviated Cooke-Fruitlands.

68. Ellen Tucker Emerson to GWC, 5 May 1881, Cooke-Fruitlands.

69. Ellen Tucker Emerson to GWC, 5 May 1881.

70. L. Maria Child to GWC, 14 May 1880, Cooke-Fruitlands.

71. William Henry Channing to GWC, 18 November 1880, Cooke-Fruitlands.

72. Alcott, "Diary for 1881," entry for 25 November 1881, MS Am 1130.12 (53). By permission of the Houghton Library, Harvard University.

73. Cooke, "Emerson's Attitude Toward Religion."

74. Unidentified newspaper clipping pasted in following entry for 30 May in Alcott, "Diary for 1882," MS Am 1130.12 (54). By permission of the Houghton Library, Harvard University.

75. JEC to Ellen Tucker Emerson, 18 February 1881, bMS Am 1280.227 (3224). Ralph Waldo Emerson Memorial Association deposit, Houghton Library, Harvard University. Not to be reproduced in whole or in part without permission.

76. Ellen Tucker Emerson to GWC, 17 May 1881, Cooke-Fruitlands.

77. Review of Cooke, *Ralph Waldo Emerson,* Boston *Commonwealth,* 29 October 1881.

78. For individual titles see Joel Myerson, *Ralph Waldo Emerson: A Descriptive Bibliography* (Pittsburgh: University of Pittsburgh Press, 1982). Cooke quotes several paragraphs (*RWE,* 137–138) from Emerson's "American Slavery" lecture, delivered in 1855 and not published in full until 2001 in *Later Lectures of Ralph Waldo Emerson* (ed. Ronald A. Bosco and Joel Myerson, 2 vols. [Athens: University of Georgia Press, 2001], 2:1). But the paragraphs that appear in Cooke *RWE* were reprinted in the Syracuse *Daily Standard* for 24 February 1855.

79. Jabez T. Sunderland, "Letter from Boston," *Unity,* 16 October 1881, 311–312.

80. Ellen Tucker Emerson to GWC, 5 May 1881.

81. Ellen Emerson seems to have overlooked Cooke's synopsis of Emerson's "Natural History of the Intellect," first given in London in 1848, later expanded for delivery at Harvard in 1870–1871. Unpublished in the first eleven volumes of the

Riverside Edition, some of the "Natural History of the Intellect" lectures were first published in 1893, the remainder not until 2001 in *Later Lectures of Emerson*. But Cooke had found detailed, near-verbatim summaries in *Douglas Jerrold's Weekly Newspaper* from 10 to 24 June 1848 (*Later Lectures of Emerson*, 1:130) and summarizes the entire series based on the newspaper accounts (Cooke *RWE*, 307–309).

82. Notebook of annual church meetings, Third Parish, Dedham, entry for 14 March 1881, Dedham Historical Society.

83. GWC to Pulpit Supply Committee, Third Parish Church, 13 June 1881, Archives, Westwood, 1st Parish, 1880–1889, Dedham Historical Society. Cooke's annual salary for preaching was $1,000, with vacation during August and three months notice of termination by either party.

84. James R. Osgood and Company, Cost Book, June 1880–February 1885, MS Am 2030.3 [8], p. 154. By permission of the Houghton Library, Harvard University.

85. "George Willis Cooke" Folder, MS Am 2346 (642).

86. Alcott, "Diary for 1881," entries for 19 October and 25 November 1881.

87. Altick, *Lives and Letters*, 163.

88. A case in point: Cooke recounts a story about the intellectual Waldo waking his wife one night, deep in thought over some lofty idea and nervously pacing the floor (Cooke *RWE*, 202). In Lidian Emerson's copy of the book, in a private collection, the entire anecdote has been delicately penciled out, presumably because it places husband and wife in the same bedroom.

89. "The Biographical Mania," *Tait's Edinburgh Magazine* n.s. 21 (January 1854): 16.

90. Warren, 208.

91. Warren, 205.

92. Warren, 199.

93. Ireland *RWE*, 291.

94. Cooke, *Poets and Problems* (Boston: Ticknor and Company, 1886), 10–12.

95. J. T. Sunderland, "Letter from Boston," *Unity* 8 (16 October 1881), 311.

96. "Emerson's Life, Writings, and Philosophy," *Critic* 1 (19 November 1881): 319.

97. "Emerson," New York *Daily Tribune*, 23 October 1881.

98. "Emerson," New York *Daily Tribune*, 23 October 1881.

99. Franklin Sanborn to GWC, 20 October 1881, Cooke-Fruitlands. Sanborn's promised review is likely the one in the Boston *Commonwealth* for 29 October 1881, which called Cooke's study "a labor of love" (1).

100. [H. W. Holland], "Mr. Emerson's Philosophy," *Nation* 33 (17 November 1881): 397.

101. "Ralph Waldo Emerson," *Century* 23 (February 1882): 622.

102. GWC to Jabez T. Sunderland, 10 January 1882, Box 2, Folder: Correspondence January–March 1882, JTS Papers.

103. Despite the similarity in title, Cooke's *George Eliot* required of him a more challenging set of judgments. He defended Eliot's common-law marriage to George Henry Lewes, claiming she was "perfectly faithful" to him (41), and found her work unimpeachably moral, though he was moderate in his appraisal of Eliot's character: "she had culture, moral power and earnestness . . . but no saintliness" (93). The book, reissued by Houghton, Mifflin in a second edition in 1884 and again in 1911, is virtually ignored by Eliot scholars today.

104. James R. Osgood and Company, Cost Book, p. 154, Houghton Library, Harvard University.

105. *Christian Union,* 20 July 1882.

106. MDC to Ellen Dana Conway, 15 March 1882, Moncure Daniel Conway Family Papers (MC 1999.6), Archives and Special Collections, Dickinson College, Carlisle, PA, hereafter abbreviated as Conway Family Papers, Dickinson.

107. GWC to EWE, 11 September 1883, bMS Am 1280.226 (3313). Ralph Waldo Emerson Memorial Association deposit, Houghton Library, Harvard University. Not to be reproduced in whole or in part without permission.

108. Notebook of annual church meetings, entries for 12 March 1883, 9 March 1885, and 8 March 1886, Records of the Third Parish, Dedham, MA, Dedham Historical Society.

109. United States Census 1900. Lucy Nash Cooke may have lost another child during these years; though the Cookes had only three children who survived infancy, in the 1900 census she reported herself as the mother of five, two of them still living.

110. GWC to Jabez T. Sunderland, 15 November [1883], Box 2, Folder: Correspondence November–December 1883, JTS Papers.

111. Cooke, "After Seventy Years," 163.

112. GWC to Sunderland, 7 March 1887, Box 3, Folder: Correspondence March 1887, JTS Papers.

113. Notebook of annual church meetings, Third Parish, Dedham, entry for 14 March 1887.

114. Cooke, "After Seventy Years," 163.

115. GWC to Sunderland, 27 April 1918, Box 5, Folder: Correspondence, 1918–1919, JTS Papers; Cooke, *The Social Evolution of Religion* (Boston: The Stratford Company, 1920), iii.

116. On Mary Leggett Cooke (1856–1938), see the *Unitarian Year Book September 1, 1939–August 31, 1940* (Boston: American Unitarian Association, [1940]), 152, and the files of the American Unitarian Association Secretary at the Andover-Harvard Theological Library, Harvard University.

117. EWE to GWC, 28 April 1882, Cooke-Fruitlands.

118. EWE to GWC, 14 November 1889, Cooke-Fruitlands.

119. Houghton, Mifflin's records show that Cooke's *Emerson* sold poorly after the firm acquired it: in 1889, 23 copies; and in 1893, after the issue of the expanded edition, 45 copies (MS Am 2030[31 and 32]). By permission of the Houghton Library, Harvard University.

120. GWC to Jabez T. Sunderland, 15 November [1883].

3. BIOGRAPHERS AND THE PORNOGRAPHER

1. "Death of Mr. Alexander Ireland," *Manchester Weekly Times,* 14 December 1894, in "Newspaper Cuttings" scrapbook, Local Studies Division, Manchester Central Library, Manchester, England, hereafter abbreviated "Newspaper Cuttings."

2. See James A. Secord, *Victorian Sensation: The Extraordinary Publication, Reception, and Secret Authorship of "Vestiges of the Natural History of Creation"* (Chicago: University of Chicago Press, 2000).

3. J. Saxon Mills, "Alexander Ireland," *Manchester City News*, 15 December 1894, in "Newspaper Cuttings." Among the other informative obituaries at the Manchester Central Library are "The Late Mr. Alexander Ireland," *Liverpool Daily Post*, 19 December 1894, and "Mr. Alexander Ireland," *Manchester Guardian*, 8 December 1894, both in "Newspaper Cuttings." See also John Mortimer, "Alexander Ireland," *Manchester Quarterly* 53 (January 1895): 1–9 and "The Late Mr. Alexander Ireland," *Manchester Faces and Places: An Illustrated Magazine* 6 (1895): 57–60.

4. AI to MDC, 30 March 1866, Alexander Ireland Papers, 1866–1893, Special Collections, University of Michigan, hereafter abbreviated Ireland Papers, Michigan.

5. EmLet, 8:96.

6. EmLet, 3:452.

7. In *English Traits* (1856) Emerson expanded his praise: "A man of sense and of letters, the editor of a powerful local journal, he added to solid virtues an infinite sweetness and *bonhommie*. There seemed a pool of honey about his heart which lubricated all his speech and action with fine jets of mead" (*Collected Works of Ralph Waldo Emerson*, ed. Robert E. Spiller et al., 8 volumes to date [Cambridge: Harvard University Press, 1971–], 5:164).

8. The source of the term is in Mrs. G. Linnaeus Banks's *The Manchester Man* (1876), but the type shows up as well as Thomas Gradgrind, a character in Dickens's *Hard Times* (1854). For my discussion of Manchester's complicated agendas of economic and social reforms, I have also relied upon Stuart Hylton, *A History of Manchester* (Chichester, UK: Phillimore & Co., 2003), and Alan Kidd, *Manchester*, third edition (Edinburgh: Edinburgh University Press, 2002).

9. Gary S. Messinger, *Manchester in the Victorian Age: The Half-known City* (Manchester: Manchester University Press, 1985), 176.

10. Thomas Carlyle to Emerson, 18 March 1847, in *The Correspondence of Emerson and Carlyle*, ed. Joseph L. Slater (New York: Columbia University Press, 1964), 419.

11. AI to Alexander Campbell, 20 October 1891, MS Gen 1662/19, Special Collections Department, Glasgow University Library, used by permission.

12. Isabel Petrie Mills, *From Tinder Box to the "Larger" Light: Threads from the Life of John Mills, Banker (Author of "Vox Humana"): Interwoven with Some Early Century Recollections by His Wife* (Manchester: Sherratt & Hughes, 1899), 140–141.

13. See for example Hylton, *History of Manchester*, 98–101 on railroads, and Kidd, *Manchester*, 13–14 on population growth.

14. Friedrich Engels, *The Condition of the Working Class in England*, trans. and ed. by W. O. Henderson and W. H. Chaloner (New York: Macmillan, 1958), 63.

15. Townsend Scudder, *The Lonely Wayfaring Man: Emerson and Some Englishmen* (London and New York: Oxford University Press, 1936), 52–53.

16. EmLet, 3:379n.

17. Lucy Brown, *Victorian News and Newspapers* (Oxford: Clarendon Press, 1985), 74.

18. Hylton, *History of Manchester*, 162–163.

19. Messinger, *Manchester in the Victorian Age*, 120; see also Brown, *Victorian News*, 72, and Kidd, *Manchester*, 160–161. Messinger points out, "By the late 1880s, large numbers of Manchester workers were also being attracted to Conservatism

through Tory exploitation of imperialistic nationalism and persuasive advocacy of protective tariffs as a means to increase working-class wages forced down by competition from Germany, France and the United States" (120).

20. AI to Alexander Campbell, 20 October 1891.

21. J. Saxon Mills, "Alexander Ireland."

22. Brian Harding, *The Ralph Waldo Emerson Collection, 1822–1903. A Brief Introduction to the Microfilm Edition of the Ralph Waldo Emerson Collection . . . From the Alexander Ireland Collection in the Manchester Central Library, Manchester England* (West Yorkshire, UK: Microform Academic Publishers, n.d.), 6.

23. Ireland wrote to Conway on 7 June 1866 that he (Ireland) had not corresponded with Emerson recently because he felt that nothing he could say would interest him. On 24 March 1867 he notes that he has written Emerson but received nothing in return. Ireland Papers, Michigan.

24. The most reliable sources of information about Conway's life are Mary Elizabeth Burtis, *Moncure Conway, 1832–1907* (New Brunswick, NJ: Rutgers University Press, 1952), and John d'Entremont, *Southern Emancipator: Moncure Conway, the American Years 1832–1865* (New York: Oxford University Press, 1987). Conway's later years are best covered in d'Entremont, *Moncure Conway 1832–1907: American Abolitionist, Spiritual Architect of "South Place," Author of "The Life of Thomas Paine"* (London: South Place Ethical Society, 1977).

25. d'Entremont, *Moncure Conway 1832–1907*, 15.

26. d'Entremont, *Moncure Conway 1832–1907*, 30.

27. Extract and all quotes in preceding paragraph are from Conway, *Autobiography, Memories and Experiences*, 1:77–78.

28. Versions of the story appear in Burtis, *Moncure Conway*, 18–19; d'Entremont, *Southern Emancipator*, 43–44; and John McAleer, *Ralph Waldo Emerson: Days of Encounter* (Boston: Little, Brown, 1984), 539.

29. EmLet, 8:292.

30. Conway, *Autobiography*, 1:139; the story of their first meeting is told in McAleer, *Ralph Waldo Emerson*, 538–548 and d'Entremont, *Southern Emancipator*, 78–79.

31. EmLet, 5:323.

32. "Overture of Mr. Conway to Mr. Mason," *New York Times*, 25 July 1863.

33. For instance, William Lloyd Garrison called Conway's offer "ill-judged and unwarrantable" and denied Conway any right to speak for the American Anti-Slavery Society.

34. Dennis Welland, "Moncure Daniel Conway and Anglo-American Relations," *Ethical Record* 81 (September 1976): 4.

35. On Hotten and his publishing career, see Simon Eliot, "Hotten: Rotten: Forgotten? An Apologia for a General Publisher," *Book History* 3 (2000): 61–93. Hotten's plan for the proposed Emerson edition is well chronicled in Dennis Welland, "John Camden Hotten and Emerson's Uncollected Essays," *Yearbook of English Studies 6*, ed. G. K. Hunter and C. J. Rawson (London: Modern Humanities Research Association, 1976), 156–175.

36. Hotten to MDC, 30 January 1870, Letter copy, Chatto & Windus Papers, outletter book 4, item 194, MS 2444/5, University of Reading, UK, hereafter abbreviated CWPapers.

37. Unidentified newspaper clipping, Alexander Ireland Collection, Manchester Central Library, quoted in Welland, "John Camden Hotten", 156.

38. Hotten to MDC, 24 January 1873, letter copy, CWPapers, out-letter book 6, MS 2444/7, item 169–170.

39. Conway, *Autobiography*, 2:395.

40. F. B. Sanborn, "Materials Concerning the Incidental Meetings of Emerson in London Collected by John Camden Hotten," *Springfield Daily Republican*, 17 November 1874.

41. Welland, "John Camden Hotten," 157–158.

42. AI to MDC, 10 June 1870 and 23 June 1870, Ireland Papers, Michigan. Once Ireland began writing about Emerson, he found it hard to stop. "My 'Reminiscences of Emerson' are about half-transcribed," he wrote to Conway on 21 June. "The subject grew under my hand, & I really do not know what will be your verdict on the paper" (AI to MDC, 21 June 1870, Box 14, Moncure Daniel Conway Papers, Rare Book and Manuscript Library, Columbia University, hereafter abbreviated Conway Papers, Columbia).

43. Welland, "John Camden Hotten," 158–159.

44. EmLet, 6:124–125.

45. EmLet, 6:134.

46. For Hotten's extensive activities in the world of Victorian pornography, see Eliot, "Hotten: Rotten: Forgotten?" 68–71; Steven Marcus, *The Other Victorians: A Study of Sexuality and Pornography in Mid-Nineteenth-Century England* (New York: Basic Books, 1966), 67–73; Peter Fryer, *Forbidden Books of the Victorians: Henry Spencer Ashbee's Bibliographies of Erotica Abridged and Edited, with an Introduction and Notes* (London: Odyssey, 1970); and Chester W. Topp, *Victorian Yellowbacks & Paperbacks, 1849–1905*, 8 vols. to date (Denver: Hermitage Antiquarian Bookshop, 1993–), 3:1–34.

47. Welland, "John Camden Hotten," 165.

48. *ETE*, 1:685.

49. *ETE*, 1:694.

50. Hotten to MDC, 21 January 1873, out-letter book 6, MS 2444/7, item 160, CWPapers. Several days later, Hotten revised his figures upward: "the loss in outlay for paper & print—will be, not £15 or £18 but £200 at least," though his expense book suggests the loss was a more modest £44 (Welland, "John Camden Hotten," 168).

51. Welland, "John Camden Hotten," 170.

52. Welland, "John Camden Hotten," 170.

53. Andrew Chatto to MDC, 16 July 1873, out-letter book 6, item 449, MS 2444/7, CWPapers.

54. Chatto to MDC, 21 July 1873, out-letter book 6, item 474, MS 2444/7, CWPapers.

55. Contract/memorandum endorsed "Conway <Aug> July 27 73/Emerson/ Introd.&c," CWPapers.

56. Welland, "John Camden Hotten," 161.

57. Welland, "John Camden Hotten," 171.

58. For a bibliography of major works, see Burtis, *Moncure Conway*, 242–254.

59. d'Entremont, *Moncure Conway 1832–1907*, 25.

60. William J. Sowder, *Emerson's Impact on the British Isles and Canada*, 146.

61. Sowder, *Emerson's Impact*, 20.

62. Sowder, *Emerson's Impact*, 156.

63. AI to MDC, 19 September 1870, Ireland Papers, Michigan. Hotten reported to Conway in 1873, "A word more about Emerson book [sic]. You speak of 'prospective revenues arising from its sale.' Permit me to say that the only English edition wch I can discover that has ever paid its expences [sic] is the little 1/− [one shilling] 'English Traits.' All the rest have eventually sold off as remainder. . . . Emerson's readers are not so numerous as you suppose. Ask at the bookstall how his *last* book sold. I took 13 copies & have *eleven* now" (Hotten to MDC, 24 January 1873, out-letter book 6, item 169–170, MS 2444/7, CWPapers).

64. Sowder, *Emerson's Impact*, 24.

65. Sowder, *Emerson's Impact*, 27.

66. Sowder, *Emerson's Impact*, 128.

67. AI to MDC, 29 December 1882, Ireland Papers, Michigan.

68. *In Memoriam* was also published in Edinburgh, Glasgow, Manchester, Liverpool, and Birmingham. The preface is dated 20 May 1882, and Conway had received and read a copy of it by 8 June, according to a letter to him from Ireland on that date (Ireland Papers, Michigan).

69. In his *Autobiography* Conway claimed that the proofs of "Emerson and His Friends" "were used by Alexander Ireland in his book on Emerson. Not unfairly used, for I had got from him many facts relating to Emerson in England as he had got from me many relating to Emerson in America" (2:395).

70. AI to MDC, 21 September 1882, Ireland Papers, Michigan.

71. AI to MDC, 8 June 1882, 19 August 1882, and 21 September 1882, Ireland Papers, Michigan.

72. AI to MDC, 19 August 1882. Lillie Langtry left polite English society to become a professional actress, causing a scandal when she first appeared on stage in late 1881.

73. Sowder, *Emerson's Impact*, 128.

74. AI to MDC, 11 August 1882 and 8 October 1882, Ireland Papers, Michigan.

75. AI to OWH, 31 December 1882, bMS Am 1241 (649), Houghton Library, Harvard University.

76. AI to MDC, 8 October 1882.

77. *Ralph Waldo Emerson. His Life, Genius, and Writings. A Biographical Sketch* was advertised for sale on 1 November in the *Manchester Examiner* for 25 October 1882. The title was apparently a late decision: in "Newspaper Cuttings" is a prospectus hand-dated "October 1882" which lists as "in the press" a "Second Edition, Largely Augmented Throughout" of *In Memoriam*. The prospectus contains 32 excerpts from reviews of the earlier version of the "first edition" of the biography.

78. William Henry Channing, "R. W. Emerson," *Modern Review* 3 (October 1882): 850–854.

79. See for instance J. M. Wheeler, "Emerson," *Progress* 1 (February 1883): 117–120, and the review of Ireland, *Ralph Waldo Emerson*, *Saturday Review*, 11 November 1882, 648–649.

80. AI to MDC, "Xmas Day 1882," Ireland Papers, Michigan.

81. AI to OWH, 31 December 1882.

82. Alcott, "Journal for 1882," entry for 20 June, p. 197, MS Am 1130.12(54), by permission of the Houghton Library, Harvard University. Characteristically for Sanborn, earlier the same day he had assured Houghton, Mifflin, "I think I can put you on the way to publishing a little book about Emerson at once, to which the family will not object if you care to do so" (Sanborn to Houghton, Mifflin, 20 June 1882, bMS Am 1925 [1564], by permission of the Houghton Library, Harvard University).

83. No sentimentalist, Ireland diversified his literary output by preparing concurrently with his Emerson biography a book that would become his best seller, *The Book-Lover's Enchiridion*, a collection of authors' comments on the joys of reading. Both books were announced together as "now ready" in the *Manchester Examiner*, 20 November 1882.

84. Margaret Oliphant, "The Ethics of Biography," *Contemporary Review* 44 (1883), 79–82.

85. "Biography," *The Spectator*, 29 July 1882, 990. Like many others, Ireland condemned Froude's disclosure of private documents as bad judgment ("or something much worse," he told Conway ominously), though later in his life he became convinced that Froude had acted according to Carlyle's wishes (AI to MDC, 8 April 1883, and AI to Ellen Dana Conway, 6 August 1886, Ireland Papers, Michigan).

86. OWH to AI, Boston, 10 January 1885, Add 34813, section D, Miscellaneous Autograph Letters, ff. 38–39, British Library.

87. Edmund Gosse, "The Custom of Biography," *Anglo-Saxon Review* 8 (1901), 195.

88. Leslie Stephen, "Biography," *National Review* 22 (1893), 181.

89. Stephen, "Biography," 174.

90. I use the pagination of Edith Emerson Forbes's bound copy of "Emerson and His Friends," *74–504, Houghton Library, Harvard University.

91. MDC to Ellen Tucker Emerson, 6 June 1882, bMS Am 1280.226 (3302). Ralph Waldo Emerson Memorial Association deposit, Houghton Library, Harvard University. Not to be reproduced in whole or in part without permission.

92. MDC to Lidian Jackson Emerson, 28 April 1882, bMS Am 1280.226 (3301). Ralph Waldo Emerson Memorial Association deposit, Houghton Library, Harvard University. Not to be reproduced in whole or in part without permission.

93. *ETE*, 1:690.

94. Quoted in d'Entremont, *Moncure Daniel Conway*, 15.

95. JMN, 15:153.

96. Slater, *Correspondence*, 586.

97. MDC to Ellen Tucker Emerson, 6 June 1882.

98. EWE to MDC, 22 July 1882, Moncure Daniel Conway Papers, Rare Book and Manuscript Library, Columbia University, Box 9. Hereafter abbreviated Conway Papers, Columbia.

99. Conway, *Autobiography* 2:407–413; Slater, *Correspondence*, 64–66.

100. Edith Emerson Forbes to MDC, 7 February [1883], Box 10, Conway Papers, Columbia; Slater, *Correspondence*, 66.

101. EWE to MDC, 22 July 1882, Box 9, Conway Papers, Columbia.

102. Conway bought the Barzillai Frost house on West Main Street in September 1862 and left for England the following April (d'Entremont, *Southern Emancipator*, 172, 183).

103. MDC to EWE, 10 May 1882, bMS Am 1280.226 (3303). Ralph Waldo Emerson Memorial Association deposit, Houghton Library, Harvard University. Not to be reproduced in whole or in part without permission.

104. Le Baron Russell to MDC, 16 July 1882, Conway Family Papers, Dickinson.

105. EWE to MDC, 15 July 1882, Box 9, Conway Papers, Columbia.

106. *ETE*, 2:476.

107. For instance, pages 1–8 of "Emerson and His Friends" appear verbatim in *EHA*, 167–172; pages 26–27 appear verbatim on p. 27 of the later book; pages 80–105 appear almost verbatim on pages 321–333.

108. AI to MDC, 2 June 1881, Ireland Papers, Michigan.

109. See for instance Chatto & Windus to MDC, 2 October 1881, out-letter book 14 (MS 2444/15), CWPapers: "We issue [usually?] half a million catalogs a year, in all of which we take care to advertise your books."

110. Chatto & Windus to MDC, 8 September 1881, out-letter book 13 (MS 2444/14), item 384, CWPapers. Ireland reported that he bought extra copies at his own expense and sent them to sympathetic editors for review (AI to MDC, 11 September 1881, Ireland Papers, Michigan).

111. Conway to "Mr. Macmillan," 2 August 1882, Macmillan Archives, Add 55256, Correspondence, vol. CDLXXI, items 207 & 208, British Library.

112. MDC to Ellen Dana Conway, 4 August 1882, Box 6, Conway Papers, Columbia.

113. MDC to Ellen Dana Conway, 13 August 1882, Box 6, Conway Papers, Columbia.

114. MDC to Ellen Dana Conway, 18 August 1882, Box 6, Conway Papers, Columbia.

115. MDC to Macmillan, 6 October 1881, Macmillan Archives, Add 55256, Correspondence, vol. CDLXXI, item 80, British Library.

116. William Dean Howells to James R. Osgood, 5 August 1882, in *Selected Letters of William Dean Howells*, ed. George Arms et al. 6 vols. (Boston: Twayne, 1979–1983), 3:25.

117. In 1863 Conway recommended Trübner to Howells, whose collection of poems had been turned down by Macmillan of London. Trübner offered to publish them only if expenses could be guaranteed. Howells eventually refused the deal (*Selected Letters of Howells*, 4:185–186). Howells later turned to Trübner, again with Conway's urging, offering the firm his *Venetian Life* (1866). Trübner offered to publish a limited number at half profits provided that Howells could find an American publisher willing to take half of the run. Howells despaired of the arrangement, and when he asked permission to shop his book to other publishers, Trübner "said Yes, almost joyously" (Howells, *Literary Friends and Acquaintance: A Personal Retrospect of American Authorship*, ed. David F. Hiatt and Edwin H. Cady [Bloomington: Indiana University Press, 1968], 88–89).

118. *Boston Daily Advertiser*, 18 November 1882; Cost Book, Records of James R. Osgood and Co. (1880–85), MS Am 2030.3 (8), Houghton Mifflin Co. Records by permission of the Houghton Library, Harvard University.

119. There is no surviving record of the size of the book's English edition, though presumably it would not have exceeded Osgood's.

120. Review of Conway, *Emerson at Home and Abroad*, Boston *Commonwealth*, 16 December 1882, 1.

121. Review of Conway, *Emerson at Home and Abroad*, *Christian Register*, 25 January 1883, 59.

122. Sowder, *Emerson's Impact*, 128.

123. His tendency toward name-dropping was widely noted, though John d'Entremont argues strenuously that the affectations of a middle-class social climber do not apply to the aristocratic Conway, who "moved with ease in high social and intellectual circles, both because he was welcome there and because he had always done so, by habit and by right" (*Southern Emancipator*, 64).

124. Review of Conway, *Emerson at Home and Abroad*, *Harper's New Monthly Magazine* 67 (June 1883): 154.

125. Thomas Wentworth Higginson, "Conway's 'Emerson at Home and Abroad,'" *Century Magazine* 25 (April 1883): 954.

126. Review of Conway, *Emerson at Home and Abroad*, *Southern Presbyterian Review* 34 (April 1883): 452–453.

127. R. C. Browne, "Two Books on Emerson," *Academy* 24 (4 August 1883): 71–72.

128. Review of Conway, *Emerson at Home and Abroad*, First Notice, *National Reformer*, 3 December 1882, 394.

129. Ellen Tucker Emerson to MDC, 29 January 1883, Box 9, Conway Papers, Columbia.

130. Edith Emerson Forbes to MDC, 6 March 1883, Box 9, Conway Papers, Columbia.

131. EWE to MDC, 6 May 1883, Box 10, Conway Papers, Columbia.

132. Review of Conway, *Emerson at Home and Abroad*, *Athenaeum*, 3 February 1883, 147.

133. Higginson, "Conway's 'Emerson at Home and Abroad,'" 955.

134. EWE to MDC, 6 May 1883. In Edward's personal copy of *EHA*, in a private collection, he has cancelled the offending passage in thick pencil.

135. Ellen Tucker Emerson to MDC, fragment, ca. 1883, Box 9, Conway Papers, Columbia.

136. *ETE*, 2:493–494.

137. AI to MDC, "Xmas Day 1882," Ireland Papers, Michigan.

138. Joel Myerson, *Ralph Waldo Emerson: A Descriptive Bibliography* (Pittsburgh: University of Pittsburgh Press, 1982), 371–372.

139. Advertisement for *Emerson at Home and Abroad* and *Ralph Waldo Emerson*, Concord Free Public Library, C.PAM.2, item 16.

140. J. M. Wheeler, "Emerson," *Progress* 1 (February 1883): 117.

141. Robert Goodbrand, "A Suggestion for a New Kind of Biography," *Contemporary Review* (London) 14 (1870): 26–27.

142. Stephen, "Biography," 180.

143. Stephen, "Biography," 180.

4. DIAGNOSING THE GENTLE ICONOCLAST

1. In its first two years Holmes's *Emerson* sold 7,925 copies, three times the average of books in the series and more than double the sales of its nearest rival in the series, the 1887 volume on Franklin (3,299 copies) (Scott E. Casper, "Defining the National Pantheon: The Making of Houghton Mifflin's Biographical Series,

1880–1900," in *Reading Books: Essays on the Material Text and Literature in America*, ed. Michele Moylan and Lane Stiles [Amherst: University of Massachusetts Press, 1996], 206–207).

2. OWH to Frank Sanborn, 15 January 1885, folder 11, Oliver Wendell Holmes (1809–1894) Papers, from the collections of the Manuscript Division at the Library of Congress, hereafter abbreviated as Holmes Papers, Library of Congress. For the continuing correction of factual errors in the book, see Thomas Franklin Currier and Eleanor M. Tilton, *A Bibliography of Oliver Wendell Holmes* (New York: New York University Press, 1953), 200.

3. OWH to John O. Sargent, 11 August 1883, John O. Sargent Papers, 1831–1893, microfilm edition, 4 reels (Boston: Massachusetts Historical Society, 1978), reel 2, Massachusetts Historical Society, partially reprinted in John T. Morse Jr., *Life and Letters of Oliver Wendell Holmes*, 2 vols. (Cambridge: Riverside Press, 1896), 2:57.

4. Rockwood Hoar to JEC, 23 September 1887, Schlesinger Library, Radcliffe Institute for Advanced Study, Harvard University, Cabot Family Papers, A-99, Box 9, vol. 13; hereafter abbreviated Cabot Papers, Radcliffe.

5. Eleanor M. Tilton, *Amiable Autocrat: A Biography of Dr. Oliver Wendell Holmes* (New York: Henry Schuman, 1947), 344.

6. Morse, *Holmes*, 2:55.

7. Thus, M. A. DeWolfe Howe in 1939 contrasts "Holmes, the realist, with his feet so firmly planted on the earth" and "Emerson . . . so much at home among the stars" (*Holmes of the Breakfast-Table* [London and New York: Oxford University Press, 1939], 150), and Miriam Rossiter Small in 1962 concludes that "any relation between the two as writers and thinkers would appear chiefly fortuitous" (*Oliver Wendell Holmes* [New York: Twayne, 1962], 138). A noticeable exception is Joel Porte's introduction to the Chelsea House reprint of *Ralph Waldo Emerson* (New York, 1980), which rightly claims for Emerson and Holmes not only a cultural kinship but also a shared faith in science and in American progress (xviii–xxv).

8. Louis Menand, *The Metaphysical Club: A Story of Ideas in America* (New York: Farrar, Straus and Giroux, 2001), 17.

9. Holmes, *A Mortal Antipathy* (1885), in *Works of Oliver Wendell Holmes* (Boston: Houghton, Mifflin, 1892), 7:10. Holmes confessed to the historian George Bancroft when the book came out, "I had a great deal to learn about Emerson for after all, though on very friendly terms with him, I did not often meet him, except at the monthly gatherings of the Saturday Club" (OWH to George Bancroft, 16 January 1885, George Bancroft Papers, Massachusetts Historical Society).

10. *Letters of John Holmes to James Russell Lowell and Others*, ed. William Roscoe Thayer (Boston: Houghton Mifflin, 1917), introduction by Alice M. Longfellow; Ralph L. Rusk, *The Life of Ralph Waldo Emerson* (New York: Charles Scribner's Sons, 1949), 116.

11. Holmes, "Poetry: A Metrical Essay" (1836), in *Works*, 12:58.

12. Morse, *Holmes*, 1:104; Rusk, *Life of Emerson*, 185.

13. For discussion of the Holmes-Emerson friendship, see also John McAleer, *Ralph Waldo Emerson: Days of Encounter* (Boston: Little, Brown, 1984), chapter 75. Like his brother Wendell, John Holmes maintained his acquaintance with Emerson, accompanying him on a famous trip to the Adirondacks in August 1858 (JMN, 13:34n).

14. Other examples of their shared participation in literary events include, in 1857, a fiftieth birthday celebration for Louis Agassiz and a kickoff dinner for the *Atlantic Monthly* magazine (JMN, 14:143–144, 146n); in 1859, the Burns centennial celebration and Holmes's own fiftieth birthday dinner (JMN, 14:269n, 315–317); in 1864, the Saturday Club's celebration of Shakespeare's birth (JMN, 15:49–50); and in 1877, the John Greenleaf Whittier seventieth birthday dinner, where the most notorious speaker was Mark Twain. In the late 1870s the two men served overlapping terms on Harvard's Board of Overseers (*Quinquennial Catalogue of the Officers and Graduates of Harvard University, 1636–1910* [Cambridge: Published by the University, 1910], 18–19; Small, *Holmes*, 138).

15. Edward Waldo Emerson, *The Early Years of the Saturday Club, 1855–1870* (Boston and New York: Houghton Mifflin, 1918), 5.

16. Howe, *Holmes of the Breakfast-Table*, 150.

17. Robert D. Richardson Jr., *Emerson: The Mind on Fire* (Berkeley: University of California Press, 1995), 404.

18. JMN, 9:381.

19. JMN, 14:316.

20. JMN, 16:112.

21. JMN, 16:188.

22. EmLet, 6:79.

23. OWH to Sargent, 11 August 1883.

24. JMN, 11:249.

25. Holmes, *A Mortal Antipathy*, in *Works*, 7:140.

26. Typed notes, no page number, Box 6, Holmes Papers, Library of Congress.

27. Holmes repeats the judgment in Holmes *RWE*, very loosely paraphrasing Emerson's "The Transcendentalist" (1844): "the '*new views*,' as they are called, are the oldest of thoughts cast in a new mould" (Holmes *RWE*, 146).

28. "At the Saturday Club" (1884), in *Works*, 13:272. Holmes makes the point that Emerson's birthplace on Summer Street, Boston, and "that of our other illustrious Bostonian, Benjamin Franklin," on Milk Street, were "within a kite-string's distance of each other" (Holmes *RWE*, 37).

29. Tilton, *Amiable*, 335.

30. Morse, *Holmes*, 2:42.

31. Holmes announced his retirement in October and gave his final lecture on 28 November. In recognition of his "many valuable services to the Medical School during the past thirty-five years," Harvard named him Emeritus Professor of Anatomy, an honorific title that carried no salary or financial benefits (*Records of the Board of Overseers of Harvard College*, vol. 12, June 28, 1882–June 24, 1891, p. 25, Harvard University Archives).

32. On the two divisive issues of faculty governance and the admission of women as students, Holmes has been aptly called "a passive sympathizer rather than an active partisan" (Thomas Francis Harrington and James Gregory Mumford, *The Harvard Medical School: A History, Narrative and Documentary, 1782–1905*, 3 vols. [New York: Lewis Publishing Company, 1905], 2:781).

33. OWH to S. Wier Mitchell, 9 October 1882, quoted in Morse, *Holmes*, 2:47.

34. OWH to Dr. Forcyce Barker, ca. October 1882, quoted in Morse, *Holmes*, 2:48.

35. Currier and Tilton, *Bibliography of Holmes*, 78–80, 146, 91–92. The reprints sold well. For instance, from 1882 through 1891 Houghton, Mifflin printed 27,000 copies of the first reissue of *The Autocrat of the Breakfast-Table*, afterward using the plates for the Riverside Edition of Holmes's *Writings* in 1891 (Currier and Tilton, *Bibliography of Holmes*, 79).

36. Tilton, *Amiable*, 335.

37. Currier and Tilton, *Bibliography of Holmes*, 186.

38. Casper, "Defining," 188.

39. Casper, "Defining," 185.

40. Gosse, "The Custom of Biography," 195.

41. Houghton, Mifflin and Company. *A Catalogue of Authors Whose Works Are Published by Houghton, Mifflin and Company* (Boston: Houghton, Mifflin, 1899), 153. The plan had remained true to H. O. Houghton's original intentions; as he wrote to Warner in 1881, "Our idea was, if possible, to have the list so made out as to include the history of American literature in the Lives of those who have been its representative authors" (Houghton to Warner, 25 April 1881, Charles Dudley Warner Papers, Watkinson Library, Trinity College, Hartford, CT; hereafter abbreviated Warner Papers, Trinity).

42. Casper, "Defining," 201.

43. Charles Dudley Warner to Houghton, Mifflin and Company, 14 January 1885, quoted in Casper, "Defining," 190 (emphasis mine). Warner became editor of the series after the death of James T. Fields in April 1881.

44. Casper, "Defining," 189.

45. Two more famous literary celebrities could scarcely be found, both of them so intimately associated with Boston that their presence there was a matter of civic pride. In 1883, the playwright and poet John Boyle O'Reilly wrote of the city: "any day you can meet great men on its streets. . . . It is only one year ago . . . that I saw Mr. Emerson and his daughter, who was always beside him, come into a horse-car that was rather crowded. There was probably not a soul on the car who did not know him. And it is sweet to remember the face of the great old philosopher and poet as he looked up and met the loving and respectful eyes around him. . . . And Oliver Wendell Holmes—every Bostonian knows him. The wise, the witty, the many-ideaed philosopher, poet, physician, novelist, essayist and professor; but best of all, the kind, the warm heart" (James Jeffrey Roche, *The Life of John Boyle O'Reilly* [New York: Cassell Publishing Company, 1891], 228–229). I am grateful to my colleague Dr. Lauren Onkey for pointing out this reference.

46. Warner to Houghton, Mifflin and Co., 19 June 1881, bMS Am 1925 (1862), folder #1, by permission of the Houghton Library, Harvard University. Warner had also contacted Thomas Wentworth Higginson, who would write the volume on Margaret Fuller, and Henry Wadsworth Longfellow, who died in March of the following year.

47. Warner to OWH, 28 September 1881, reel 3, item 4983–4984, Holmes Papers, Library of Congress.

48. Warner to OWH, 28 September 1881.

49. Warner to Frank Sanborn, 2 October 1881, in *Correspondence of Benjamin Franklin Sanborn*, ed. Kenneth Walter Cameron (Hartford, CT: Transcendental Books, 1982), item #2361.

50. Warner to Houghton, Mifflin Co., 29 June 1882, bMS Am 1925 (1862), by permission of the Houghton Library, Harvard University.

51. H. O. Houghton to Warner, 27 February 1883, Warner Papers, Trinity.

52. Holmes's original contract with Osgood was amended on 1 May 1877 to guarantee him an annuity of $750 in lieu of royalties, to increase to $1,000 from 1880 to 1887. The contract was transferred to Houghton, Mifflin on 1 May 1880. A memorandum dated 1 December 1882 between Holmes and Houghton, Mifflin specified an additional $3,000 annuity (for a total of $4,000) for the next three years, to cover royalties on Holmes's existing titles; for any new work he would receive royalties of 10 percent on the trade price for the first eight months of sales, after which those new books would be covered under the existing annuity (MS Am 2346 [1408]. By permission of the Houghton Library, Harvard University).

53. Though the exact date of his move is uncertain, Holmes began renting the new "summer cottage" on Hale Street soon after his retirement, according to Joseph E. Garland, *Boston's North Shore: Being an Account of Life Among the Noteworthy, Fashionable, Wealthy, Eccentric and Ordinary 1823–1890* (Boston: Little, Brown, 1978), 257.

54. OWH to Sargent, 11 August 1883.

55. OWH, Research notes on Emerson, bMs Am 1234.10, Houghton Library, Harvard University.

56. Holmes reported that he already owned *Nature, Addresses & Lectures* (1849), *Conduct of Life* (1860), *Letters and Social Aims* (1870), *Society and Solitude* (1870), *Poems*, and *May Day* (these last two in the Riverside edition of 1883). On the reverse of his letter, the firm acknowledged sending him on 20 June *Representative Men, Essays* (First Series), *Essays* (Second Series), and *English Traits* (OWH to Houghton, Mifflin and Co., 18 June 1883, bMS Am 1925 [859]. By permission of the Houghton Library, Harvard University).

57. OWH to Ebenezer Rockwood Hoar, 21 June 1883, Hoar Family Papers, 1738–1958, Vault A45 Hoar Unit 1, Box 2, Series II. Ebenezer Rockwood Hoar Papers, [182-]–1895, Concord Free Public Library; hereafter abbreviated Hoar Papers, Concord.

58. OWH to Ebenezer Rockwood Hoar, 8 July 1883, Hoar Papers, Concord.

59. OWH to Sargent, 11 August 1883.

60. OWH to James Russell Lowell, 29 August 1883, in Morse, *Holmes*, 2:132.

61. Holmes Papers, Library of Congress, Box 6.

62. "Emerson manuscript," Box 5, Holmes Papers, Library of Congress.

63. Quoted in Morse, *Holmes*, 1:321. The usually amiable Holmes complained about the burden of literary celebrity in 1886, particularly the imposition of thousands of letters he received annually from autograph hunters, would-be poets, and advice-seekers, each expecting a personal reply. He joked bitterly about hanging a sign outside his home: "Professional Correspondent, attends to letters on all subjects, from all persons and all quarters. Autographs in quantity at short notice" (Holmes, "A Cry from the Study," *Atlantic Monthly* 52 [January 1886]: 91–98).

64. EWE to OWH, 9 December 1883, Box 6, Holmes Papers, Library of Congress.

65. Caroline Tappan to OWH, 3 January 1884, Box 6, Holmes Papers, Library of Congress.

66. Le Baron Russell to OWH, 22–24 February 1884, Box 6, Holmes Papers, Library of Congress.

67. Frank Sanborn to OWH, 20 March 1854, Box 6, Holmes Papers, Library of Congress, listed in John Wheeler Clarkson Jr., "Mentions of Emerson and Thoreau in the Letters of Franklin Benjamin Sanborn," *Studies in the American Renaissance 1978*, ed. Joel Myerson (Boston: Twayne, 1978), 387–420. Whitman's recollections appear in chapter 15 of Holmes *RWE*, 344–345, where Holmes identifies them as reprinted from Alexander Ireland.

68. OWH to JEC, 6 February 1884, A-99, Box 3, Cabot Papers, Radcliffe. Cabot and his family also summered at Beverly Farms, so there were very likely face-to-face discussions not in the written record.

69. JEC to OWH, 7 February 1884, Box 6, Holmes Papers, Library of Congress. Cabot made a revealing remark about Emerson's German influences: Emerson "knew little or nothing at first hand of any of the German metaphysicians. Kant he respected and quoted at second hand. I tried to get him to look into Hagel [sic] but unsuccessfully though he read or read in Sterling's book about Hagel being more attracted by S's positive tone than by his matter. Schopenhauer he detested (also at second-hand) from his pessimistic results."

70. Tilton, *Amiable*, 348–349.

71. OWH to James Freeman Clarke, 9 February 1884, in Morse, *Holmes*, 2:59.

72. OWH to Clarke, 19 February 1884, bMS Am 1569.7 (349), Houghton Library, Harvard University.

73. OWH to Houghton, Mifflin and Company, 22 March 1884, bMS Am 1925 (859), folder 5, by permission of the Houghton Library, Harvard University.

74. OWH to Sanborn, 16 March 1884, in Cameron, *Correspondence of Sanborn*, item #2439.

75. Tilton, *Amiable*, 435 n.24.

76. Charles Dudley Warner to Houghton, Mifflin, 4 July 1884, bMS Am 1925 (1862), folder 3, by permission of the Houghton Library, Harvard University.

77. H. O. Houghton to Warner, 8 July 1884, Warner Papers, Trinity.

78. OWH to Warner, 11 July 1884, in Morse, *Holmes*, 2:60–61.

79. OWH to Houghton, Mifflin and Company, 28 August 1884, bMS Am 1925 (859), folder 6, by permission of the Houghton Library, Harvard University.

80. OWH to Houghton, Mifflin and Company, 5 September 1884, bMS Am 1925 (859), folder 6, by permission of the Houghton Library, Harvard University.

81. OWH to Houghton, Mifflin and Company, 4 December 1884, bMS Am 1925 (859), folder 6, by permission of the Houghton Library, Harvard University.

82. Currier and Tilton, *Bibliography of Holmes*, 199.

83. *Boston Daily Advertiser*, 10 December 1884.

84. Contract for *Ralph Waldo Emerson*, dated 6 December 1884, MS Am 2346 (1408). By permission of the Houghton Library, Harvard University.

85. Morse, *Holmes*, 2:63.

86. On biography, Morse maintains Holmes had "no very high or rare degree of aptitude for that kind of work. There were too many fences in such fields, and he could not move discursively enough" (Morse, *Holmes*, 2:64).

87. In a self-reflective aside, Holmes compared his own work as a memoirist to Cabot, "a future and better equipped laborer in the same field" (Holmes *RWE*, 358).

88. OWH to AI, 4 January 1884, Add 34813, Section D, Miscellaneous Autograph Letters, ff. 34–35, British Library.

89. OWH to Ellen Tucker Emerson, 25 September 1884, bMS Am 1280.226 (3656). Ralph Waldo Emerson Memorial Association deposit, Houghton Library, Harvard University. Not to be reproduced in whole or in part without permission. The information about Emerson's habits and physical presence—including his height, weight, and the circumference of his head—appears in the final chapter of Holmes *RWE*, "Emerson.—A Retrospect," 359–360.

90. OWH to Ellen Tucker Emerson, 9 October 1884, in Morse, *Holmes*, 2:60.

91. OWH to AI, 10 January 1885, Add 34813, section D, Miscellaneous Autograph Letters, ff. 38–39, British Library.

92. Joel Benton, *Emerson as a Poet* (New York: M. L. Holbrook, 1883), 49.

93. Holmes could have read similar appraisals of Emerson as a poet soon after Emerson's death in William T. Harris, "Ralph Waldo Emerson," *Atlantic Monthly* 50 (August 1882): 238–252 or Edwin P. Whipple, "Emerson as a Poet," *North American Review* 135 (July 1882): 68–71, an essay Holmes cites several times. Holmes did not attend the 1882 Emerson commemoration at the Concord School of Philosophy on 22 July, where George Willis Cooke read Benton's paper, although there was some speculation that he had been invited to give the dedicatory poem (unidentified newspaper clipping, Scrapbook, "Proceedings of Concord School 1882," pp. 36–43, 167, William Torrey Harris Concord School of Philosophy scrapbook, 1879–1887, folder 4, Vault A35, W. T. Harris Unit 2, Concord Free Public Library).

94. Joel Porte, in "Holmes's Emerson," states, "Transcendentalism, which forty years earlier had elicited public derision and execration, now found itself invested with the dignity of an ancestral creed" (*Consciousness and Culture: Emerson and Thoreau Reviewed* [New Haven: Yale University Press, 2004], 88–89). The sentiment may have been true among latter-day sympathizers, but as I argue in chapter 1, among the general literate public the movement's reputation was less than positive.

95. [H. W. Holland], "Mr. Emerson's Philosophy," *Nation*, 17 November 1881, 397.

96. Charles E. Mitchell, *Individualism and Its Discontents: Appropriations of Emerson, 1880–1950* (Amherst: University of Massachusetts Press, 1997), 26, 35, 7, 5.

97. T. S. McMillin, *Our Preposterous Use of Literature: Emerson and the Nature of Reading* (Urbana: University of Illinois Press, 2000), 89.

98. Randall Fuller, *Emerson's Ghosts: Literature, Politics, and the Making of Americanists* (New York: Oxford University Press, 2007), 35.

99. Fuller, *Emerson's Ghosts*, 35.

100. Holmes, *Mortal Antipathy*, 7:17.

101. McMillin also develops the therapeutic possibilities of Emerson's prose in *Our Preposterous Use of Literature*, 89–90.

102. McMillin, *Our Preposterous Use of Literature*, 90–91.

103. The durable equation of Transcendentalism with craziness persisted into the twentieth century. See, for instance, Henry David Gray, who in 1917 contrasted the "half-mad representatives of what they called 'the Newness'" with Emerson, "the most conspicuously sane man among them all" (*Emerson: A Statement of New England Transcendentalism as Expressed in the Philosophy of Its Chief Exponent* [Stanford, CA: Stanford University Press, 1917], 8).

104. Morse, *Holmes*, 2:58.

105. Roy Porter, *Madness: A Brief History* (New York: Oxford University Press, 2002), 52–58. See also the American Psychiatric Association, *One Hundred Years of American Psychiatry* (New York: Columbia University Press for the American Psychiatric Association, 1944) and Gerald N. Grob, *The Mad Among Us: A History of the Care of America's Mentally Ill* (Cambridge: Harvard University Press, 1994).

106. See Henry K. Beecher and Mark D. Altschule, *Medicine at Harvard: The First Three Hundred Years* (Hanover, NH: University Press of New England, 1977), 157–162, for a brief history of the development of psychiatry as an academic discipline at Harvard in the late nineteenth century. See also Harrington, *The Harvard Medical School*.

107. Tilton, *Amiable*, 353.

108. Bronson Alcott to OWH, 12 December 1884, box 1, item 4305, Holmes Papers, Library of Congress.

109. Matthew Arnold to OWH, 26 December 1884, box 1, item 4317, Holmes Papers, Library of Congress.

110. Herbert Spencer to OWH, 16 April 1885, reel 3, item 4918, Holmes Papers, Library of Congress.

111. Henry James Sr. to OWH, 5 March [1885], vol. 2, sheets 629, 4629–4633, Holmes Papers, Library of Congress.

112. James Russell Lowell to OWH, 28 December 1884, in *Letters of James Russell Lowell*, ed. Charles Eliot Norton, 2 vols. (New York: Harper and Brothers, 1894), 2:292.

113. Christopher Cranch to OWH, 3 February 1885, box 1, item 4452, Holmes Papers, Library of Congress.

114. Octavius Frothingham to OWH, 11 December 1884, box 1, item 4522–4523, Holmes Papers, Library of Congress.

115. Rockwood Hoar to OWH, 28 December 1884, in Morse, *Holmes*, 2:64.

116. Rutherford B. Hayes to OWH, 21 November 1885, vol. 2, Holmes Papers, Library of Congress.

117. OWH to AI, 10 January 1885. In fact, Ireland had already read the book, "with deep interest," as he reported to Mrs. Conway in a letter of 29 December 1884 (Ireland Papers, Special Collections Library, University of Michigan).

118. OWH to Frank Sanborn, 27 January 1885, in Cameron, *Correspondence of Sanborn*, item 2493.

119. Houghton, Mifflin Co., "Record of Book Sales, 1880–1891," MS Am 2030 (31), sec. 1, p. 6, by permission of the Houghton Library, Harvard University.

120. OWH to Henry Houghton, 20 August 1885, bMS Am 1925 (859), folder 6, by permission of the Houghton Library, Harvard University.

121. Casper, "Defining," 183.

122. According to Currier and Tilton, some 9,000 copies were printed in the first three months (*Bibliography of Holmes*, 200).

123. Henry O. Houghton to Charles Dudley Warner, 17 February 1885, Warner Papers, Trinity.

124. For an overview of commentary on the book, see Robert E. Burkholder and Joel Myerson, *Emerson: An Annotated Secondary Bibliography* (Pittsburgh: University of Pittsburgh Press, 1985), particularly items A1950–A1975.

125. MDC, "The Life of Emerson, by Oliver Wendell Holmes," *Our Corner* 5 (1 March 1885): 138–141.

126. GWC, "Dr. Holmes' Life of Emerson," *Unitarian Review* 23 (March 1885): 279–281.

127. OWH to Frank Sanborn, 9 October 1884, in Cameron, *Correspondence of Sanborn*, item 2473.

128. OWH to James Freeman Clarke, 21 December 1884, bMS Am 1569.7 (352), Houghton Library, Harvard University.

129. OWH to Sanborn, 19 December 1884, in Cameron, *Correspondence of Sanborn*, item 2489.

130. Frederic Henry Hedge to OWH, 22 December [1884], bMS Am 1241.1 (374), by permission of the Houghton Library, Harvard University.

131. OWH to George Bancroft, 16 January 1885.

132. Tilton, *Amiable*, 344.

5. AUTHORIZING EMERSON'S BIOGRAPHY

1. Edward W. Emerson, *Early Years of the Saturday Club, 1855–1870* (Boston: Houghton Mifflin, 1918), 267. I am indebted throughout this chapter to the thorough work of Nancy Craig Simmons in her doctoral dissertation, "Man Without a Shadow: The Life and Work of James Elliot Cabot, Emerson's Biographer and Literary Executor" (Ph.D. dissertation, Princeton University, 1980). Two relevant sections of Simmons's dissertation have been published: "Arranging the Sibylline Leaves: James Elliot Cabot's Work as Emerson's Literary Executor," *Studies in the American Renaissance 1983*, ed. Joel Myerson (Charlottesville: University Press of Virginia, 1983), 335–389, and "Philosophical Biographer: James Elliot Cabot and *A Memoir of Ralph Waldo Emerson*," *Studies in the American Renaissance 1987*, ed. Joel Myerson (Charlottesville: University Press of Virginia, 1987), 365–392. Simmons has also edited "The 'Autobiographical Sketch' of James Elliot Cabot," *Harvard Library Bulletin* 30 (April 1982), 117–152.

2. *ETE*, 2:414–415.

3. JEC to EWE, 13 November 1877, bMS Am 1280.226 (3243); JEC to Ellen Tucker Emerson, 18 February 1881, bMS Am 1280.226 (3224). Ralph Waldo Emerson Memorial Association deposit, Houghton Library, Harvard University. Not to be reproduced in whole or in part without permission.

4. Simmons, "Autobiographical Sketch," 135.

5. Simmons, "Autobiographical Sketch," 142.

6. Simmons, "Philosophical Biographer," 366.

7. EmLet, 3:286.

8. Simmons, "Philosophical Biographer," 369. In point of fact, the families were distantly related by marriage. James Elliot Cabot's mother was Eliza Perkins; her sister Margaret was the mother of John Murray Forbes, Edith Emerson Forbes's father-in-law.

9. Channing wrote Lidian Emerson on 6 May 1882, less than two weeks after Waldo's death, offering his condolences and advising her in great detail about the publication of her husband's works in England (bMS Am 1280.226 [3266]. Ralph Waldo Emerson Memorial Association deposit, Houghton Library, Harvard University. Not to be reproduced in whole or in part without permission). For a fuller discussion of Channing's critique of Cabot, see Robert D. Habich, "Channing Re-

members Emerson: Visits to Concord in 1870 and 1877," *New England Quarterly* 73 (September 2000): 495–506.

10. Elizabeth Dwight Cabot to JEC, 22 July 1882.

11. Elizabeth Dwight Cabot to JEC, 25[?] July 1882, Cabot Papers, Radcliffe, A-99, Box 3, folder 41.

12. Channing to JEC, 27 July 1882, bMS Am 1280.226 (3267). Ralph Waldo Emerson Memorial Association deposit, Houghton Library, Harvard University. Not to be reproduced in whole or in part without permission.

13. In "Ralph Waldo Emerson," *Inquirer* [London], 6 May 1882, Channing listed a number of topics he was working on that were "too vast and rich for meager treatment [and] must be deferred to a later time and another place" (285), and in "R. W. Emerson," *Modern Review* 3 (October 1882), Channing claimed to have written "a voluminous heap of MSS." that indicates "my notice was planned on the scale of a book" (850). Among the others who projected biographies of Emerson but did not write them are Julius H. Ward, a minister whose book was announced in the *Christian Union* for 8 June 1882, and Louisa May Alcott, who was so dissatisfied with Cabot's treatment of Emerson's relationship with her father that she vowed to write her own version (Louisa May Alcott to A. Bronson Alcott, 13 October 1887, in *The Selected Journals of Louisa May Alcott*, ed. Joel Myerson and Daniel Shealy, associate ed. Madeleine B. Stern [Boston: Little, Brown, 1987], 321).

14. Thomas Wentworth Higginson, *Carlyle's Laugh and Other Surprises* (Boston: Houghton, Mifflin, 1909), 243–244. In his *Cheerful Yesterdays* (Boston and New York: Houghton, Mifflin, 1898), Higginson recalled Cabot from his Harvard days, "fresh from a German university . . . however, most un-German in clearness and terseness" (105).

15. EWE to MDC, 6 May 1883, Conway Papers, Columbia.

16. Simmons, "Man Without a Shadow," 429–430. Edward Twistleton (Ted) Cabot (1861–1893), the second of the Cabots' seven sons, was a Harvard graduate, class of 1883 (L. Vernon Briggs, *History and Genealogy of the Cabot Family, 1475–1927* 2 vols. [Boston: Charles E. Goodspeed, 1927], 1:696; *Quinquennial Catalogue of the Officers and Graduates of Harvard University, 1636–1910* [Cambridge, MA: Published by the University, 1910], 276).

17. Simmons, "Philosophical Biographer," 372.

18. JEC, [Notes on Emerson], bMS Am 1280.235 (711). Ralph Waldo Emerson Memorial Association deposit, Houghton Library, Harvard University. Not to be reproduced in whole or in part without permission. For an apt discussion of the way Cabot's research methods reflected his philosophy and personality, see Simmons, "Philosophical Biographer," 371–372.

19. Edith Emerson Forbes to Elizabeth Dwight Cabot, 29 April 1885, bMS Am 1280.226 (3500). Ralph Waldo Emerson Memorial Association deposit, Houghton Library, Harvard University. Not to be reproduced in whole or in part without permission.

20. JEC to Elizabeth Dwight Cabot, 24 July 1885, Cabot Papers, Radcliffe, A-99, Box 5, folder 83.

21. *ETE*, 2:552.

22. *ETE*, 2:564.

23. Simmons, "Man Without a Shadow," 434.

24. *Boston Daily Advertiser*, 17 September 1887. Cabot negotiated very favorable publication terms. According to his contract with Houghton, Mifflin, dated 9 February 1887, he would receive 20 percent royalty on the retail price of all domestic sales and 50 percent royalty on the sales of any foreign edition. He also specified that "no advertisement of any nature shall be inserted in any edition of said work," perhaps to avoid the mention of Conway's and Holmes's biographies of Emerson, which were also being sold by Houghton, Mifflin at this time ("Cabot, James Elliot. A Memoir of Ralph Waldo Emerson," MS Am 2346 [458], by permission of the Houghton Library, Harvard University.)

25. Edward W. Forbes, "Edward Waldo Emerson," in *The Saturday Club: A Century Completed 1920–1956*, ed. Forbes and John H. Finley Jr. (Boston: Houghton Mifflin, 1958), 28, 31, 32.

26. Ellen Tucker Emerson, *The Life of Lidian Jackson Emerson*, ed. Delores Bird Carpenter (Boston: Twayne, 1980), 157; Benjamin Kendall Emerson, *The Ipswich Emersons* (Boston: privately printed, 1900), 371. Edward reported that his poor eyesight caused him to return from a business venture in Iowa after his graduation in 1866 (*Harvard College Class of 1866 Class Report, July, 1866 to June, 1869* [Boston, 1869], 17). For other biographical information I have relied upon Bliss Perry, "Dr. Edward Waldo Emerson," *Concord Journal*, 6 February 1930; Allen French, "Edward Waldo Emerson: A Memoir," *Proceedings of the Massachusetts Historical Society*, 3rd Series, 65 (February 1935), 387–390, expanded as "Edward Waldo Emerson," in *Memoirs of Members of the Social Circle in Concord, Fifth Series, from 1900 to 1939* (Cambridge, MA: Privately printed, The University Press, 1940), 293–311; and Edward W. Forbes, "Edward Waldo Emerson."

27. Perry, "Dr. Edward Waldo Emerson," 2.

28. Edward Waldo Emerson, printed information sheet for the Social Circle in Concord, n.d., bMS Am 1280.235 (355). Ralph Waldo Emerson Memorial Association deposit, Houghton Library, Harvard University. Not to be reproduced in whole or in part without permission.

29. EmLet, 5:290–291.

30. The anecdote about Edward Emerson's enlistment and subsequent return appears in two versions. Edward claimed that his sister Edith had dissuaded him from serving (see EmLet, 9:149n82). Lidian Emerson recalled that John Murray Forbes had convinced Edward that his military service was not worth the risk to his father's health (*Life of Lidian Emerson*, 142). Jessie Bray recounts Edward's military aspirations in "'Not a *pure* idealist': Ralph Waldo Emerson, Edward Waldo Emerson, and the Civil War," *Resources for American Literary Study* 32 (2007): 85–97.

31. On Edward's decision to forego painting and enter medical school, see Perry, "Dr. Edward Waldo Emerson," 2, and H. Winthrop Peirce, *The History of the School of the Museum of Fine Arts, Boston, 1877–1927* (Boston: Museum of Fine Arts, 1930), 55–56.

32. Only four years separated Edward from his brother-in-law William Hathaway Forbes (1840–1897), who entered the war in 1861 and rose to the rank of Lieutenant Colonel in the 2nd Massachusetts Cavalry. He was taken prisoner during a skirmish in Virginia in 1864, "standing in his stirrups with saber drawn, fighting desperately," according to one eyewitness. Forbes married Edith Emerson in 1865. A successful

industrialist and later president of the American Bell Telephone Company, Forbes was a trusted financial advisor to other members of the Emerson family. See Arthur S. Pier, *Forbes: Telephone Pioneer* (New York: Dodd, Mead, 1953).

33. EWE to MDC, 15 July 1882, Conway Papers, Columbia; Edward W. Forbes, "Edward Waldo Emerson," 35.

34. For a detailed account of Cabot's role as literary executor, see chapters 7 and 8 of Simmons's dissertation, especially pp. 348–428. This material is condensed in Simmons, "Arranging the Sibylline Leaves."

35. *ETE*, 2:486.

36. EWE to JEC, 27 May 1887, Cabot Papers, Radcliffe, A-99, Box 9, volume 13.

37. Edward Waldo Emerson, *Early Years of the Saturday Club*, 268.

38. Simmons, "Arranging the Sibylline Leaves," 362.

39. EWE to MDC, 6 May 1883.

40. Edward Waldo Emerson, *Early Years of the Saturday Club*, 267.

41. Around this time Cabot asked for clarification of the terms of his appointment, and Edward quoted him the entire paragraph from his father's revised will: "I appoint my friend James Elliot Cabot to be my literary executor giving him authority, acting in cooperation with my children, or the survivors or survivor of them, to publish or withhold from publication any of my unpublished papers." EWE to JEC, 27 January 1883, bMS Am 1280.226 (261). Ralph Waldo Emerson Memorial Association deposit, Houghton Library, Harvard University. Not to be reproduced in whole or in part without permission.

42. Contract, "Emersons [sic] Works March 15th 1883, Old & New Editions," MS Am 2346 (914), folder 4, by permission of the Houghton Library, Harvard University.

43. Edith Emerson Forbes to Elizabeth Dwight Cabot, fragment, ca. July 1886, bMS Am 1280.226 (3501). Ralph Waldo Emerson Memorial Association deposit, Houghton Library, Harvard University. Not to be reproduced in whole or in part without permission.

44. Edith Emerson Forbes to EWE, 14 July 1886, Edith Emerson Forbes and William Hathaway Forbes Papers and Additions, Massachusetts Historical Society, hereafter abbreviated Forbes Papers, Massachusetts Historical Society.

45. Simmons, "Philosophical Biographer," 372–373.

46. Edith Emerson Forbes to EWE, 14 July 1886, Forbes Papers, Massachusetts Historical Society.

47. Edith Emerson Forbes to Ellen Tucker Emerson, 17 July 1886, Forbes Papers, Massachusetts Historical Society. In the Cabot Papers, Radcliffe, folder 126, is an undated manuscript in Edith's hand, 9 small leaves, pencil-written, of miscellaneous recollections of her father when she was a small child.

48. The family's strategizing makes clear that the money was indeed a way to show their gratitude to Cabot. Edith wrote to Ellen on 9 July 1882, "Will suggested that a good argument to use would be to mention the ever recurring pleasure we have had in Uncle Adams's legacy to us and that it would please us to have the Cabot boys so reminded of Father's affection for their father" (Forbes Papers, Massachusetts Historical Society).

49. JEC to EWE, 18 November 1887, bMS Am 1280.226 (3249). Ralph Waldo Emerson Memorial Association deposit, Houghton Library, Harvard University. Not to be reproduced in whole or in part without permission.

50. *ETE*, 2:503.

51. EWE to Ellen Tucker Emerson, 18 July [1883], bMS Am 1280.226 (305). Ralph Waldo Emerson Memorial Association deposit, Houghton Library, Harvard University. Not to be reproduced in whole or in part without permission.

52. Simmons, "Man Without a Shadow," 416, 411.

53. Ellen Tucker Emerson to Elizabeth Dwight Cabot, 13 August 1883, Cabot Papers, Radcliffe, A-99, Box 6, folder 125.

54. Simmons, "Arranging the Sibylline Leaves," 372. Simmons contrasts Edward's "indecision, circular discussions, and fretting about minor questions" over the projected volume of *Poems* with Cabot's decisiveness and argues that Cabot "was happy to keep Edward occupied" with the volume ("Man Without a Shadow," 412).

55. EWE to JEC, 19 October 1883, bMS Am 1280.226 (295). Ralph Waldo Emerson Memorial Association deposit, Houghton Library, Harvard University. Not to be reproduced in whole or in part without permission. Joseph M. Thomas analyzes Edward's contributions as editor of his father's poetry in "The Familial Canon of Emerson's Poetry" (unpublished paper, American Literature Association meeting, 25 May 2007).

56. For specific information about the activities of the Social Circle, I rely upon two manuscript sources at the Concord Free Public Library, quoted by permission: the "Copy of Records 1795–1882," which contains minutes, membership rolls, and the group's constitution, and the "Record Book Social Circle in Concord," Deposit Collection, which contains minutes for meetings from 1882 through 1922.

57. "Record Book Social Circle in Concord," 54–55; Frank Sanborn to William T. Harris, 25 February 1887, in *Correspondence of Benjamin Franklin Sanborn*, ed. Kenneth Walter Cameron (Hartford, CT: Transcendental Books, 1982), item 2559. John Shepard Keyes, Edward's father-in-law, recorded in his diary for the meeting of 1 March, "Edward going on with his memoir of his Father[.] Sanborn kept interrupting until I protested to the Chairman and squelched his impertinence, much to the clubs amusement." Of the 8 March reading, Keyes noted, "The Judge [Rockwood Hoar] and I agreed that it was like having Mr Emerson back talking to us for the evening" (John Shepard Keyes Papers, 1837–1908, Vault A45, Keyes, Unit 2, volume 10, Diary 1882–1887, 274–275, Concord Free Public Library). Edward Waldo Forbes records that the manuscript was also read in May at Edith and Will Forbes's home ("Edward Waldo Emerson," 37).

58. Cabot in fact published the first chapter of the *Memoir* in the *Atlantic Monthly* in May 1887.

59. "Record Book Social Circle in Concord," 69–73. *Emerson in Concord* was first advertised for sale in the Boston *Daily Advertiser* on 4 May 1889.

60. Simmons, "Philosophical Biographer," 385.

61. Cabot's own attitude toward the other members of the movement is perhaps best reflected in Simmons's "Autobiographical Sketch," where he claims to have been "something of a 'Transcendentalist'" as a student at Harvard in his admiration for Carlyle, his contempt for the "working day world," and his inattention to his studies (135).

62. Simmons, "Arranging the Sibylline Leaves," 383.

63. Quoted in Simmons, "Philosophical Biographer," 371.

64. *ETE*, 2:473.

65. *ETE*, 2:564.

66. Simmons, "Philosophical Biographer," 373.

67. JEC to Ellen Tucker Emerson, 18 February 1881.

68. Simmons, "Philosophical Biographer," 377.

69. Simmons, "Philosophical Biographer," 368.

70. *ETE*, 2:579.

71. In addition, Edward points out, Emerson was famously inept with tools (*E in C*, 129).

72. Annie Keyes Emerson to Mildred Conway Sawyer, 17 December n.y., Conway Papers, Columbia, box 9.

73. Quoted in Edward W. Forbes, "Edward Waldo Emerson," 36.

74. *ETE*, 2:473.

75. Houghton, Mifflin Co., "Record of Book Sales, 1880–1891," MS Am 2030 (31), sec. 2, p. 8 [*Memoir*] and sec. 3, pp. 10–11 [*Emerson in Concord*], by permission of the Houghton Library, Harvard University. Figures for *Emerson in Concord* do not include the 261 copies privately printed for distribution to members and friends of the Social Circle in Concord.

76. Sarah S. Storer to JEC, 28 May 1887. Cabot papers, Radcliffe, A-99, Box 9, Vol. 13.

77. George W. Curtis to JEC, 25 October 1887. Cabot papers, Radcliffe, A-99, Box 9, Vol. 13.

78. Rockwood Hoar to JEC, 23 September 1887. Cabot papers, Radcliffe, A-99, Box 9, Vol. 13.

79. James Freeman Clarke to JEC, 31 May 1887. Cabot papers, Radcliffe, A-99, Box 9, Vol. 13.

80. Review of *A Memoir of Ralph Waldo Emerson*, *Athenaeum*, 29 October 1887, 561.

81. [Horace E. Scudder,] "Emerson's Genius," *Atlantic* 60 (October 1887): 567.

82. Hedge, "Cabot's Memoir of Emerson," *Unitarian Review* 28 (November 1887): 416, 418.

83. [William Henry Thorne], "Emerson and His Biographers," *Globe* 1 (October–December 1889): 37, 50.

84. Simmons, "Autobiographical Sketch," 151.

85. [George Edward Woodberry,] "Emerson's Concord Life," *Atlantic Monthly* 64 (August 1889): 270, 273.

86. "Emerson in Concord," *Christian Union*, 23 May 1889, 670.

87. [F. B. Sanborn,] "Carlyle and Emerson Once More," *Springfield Daily Republican*, 3 June 1889, 8. Sanborn's relationship with other members of the Social Circle was strained at this time—he would be dropped from its membership in 1890—so he may have been excessively critical of a book they sponsored.

88. A notable exception was Walt Whitman, who was outraged over a footnote in *Emerson in Concord* about Emerson's eventual disenchantment with the catalogue style of *Leaves of Grass* (*E in C*, 228n). Whitman said the note was "as dirty and lying a paragraph as ever was written," labeled Edward Emerson "constitutionally

my enemy," and called the Emerson siblings "a bad lot" for manipulating and controlling their father. There is no evidence that the Emersons knew of Whitman's tirade (Horace Traubel and William White, *With Walt Whitman in Camden*, vol. 6, ed. Gertrude Traubel [Carbondale: Southern Illinois University Press, 1982], 122). For the complete episode, see Jerome Loving, "Emerson's 'Constant Way of Looking at Whitman's Genius,'" *American Literature* 51 (November 1979): 399–403.

89. [Sanborn,] "Carlyle and Emerson," 8.

90. "Emerson in Concord," *Christian Union*, 670.

91. "Our Library Table," *Athenaeum*, 1 June 1889, 695.

6. SHELF LIFE

1. Randall Fuller, *Emerson's Ghosts: Literature, Politics, and the Making of Americanists* (New York: Oxford University Press, 2007), 27.

2. For an overview of Houghton, Mifflin and Company's progress in the late Gilded Age, see John Tebbel, *A History of Book Publishing in the United States*, 4 vols. (New York: R. R. Bowker, 1972–1981), 2:247–259. For a more detailed history, see Ellen B. Ballou, *The Building of the House: Houghton Mifflin's Formative Years* (Boston: Houghton Mifflin, 1970). Following the firm's incorporation in 1908, its name changed to the comma-less Houghton Mifflin Company.

3. Houghton Mifflin Company to Mrs. Florence Cooke [sic], 16 October 1926, MS Am 2346 (642), by permission of the Houghton Library, Harvard University.

4. AI to MDC, 26 June 1870, Ireland Papers, Michigan.

5. AI to Alexander Campbell, 20 October 1891, Special Collections, Glasgow University Library.

6. Petition dated November 1893, Local Studies Division, Manchester Central Library, Manchester, England.

7. Folder for "Conway, Moncure D." MS Am 2346 (637), by permission of the Houghton Library, Harvard University.

8. Charles H. Pearson, "Emerson" (1883), in *Reviews and Critical Essays* (London: Methuen, 1896), 185.

9. Conway, *Ellen Dana Conway* [New York: Privately printed, 1898?], 4.

10. Quoted in John d'Entremont, *Moncure Conway 1832–1907*, 30.

11. Moncure D. Conway, "Emerson: The Teacher and the Man," *Critic* 42 (May 1903): 404–411. An abbreviated version appears in Conway *EHA*, 3–4.

12. "Emerson Extolled at Authors' Dinner," *New York Times*, 26 May 1903.

13. John Torrey Morse Jr., *Holmes*, 2:71.

14. Add to this number the 5,520 copies shipped to Kegan Paul for sale in England; an additional 3,310 copies of a combined Emerson/Motley volume, which was sold from 1892 to 1918 as volume 14 (later volume 11) of the Riverside Edition of Holmes's works; and an unknown number of copies sold as part of the "Riverside Popular Biographies" series beginning in 1912, and Holmes's *Emerson* emerges as easily the best-selling of the original six biographies (Casper, "Defining," 183). According to Thomas Franklin Currier and Eleanor M. Tilton, some 9,000 copies of Holmes *RWE* were printed in the first three months. The last copies were bound

in February 1930; the plates were finally destroyed in 1942 (*A Bibliography of Oliver Wendell Holmes*, 200).

15. Houghton, Mifflin to George Leverett, 23 October 1888, MS Am 2346 (911), by permission of the Houghton Library, Harvard University.

16. Houghton Mifflin to Raymond Emerson, 18 May 1932, by permission of the Houghton Library, Harvard University.

17. Internal memorandum from "Trade Department BO," 29 June 1939, MS Am 2346 (911), by permission of the Houghton Library, Harvard University.

18. Joel Myerson, *Ralph Waldo Emerson: A Descriptive Bibliography* (Pittsburgh: University of Pittsburgh Press, 1982), 549.

19. Edward Waldo Emerson, ed., *Complete Works of Ralph Waldo Emerson* [Centenary Edition] (Boston: Houghton, Mifflin, 1903–1904), 1:xxxix, xiii.

20. Myerson, Introduction to the AMS Reprint Edition, Second Edition, *Complete Works of Ralph Waldo Emerson* (New York: AMS Press, 1979), 1:n.p.

21. "Dr. E. W. Emerson Dead at Age of 85," *New York Times*, 28 January 1930.

22. Myerson, *Descriptive Bibliography*, 551.

23. Moses Williams to Houghton Mifflin, 16 November 1933, MS Am 2346 (458), by permission of the Houghton Library, Harvard University.

24. Ballou, *Building of a House*, 488–489.

25. Tebbel, *History of Book Publishing*, 2:258.

26. For the most comprehensive treatment of Emerson's later reputation, see Sarah Ann Wider, *The Critical Reception of Emerson: Unsettling All Things* (Rochester, NY: Camden House, 2000). Surveys of Emerson's later appropriation also appear in Charles E. Mitchell, *Individualism and Its Discontents: Appropriations of Emerson, 1880–1950* (Amherst: University of Massachusetts Press, 1997), and Randall Fuller, *Emerson's Ghosts*. An excellent treatment of the ways Emersonian self-reliance has been adapted to later use is Wesley T. Mott, "'The Age of the First Person Singular': Emerson and Individualism," in *A Historical Guide to Ralph Waldo Emerson*, ed. Joel Myerson (New York: Oxford University Press, 2000), 61–100.

27. See, for example, Leo Braudy, *The Frenzy of Renown: Fame and Its History* (New York: Oxford University Press, 1986); P. David Marshall, *Celebrity and Power: Fame in Contemporary Culture* (Minneapolis: University of Minnesota Press, 1997); James Monaco, *Celebrity: The Media as Image Makers* (New York: Delta, 1978); and especially Daniel J. Boorstin, *The Image: A Guide to Pseudo-Events in America* (New York: Harper, 1964).

28. Monaco, "Celebration," in *Celebrity*, 10.

29. Braudy, *Frenzy of Renown*, 464. For the persistence of this myth into the twentieth century, see Joyce Piell Wexler, *Who Paid for Modernism? Art, Money, and the Fiction of Conrad, Joyce, and Lawrence* (Fayetteville: University of Arkansas Press, 1997), which skillfully examines how modernist authors negotiated "an ideological contradiction between art and money that pervaded their culture" (xii).

30. Braudy, *Frenzy of Renown*, 468. In *Authors Inc.: Literary Celebrity in the Modern United States, 1880–1980* (New York: New York University Press, 2004), Loren Daniel Glass astutely situates the growth of literary celebrity from 1880 to 1980 in an emergent dialectic between the success in mass culture associated with the female and the achievement of isolated artists associated with masculinity. It is a theory rich

in possibilities for *describing* Emerson, whose iconization in some ways hinged upon a kind of eviscerated disengagement with the world, but less so as a way of *accounting* for him, since Glass's approach focuses on the conscious self-promotion of, say, a Twain or a Hemingway, not the cultural shanghaiing that occurred after Emerson's death. David Haven Blake's *Walt Whitman and the Culture of American Celebrity* (New Haven: Yale University Press, 2006) explores the conscious ways in which Whitman responded to the contemporary pursuit of fame with his self-celebrating poetry.

31. The commemorative nature of photography during Emerson's lifetime meant that subjects routinely look posed and serious; not until after the advent of an inexpensive Kodak camera and the impromptu "snapshot" do subjects begin to appear relaxed and casual in photographs. For the most comprehensive collection of Emerson visual iconography, from photographs to calendars to commercial products that bore his name, consult the web site of the Ralph Waldo Emerson Society, www.emersonsociety.org, based on the collections of Joel Myerson. Sean Ross Meehan explores the response of Emerson and some of his contemporaries to the relationship between the photograph and life-writing in *Mediating American Autobiography: Photography in Emerson, Thoreau, Douglass, and Whitman* (Columbia: University of Missouri Press, 2008).

32. Mutlu Konuk Blasing, *The Art of Life: Studies in American Autobiographical Literature* (Austin and London: University of Texas Press, 1977), xv.

33. Bonnie Carr O'Neill, "'The Best of Me Is There': Emerson as Lecturer and Celebrity," *American Literature: A Journal of Literary History, Criticism, and Bibliography* 80 (December 2008): 759, 761.

34. Monaco, "Celebration," 6–7.

35. Tebbel, *History of Book Publishing*, 2:47.

36. Todd H. Richardson, "Emerson's Canonization and the Boston Periodical Press: 1872–1903" (Ph.D. dissertation, University of South Carolina, 2002), 15, 17.

37. Todd H. Richardson, "Emerson's Canonization," 25.

38. Len Gougeon, "Looking Backwards: Emerson in 1903," *Nineteenth-Century Prose* 30 (Spring/Fall 2003): 50, 61–62, 54.

39. OWH to AI, 10 January 1885, Add 34813, section D, Miscellaneous Autograph Letters, ff. 38–39, British Library, printed in Morse, *Holmes*, 2:63, who misdates it as 15 January.

40. Frederic Henry Hedge to OWH, 22 December [1884], bMS Am 1241.1 (374).

41. William Henry Channing to JEC, 27 August 1882.

42. Alcott, "Journal 1881," entry for 25 November, MS Am 1130.12 (53), vol. 58 (emphasis added), by permission of the Houghton Library, Harvard University.

43. *ETE*, 2:590.

44. OWH to Ellen Tucker Emerson, 9 October 1884, in Morse, *Holmes*, 2:60.

45. Quoted in Edward W. Forbes, "Edward Waldo Emerson," 36.

46. Typescript notes of Edith Emerson Forbes to Elizabeth Cabot, undated [penciled "July? 1886"], collection of Beatrice Forbes Manz, quoted by permission.

BIBLIOGRAPHY

BOOKS AND ARTICLES

"Actresses for the Album: Popular Artists Whose Pictures Sell Readily." *New York Times*, November 5, 1882.

Alcott, A. Bronson. *Journals of Bronson Alcott*. Edited by Odell Shepard. Boston: Little, Brown, 1938.

———. *Ralph Waldo Emerson: An Estimate of His Character and Genius, in Prose and Verse*. Boston: A. Williams, 1882.

Alcott, Louisa May. *The Selected Journals of Louisa May Alcott*. Edited by Joel Myerson and Daniel Shealy, associate ed. Madeleine B. Stern. Boston: Little, Brown, 1987.

Althusser, Louis. "Ideology and Ideological State Apparatuses." *Lenin and Philosophy and Other Essays*, 127–186. Translated by Ben Brewster. New York and London: Monthly Review Press, 1971.

Altick, Richard D. *Lives and Letters: A History of Literary Biography in England and America*. New York: Knopf, 1965.

American Psychiatric Association. *One Hundred Years of American Psychiatry*. New York: Columbia University Press for the American Psychiatric Association, 1944.

Ballou, Ellen B. *The Building of the House: Houghton Mifflin's Formative Years*. Boston: Houghton Mifflin, 1970.

Beecher, Henry K., and Mark D. Altschule. *Medicine at Harvard: The First Three Hundred Years*. Hanover, NH: University Press of New England, 1977.

Benton, Joel. *Emerson as a Poet*. New York: M. L. Holbrook, 1883.

"The Biographical Mania." *Tait's Edinburgh Magazine*, n.s. 21 (January 1854): 16–23.

"Biography." *The Spectator*, July 29, 1882.

Blake, David Haven: *Walt Whitman and the Culture of American Celebrity*. New Haven, CT: Yale University Press, 2006.

Blasing, Mutlu Konuk. *The Art of Life: Studies in American Autobiographical Literature*. Austin and London: University of Texas Press, 1977.

Boorstin, Daniel. *The Image: A Guide to Pseudo-Events in America*. New York: Harper, 1964.

Bosco, Ronald A. "We Find What We Seek: Emerson and His Biographers." *A Historical Guide to Ralph Waldo Emerson*, 269–290. Edited by Joel Myerson. New York and Oxford: Oxford University Press, 2000.

Bosco, Ronald A., and Joel Myerson, eds. *Later Lectures of Ralph Waldo Emerson, 1843–1871*. 2 vols. Athens: University of Georgia Press, 2001.

Brake, Laurel. "The Serialisation of Books: Macmillan's English Men of Letters Series and the New Biography." *Print in Transition 1850–1910: Studies in Media and Book History*, 52–66. Basingstoke, UK, and New York: Palgrave, 2001.

Braudy, Leo. *The Frenzy of Renown: Fame and Its History*. New York: Oxford University Press, 1986.

Bray, Jessie. "'Not a *pure* idealist': Ralph Waldo Emerson, Edward Waldo Emerson, and the Civil War." *Resources for American Literary Study* 32 (2007): 85–97.

Briggs, L. Vernon. *History and Genealogy of the Cabot Family, 1475–1972*. 2 vols. Boston: Charles E. Goodspeed, 1927.

Brodhead, Richard H. *Cultures of Letters: Scenes of Reading and Writing in Nineteenth-Century America*. Chicago and London: University of Chicago Press, 1993.

Broughton, Trev Lynn. *Men of Letters, Writing Lives: Masculinity and Literary Auto/Biography in the Late Victorian Period*. London: Routledge, 1999.

Brown, Lucy. *Victorian News and Newspapers*. Oxford: Clarendon Press, 1985.

Browne, R. C. "Two Books on Emerson." *Academy* 24 (August 4, 1883): 71–72.

Burkholder, Robert E. "George Willis Cooke." *American Literary Critics and Scholars, 1880–1900*, 50–57. Edited by John W. Rathbun and Monica M. Grecu. Detroit: Gale, 1988.

Burkholder, Robert E., and Joel Myerson. *Emerson: An Annotated Secondary Bibliography*. Pittsburgh: University of Pittsburgh Press, 1985.

Burtis, Mary Elizabeth. *Moncure Conway, 1832–1907*. New Brunswick, NJ: Rutgers University Press, 1952.

Cabot, James Elliot. *Memoir of Ralph Waldo Emerson*. 2 vols. Boston and New York: Houghton, Mifflin, 1887.

"The Camera Epidemic." *New York Times*, August 20, 1884.

Cameron, Kenneth Walter, ed. *Concord Harvest: Publications of the Concord School of Philosophy and Literature with Notes on Its Successors and Other Resources for Research in Emerson, Thoreau, Alcott and the Later Transcendentalists*. 2 vols. Hartford, CT: Transcendental Books, 1970.

———. *Response to Transcendental Concord: The Last Decades of the Era of Emerson, Thoreau, and the Concord School as Recorded in Newspapers*. Hartford, CT: Transcendental Books, 1974.

Casper, Scott E. *Constructing American Lives: Biography and Culture in Nineteenth-Century America*. Chapel Hill: University of North Carolina Press, 1999.

———. "Defining the National Pantheon: The Making of Houghton Mifflin's Biographical Series, 1880–1900." *Reading Books: Essays on the Material Text and Literature in America*, 179–222. Edited by Michele Moylan and Lane Stiles. Amherst: University of Massachusetts Press, 1996.

Channing, William Henry. "R. W. Emerson." *Modern Review* 3 (October 1882): 850–854.

———. "Ralph Waldo Emerson." *Inquirer* (London), May 6, 1882.

Clarkson, John Wheeler, Jr. "Mentions of Emerson and Thoreau in the Letters of Franklin Benjamin Sanborn." *Studies in the American Renaissance 1978*, 387–420. Edited by Joel Myerson. Boston: Twayne, 1978.

Cockshut, A. O. J. *Truth to Life: The Art of Biography in the Nineteenth Century.* London: Collins, 1974.

Conway, Moncure Daniel. *Autobiography, Memories and Experiences.* 2 vols. Boston: Houghton, Mifflin, 1904.

———. *Ellen Dana Conway.* New York: Privately printed, [1898?].

———. *Emerson at Home and Abroad.* Boston: James R. Osgood and Co., 1882; London: Trübner, 1883.

———. "Emerson: The Teacher and the Man." *Critic* 42 (May 1903): 404–411.

———. "The Life of Emerson, by Oliver Wendell Holmes." *Our Corner* 5 (March 1, 1885): 138–141.

———. "Ralph Waldo Emerson." *Fortnightly Review*, June 1, 1882, 20–28.

Cooke, George Willis. "After Seventy Years—an Optimist." *Unity* 81 (May 9, 1918): 163–165.

———. "Dr. Holmes' Life of Emerson." *Unitarian Review* 23 (March 1885): 279–281.

———. "Emerson's Attitude Toward Religion." *Saturday Herald*, February 14, 1880.

———. *George Eliot: A Critical Study of Her Life, Writings and Philosophy.* Boston: J. R. Osgood and Company, 1883; London: Sampson Low, 1883.

———. *A History of the Clapboard Trees or Third Parish, Dedham, Mass. Now the Unitarian Parish, West Dedham 1736–1886.* Boston: Geo. H. Ellis, 1887.

———. *Poets and Problems.* Boston: Ticknor and Company, 1886.

———. *Ralph Waldo Emerson: His Life, Writings, and Philosophy.* Boston: James R. Osgood and Co., 1881; London: Sampson Low, Marston Searle, & Rivington, 1882.

———. *The Social Evolution of Religion.* Boston: The Stratford Company, 1920.

———. "Unity Church." *Saturday Herald*, February 14, 1880.

"The Craze for Biographies." *Spectator*, April 14, 1888.

Currier, Thomas Franklin, and Eleanor M. Tilton. *A Bibliography of Oliver Wendell Holmes.* New York: New York University Press, 1953.

d'Entremont, John. *Moncure Conway 1832–1907: American Abolitionist, Spiritual Architect of "South Place," Author of "The Life of Thomas Paine."* London: South Place Ethical Society, 1977.

———. *Southern Emancipator: Moncure Conway, the American Years 1832–1865.* New York: Oxford University Press, 1987.

Dodge, M. A. "The New School of Biography." *Atlantic Monthly* 14 (November 1864): 579–589.

Dole, Nathan Haskell. "Life of Ralph Waldo Emerson." *The Early Poems of Ralph Waldo Emerson*, vii–xli. New York: Thomas Y. Crowell, 1899.

"Dr. E. W. Emerson Dead at Age 85." *New York Times*, January 28, 1930.

Dunn, Waldo Hillary. *James Anthony Froude: A Biography.* 2 vols. Oxford: Clarendon Press, 1961, 1963.

Eliot, George. *The George Eliot Letters*. Edited by Gordon S. Haight. 9 vols. New Haven, CT: Yale University Press, 1954–1978.

Eliot, Simon. "Hotten: Rotten: Forgotten? An Apologia for a General Publisher." *Book History* 3 (2000): 61–93.

"Emerson." New York *Daily Tribune*, October 23, 1881.

Emerson, Benjamin Kendall. *The Ipswich Emersons, A.D. 1636–1900*. Boston: privately printed, 1900.

Emerson, Edward Waldo. *The Early Years of the Saturday Club, 1855–1870*. Boston and New York: Houghton Mifflin, 1918.

———. *Emerson in Concord: A Memoir*. Boston and New York: Houghton, Mifflin, 1889.

———. "Emerson vs. Cook." *Saturday Herald*, March 6, 1880.

Emerson, Ellen Tucker. *The Letters of Ellen Tucker Emerson*. 2 vols. Edited by Edith E. W. Gregg. Kent, OH: Kent State University Press, 1982.

———. *The Life of Lidian Jackson Emerson*. Edited by Delores Bird Carpenter. Boston: Twayne, 1980.

"Emerson Extolled at Authors' Dinner." *New York Times*, May 26, 1903.

Emerson, Ralph Waldo. *Collected Works of Ralph Waldo Emerson*. Edited by Robert E. Spiller et al. 8 vols. to date. Cambridge, MA: Harvard University Press, 1971–.

"Emerson's Life, Writings, and Philosophy." *Critic* 1 (November 19, 1881): 319–320.

Engels, Friedrich. *The Condition of the Working Class in England*. Translated and edited by W. O. Henderson and W. H. Chaloner. New York: Macmillan, 1958.

"Faces of Noted People: The Popular Craze for Photographs of Celebrities." *New York Times*, February 25, 1883.

Fischer, David Hackett. *Paul Revere's Ride*. New York: Oxford University Press, 1994.

Fish, Stanley. "Just Published: Minutiae without Meaning." *New York Times*, September 7, 1999.

Folsom, Ed. *Walt Whitman's Native Representations*. New York: Cambridge University Press, 1994.

Forbes, Edward W. "Edward Waldo Emerson." *The Saturday Club: A Century Completed 1920–1956*, 27–41. Edited by Edward W. Forbes and John H. Finley Jr. Boston: Houghton Mifflin, 1958.

French, Allen. "Edward Waldo Emerson: A Memoir." *Proceedings of the Massachusetts Historical Society*, 3rd Series, 65 (February 1935): 387–390.

Froude, James Anthony. *My Relations with Carlyle*. London: Longmans, Green, 1903.

———. *Thomas Carlyle: A History of His Life in London, 1834–1881*. London: Longmans, Green, 1884.

———. *Thomas Carlyle: A History of the First Forty Years of His Life, 1795–1835*. London: Longmans, Green, 1882.

Fryer, Peter. *Forbidden Books of the Victorians: Henry Spencer Ashbee's Bibliographies of Erotica Abridged and Edited, with an Introduction and Notes*. London: Odyssey, 1970.

Fuller, Randall. *Emerson's Ghosts: Literature, Politics, and the Making of Americanists*. New York: Oxford University Press, 2007.

Garland, Joseph E. *Boston's North Shore: Being an Account of Life Among the Note-worthy, Fashionable, Wealthy, Eccentric and Ordinary 1823–1890*. Boston: Little, Brown, 1978.

Garnett, Richard. *Life of Ralph Waldo Emerson*. London: Walter Scott, 1888.

Glass, Loren Daniel. *Authors Inc.: Literary Celebrity in the Modern United States, 1880–1980*. New York: New York University Press, 2004.

Goodbrand, Robert. "A Suggestion for a New Kind of Biography." *Contemporary Review* 14 (1870): 20–28.

Gosse, Edmund. "The Custom of Biography." *Anglo-Saxon Review* 8 (1901): 195–208.

Gougeon, Len. "Looking Backwards: Emerson in 1903." *Nineteenth-Century Prose* 30 (Spring/Fall 2003): 50–73.

———. *Virtue's Hero: Emerson, Antislavery, and Reform*. Athens: University of Georgia Press, 1990.

Gould, Elizabeth Porter. "The Biography of the Future." *Literary World* 16 (May 16, 1885): 171.

Gray, Henry David. *Emerson: A Statement of New England Transcendentalism as Expressed in the Philosophy of Its Chief Exponent*. Stanford, CA: Stanford University Press, 1917.

Green, Rev. Walter Cox, comp. *General Catalogue of the Meadville Theological School, Meadville, Pennsylvania, 1844–1910*. Meadville: Privately printed, 1910.

Grob, Gerald N. *The Mad Among Us: A History of the Care of America's Mentally Ill*. Cambridge, MA: Harvard University Press, 1994.

Guernsey, Alfred Hudson. *Ralph Waldo Emerson: Philosopher and Poet*. New York: D. Appleton and Company, 1881.

Habich, Robert D. "Biography, Memoir, and Reminiscence." *Oxford Handbook of Transcendentalism*, 426–437. Edited by Joel Myerson, Sandra Harbert Petrulionis, and Laura Dassow Walls. New York: Oxford University Press, 2010.

———. "Channing Remembers Emerson: Visits to Concord, 1870 and 1877." *New England Quarterly* 73 (September 2000): 495–506.

———. "Holmes, Cabot, and Edward Emerson and the Challenges of Writing Emerson's Biography in the 1880s." *Emerson Bicentennial Essays*, 3–32. Edited by Ronald A. Bosco and Joel Myerson. Boston: Massachusetts Historical Society, 2006.

———. *Transcendentalism and the "Western Messenger": A History of the Magazine and Its Contributors, 1835–1841*. Rutherford, NJ: Fairleigh Dickinson University Press, 1985.

Hamilton, Nigel. *Biography: A Brief History*. Cambridge and London: Harvard University Press, 2007.

Harding, Brian. *A Brief Introduction to the Microfilm Edition of the Ralph Waldo Emerson Collection . . . From the Alexander Ireland Collection in the Manchester Central Library, Manchester England*. West Yorkshire, UK: Microform Academic Publishers, n.d.

Harrington, Thomas Francis, and James Gregory Mumford. *The Harvard Medical School: A History, Narrative and Documentary, 1782–1905*. 3 vols. New York: Lewis Publishing Company, 1905.

Harris, William T. "Ralph Waldo Emerson." *Atlantic Monthly* 50 (August 1882): 238–252.

Harrison, Frederic. "Froude's Life of Carlyle." *North American Review* 140 (January 1885): 9–21.

Harvard College Class of 1866 Class Report, July, 1866 to June, 1869. Boston: Rand, Avery, & Frye, 1869.

Hedge, Frederic Henry. "Cabot's Memoir of Emerson." *Unitarian Review* 28 (November 1887): 416–420.

Higginson, Thomas Wentworth. *Carlyle's Laugh and Other Surprises.* Boston: Houghton, Mifflin, 1909.

———. *Cheerful Yesterdays.* Boston and New York: Houghton, Mifflin, 1898.

———. "Conway's 'Emerson at Home and Abroad.'" *Century Magazine* 25 (April 1883): 954–956.

———. *Margaret Fuller Ossoli.* Boston: Houghton, Mifflin, 1885.

History of Jefferson County, Wisconsin. Chicago: Western Historical Co., 1879.

Hoagland, N. S. "Correspondence: Seventieth Birthday Reception of George Willis Cooke." *Unity* 81 (May 23, 1918): 200.

[Holland, H. W.] "Mr. Emerson's Philosophy." *Nation* 33 (November 17, 1881): 396–397.

Holmes, Oliver Wendell. "A Cry from the Study." *Atlantic Monthly* 52 (January 1886): 91–98.

———. "Doings of the Sunbeam." *Atlantic Monthly* 7 (July 1863): 1–15.

———. *A Mortal Antipathy.* Vol. 7 of *Works of Oliver Wendell Holmes.* Boston: Houghton, Mifflin, 1892.

———. "Poetry: A Metrical Essay." *Works of Oliver Wendell Holmes*, 12:35–59. 13 vols. Boston: Houghton, Mifflin, 1892.

———. "The Stereoscope and the Stereograph." *Atlantic Monthly* 3 (June 1859): 738–748.

Houghton, Mifflin and Company. *A Catalogue of Authors Whose Works Are Published by Houghton, Mifflin and Company.* Boston: Houghton, Mifflin, 1899.

Howe, M. A. DeWolfe. *Holmes of the Breakfast-Table.* London and New York: Oxford University Press, 1939.

Howells, William Dean. *Literary Friends and Acquaintance: A Personal Retrospect of American Authorship.* Edited by David F. Hiatt and Edwin H. Cady. Bloomington: Indiana University Press, 1968.

———. *Selected Letters of William Dean Howells.* Edited by George Arms et al. 6 vols. Boston: Twayne, 1979–1983.

Hylton, Stuart. *A History of Manchester.* Chichester, UK: Phillimore & Co., 2003.

Indianapolis Directory for 1880. Indianapolis: R. L. Polk, 1880.

Indianapolis Directory for 1881. Indianapolis: R. L. Polk, 1881.

Indianapolis Woman's Club, 1875–1940. Greenfield, IN: Wm. Mitchell Printing Co., Old Swimming Hole Press, 1944.

Ireland, Alexander. *Ralph Waldo Emerson. His Life, Genius, and Writings. A Biographical Sketch.* London: Simpkin, Marshall, 1882.

James, Henry. *Hawthorne.* London: Macmillan, 1879.

Kendall, Paul Murray. *The Art of Biography.* New York: Norton, 1965.

Kidd, Alan. *Manchester.* 3rd Edition. Edinburgh: Edinburgh University Press, 2002.

Kleinfield, H. L. "The Structure of Emerson's Death." *Bulletin of the New York Public Library* 65 (1961): 47–64.

"The Late Mr. Alexander Ireland." *Manchester Faces and Places: An Illustrated Magazine* 6 (1895): 57–60.

Loving, Jerome. "Emerson's 'Constant Way of Looking at Whitman's Genius.'" *American Literature* 51 (November 1979): 399–403.

Lowell, James Russell. *Letters of James Russell Lowell.* Edited by Charles Eliot Norton. 2 vols. New York: Harper and Brothers, 1894.

Lyttle, Charles Harold. *Freedom Moves West: A History of the Western Unitarian Conference, 1852–1952.* Boston: Beacon, 1952.

Marcus, Steven. *The Other Victorians: A Study of Sexuality and Pornography in Mid-Nineteenth-Century England.* New York: Basic Books, 1966.

Markus, Julia. *J. Anthony Froude: The Last Undiscovered Great Victorian.* New York: Scribners, 2005.

Marshall, P. David. *Celebrity and Power: Fame in Contemporary Culture.* Minneapolis: University of Minnesota Press, 1997.

McAleer, John. *Ralph Waldo Emerson: Days of Encounter.* Boston: Little, Brown, 1984.

McGann, Jerome J. *The Textual Condition.* Princeton, NJ: Princeton University Press, 1991.

McMillin, T. S. *Our Preposterous Use of Literature: Emerson and the Nature of Reading.* Urbana: University of Illinois Press, 2000.

Meehan, Sean Ross. *Mediating American Autobiography: Photography in Emerson, Thoreau, Douglass, and Whitman.* Columbia: University of Missouri Press, 2008.

Menand, Louis. *The Metaphysical Club: A Story of Ideas in America.* New York: Farrar, Straus and Giroux, 2001.

Messinger, Gary S. *Manchester in the Victorian Age: The Half-known City.* Manchester, UK: Manchester University Press, 1985.

Mills, Isabel Petrie. *From Tinder Box to the "Larger" Light: Threads from the Life of John Mills, Banker (Author of "Vox Humana"): Interwoven with Some Early Century Recollections by His Wife.* Manchester, UK: Sherratt & Hughes, 1899.

Mills, J. Saxon. "Alexander Ireland." *Manchester City News,* December 15, 1894.

Mitchell, Charles E. *Individualism and Its Discontents: Appropriations of Emerson, 1880–1950.* Amherst: University of Massachusetts Press, 1997.

Monaco, James. *Celebrity: The Media as Image Makers.* New York: Delta, 1978.

Morse, John Torrey, Jr. *Life and Letters of Oliver Wendell Holmes.* 2 vols. Cambridge: Riverside Press, 1896.

Mortimer, John. "Alexander Ireland." *Manchester Quarterly* 53 (January 1895): 1–9.

Mott, Frank Luther. *American Journalism: A History, 1690–1960.* Third Edition. New York: Macmillan, 1962.

Mott, Wesley T. "'The Age of the First Person Singular': Emerson and Individualism." *A Historical Guide to Ralph Waldo Emerson,* 61–100. Edited by Joel Myerson. New York: Oxford University Press, 2000.

Myerson, Joel. "Introduction to the AMS Edition." *Complete Works of Ralph Waldo Emerson.* Second Edition. New York: AMS Press, 1979.

———. *Ralph Waldo Emerson: A Descriptive Bibliography.* Pittsburgh: University of Pittsburgh Press, 1982.

Oehlschlaeger, Fritz, and George Hendrick, eds. *Toward the Making of Thoreau's Modern Reputation: Selected Correspondence of S. A. Jones, A. W. Hosmer, H. S. Salt, H. G. O. Blake, and D. Ricketson.* Urbana: University of Illinois Press, 1979.

Oliphant, Margaret O. W. "The Ethics of Biography." *Contemporary Review* 44 (1883): 76–93.

O'Neill, Bonnie Carr. "'The Best of Me Is There': Emerson as Lecturer and Celebrity." *American Literature: A Journal of Literary History, Criticism, and Bibliography* 80 (December 2008): 739–767.

"Our Library Table." *Athenaeum* (June 1, 1889): 695.

Pearson, Charles H. "Emerson." *Reviews and Critical Essays*, 171–186. London: Methuen, 1896.

Peirce, H. Winthrop. *The History of the School of the Museum of Fine Arts, Boston, 1877–1927*. Boston: Museum of Fine Arts, 1930.

Perry, Bliss. "Dr. Edward Waldo Emerson." *Concord Journal*, February 6, 1930.

Pier, Arthur S. *Forbes: Telephone Pioneer*. New York: Dodd, Mead, 1953.

Porte, Joel. "Holmes's Emerson." *Consciousness and Culture: Emerson and Thoreau Reviewed*, 88–95. New Haven, CT: Yale University Press, 2004.

Porter, Roy. *Madness: A Brief History*. New York: Oxford University Press, 2002.

Quinquennial Catalogue of the Officers and Graduates of Harvard University, 1636–1910. Cambridge, MA: Published by the University, 1910.

"Ralph Waldo Emerson." *Century* 23 (February 1882): 622–623.

"Reminiscences." *New-York Times*. May 2, 1882.

Richardson, Robert D., Jr. *Emerson: The Mind on Fire*. Berkeley: University of California Press, 1995.

———. "The Perils of Writing Biography." *Lives Out of Letters: Essays on American Literary Biography and Documentation, in Honor of Robert N. Hudspeth*, 253–260. Edited by Robert D. Habich. Madison, NJ: Fairleigh Dickinson University Press, 2004.

Richardson, Todd H. "Emerson's Canonization and the Boston Periodical Press: 1872–1903." PhD diss., University of South Carolina, 2002.

Ricoeur, Paul. "Objectivity and Subjectivity in History." *History and Truth*, 21–40. Translated by Charles A. Kelbley. Evanston, IL: Northwestern University Press, 1965.

Robinson, David. "Jenkin Lloyd Jones." *Unitarianism in America*. http://www.harvardsquarelibrary.org/UIA%20Online/47jones.html.

Roche, James Jeffrey. *The Life of John Boyle O'Reilly*. New York: Cassell Publishing Company, 1891.

Ronda, Bruce. "The Concord School of Philosophy and the Legacy of Transcendentalism." *New England Quarterly* 82 (December 2009): 575–607.

Rusk, Ralph L. *The Life of Ralph Waldo Emerson*. New York: Charles Scribner's Sons, 1949.

Salt, Henry Stephens. *Life of Henry David Thoreau*. 1890. London: Scott, 1896.

Sanborn, F. B. "Materials Concerning the Incidental Meetings of Emerson in London Collected by John Camden Hotten." *Springfield Daily Republican*, November 17, 1874.

Sanborn, Franklin Benjamin. *Correspondence of Franklin Benjamin Sanborn*. Compiled by Kenneth Walter Cameron. Hartford, CT: Transcendental Books, 1982.

Sandler, Martin W. *Photography: An Illustrated History*. New York: Oxford University Press, 2002.

Scharnhorst, Gary. *Henry David Thoreau: A Case Study in Canonization*. Columbia, SC: Camden House, 1993.

[Scudder, Horace E.] "Emerson's Genius." *Atlantic Monthly* 60 (October 1887): 566–572.

Scudder, Townsend. *The Lonely Wayfaring Man: Emerson and Some Englishmen*. London and New York: Oxford University Press, 1936.

Secord, James A. *Victorian Sensation: The Extraordinary Publication, Reception, and Secret Authorship of "Vestiges of the Natural History of Creation."* Chicago: University of Chicago Press, 2000.

Simmons, Nancy Craig. "Arranging the Sibylline Leaves: James Elliot Cabot's Work as Emerson's Literary Executor." *Studies in the American Renaissance 1983*, 335–389. Edited by Joel Myerson. Charlottesville: University Press of Virginia, 1983.

———. "Man Without a Shadow: The Life and Work of James Elliot Cabot, Emerson's Biographer and Literary Executor." PhD diss., Princeton University, 1980.

———. "Philosophical Biographer: James Elliot Cabot and *A Memoir of Ralph Waldo Emerson*." *Studies in the American Renaissance 1987*, 365–392. Edited by Joel Myerson. Charlottesville: University Press of Virginia, 1987.

Simmons, Nancy Craig, ed. "The 'Autobiographical Sketch' of James Elliot Cabot." *Harvard Library Bulletin* 30 (April 1982): 117–152.

Slater, Joseph, ed. *The Correspondence of Emerson and Carlyle*. New York: Columbia University Press, 1964.

Small, Miriam Rossiter. *Oliver Wendell Holmes*. New York: Twayne, 1962.

Sowder, William J. *Emerson's Impact on the British Isles and Canada*. Charlottesville: University Press of Virginia, 1966.

Stephen, Sir Leslie. "Biography." *National Review* 23 (1893): 171–183.

———. "National Biography." *Studies of a Biographer*, 1: 1–34. 4 vols. London: Duckworth, 1902–1907.

Strachey, Lytton. *Portraits in Miniature and Other Essays*. New York: Harcourt, 1931.

Sulgrove, Berry R. *History of Indianapolis and Marion County, Indiana*. Philadelphia: L. H. Everts & Co., 1884.

Sunderland, J. T. "George Willis Cooke: An Appreciation." *Unity* 91 (June 14, 1923): 249–254.

———. "Letter from Boston." *Unity* 8 (October 16, 1881): 311.

Tebbel, John. *A History of Book Publishing in the United States*. 4 vols. New York: R. R. Bowker, 1972–1981.

Thayer, William Roscoe, ed. *Letters of John Holmes to James Russell Lowell and Others*. Boston: Houghton Mifflin, 1917.

Thomas, Joseph M. "The Familial Canon of Emerson's Poetry." Paper presented at the annual American Literature Association meeting, Boston, Massachusetts, May 25, 2007.

Thoreau, Henry David. *Walden*. Edited by J. Lyndon Shanley. Princeton, NJ: Princeton University Press, 1971.

[Thorne, William Henry.] "Emerson and His Biographers." *Globe* 1 (October–December 1889): 37–55.

Tilton, Eleanor M. *Amiable Autocrat: A Biography of Dr. Oliver Wendell Holmes*. New York: Henry Schuman, 1947.

Tomsich, John. *A Genteel Endeavor: American Culture and Politics in the Gilded Age*. Stanford, CA: Stanford University Press, 1971.

Topp, Chester W. *Victorian Yellowbacks & Paperbacks, 1849–1905*. 8 vols. to date. Denver: Hermitage Antiquarian Bookshop, 1993–.

Traubel, Horace. *With Walt Whitman in Camden*. Vol. 6. Edited by Gertrude Traubel and William White. Carbondale: Southern Illinois University Press, 1982.

Tridgell, Susan. *Understanding Our Selves: The Dangerous Art of Biography*. Oxford and Bern: Peter Lang, 2004.

Unitarian Year Book September 1, 1939–August 31, 1940. Boston: American Unitarian Association, 1940.

Warren, Austin. "The Concord School of Philosophy." *New England Quarterly* 2 (April 1929): 199–233.

Welland, Dennis. "John Camden Hotten and Emerson's Uncollected Essays." *Yearbook of English Studies* 6, 156–175. Edited by G. K. Hunter and C. J. Rawson. London: Modern Humanities Research Association, 1976.

———. "Moncure Daniel Conway and Anglo-American Relations." *Ethical Record* 81 (September 1976): 4–7.

Welling, William. *Photography in America: The Formative Years, 1839–1900*. New York: Thomas Y. Crowell, 1978.

Wexler, Joyce Piell. *Who Paid for Modernism? Art, Money, and the Fiction of Conrad, Joyce, and Lawrence*. Fayetteville: University of Arkansas Press, 1997.

Wheeler, J. M. "Emerson." *Progress* 1 (February 1883): 117–120.

Whipple, Edwin P. "Emerson as a Poet." *North American Review* 135 (July 1882): 68–71.

Wider, Sarah Ann. *The Critical Reception of Emerson: Unsettling All Things*. Rochester, NY: Camden House, 2000.

[Woodberry, George E.] "Emerson's Concord Life." *Atlantic Monthly* 64 (August 1889): 270–273.

Woolf, Virginia. "The Art of Biography." *The Death of the Moth and Other Essays*, 187–197. San Diego: Harcourt Brace Jovanovich, 1942.

Worthen, John. "The Necessary Ignorance of a Biographer." *The Art of Literary Biography*, 227–244. Edited by John Batchelor. Oxford: Clarendon Press, 1995.

MANUSCRIPT COLLECTIONS (ALPHABETIZED BY LAST NAME)

Amos Bronson Alcott Papers (MS Am 1130.9–1130.12). By permission of the Houghton Library, Harvard University.

George Bancroft Papers, Massachusetts Historical Society. Used by permission.

Cabot Family Papers, A-99, Schlesinger Library, Radcliffe Institute for Advanced Study, Harvard University.

Chatto & Windus Archives, Centre for Writing, Publishing and Printing History, MS 2444/5, Special Collections, University of Reading, UK. By permission of the Random House Group Ltd.

James Freeman Clarke Additional Correspondence, 1787–1886 (MS Am 1569.7). Houghton Library, Harvard University.

Class Book of 1829, Harvard University Archives, HUD 229.714 f.

Class Book of 1866, Harvard University Archives, HUD 266.714 f.

Moncure Daniel Conway Family Papers, MC1999.6, Archives and Special Collections, Dickinson College, Carlisle, PA. Used by permission.

Moncure Daniel Conway Papers, Rare Book and Manuscript Library, Columbia University. Used by permission.

George Willis Cooke Manuscript Collection, Courtesy of Fruitlands Museum, Harvard, Massachusetts.

Emerson Family Correspondence (MS Am 1280.226). Ralph Waldo Emerson Memorial Association deposit, Houghton Library, Harvard University. Not to be reproduced in whole or in part without permission.

Emerson Family Papers (MS Am 1280.235). Ralph Waldo Emerson Memorial Association deposit, Houghton Library, Harvard University. Not to be reproduced in whole or in part without permission.

Edith Emerson Forbes and William Hathaway Forbes Papers and Additions, Massachusetts Historical Society. Used by permission of the Forbes Archive Committee.

Letters to Ralph Waldo Emerson (bMS Am 1280). Ralph Waldo Emerson Memorial Association deposit, Houghton Library, Harvard University. Not to be reproduced in whole or in part without permission.

William Torrey Harris Concord School of Philosophy scrapbooks, 1879–1887. Vault A35, W. T. Harris Unit 2, Concord Free Public Library. Used by permission.

Hoar Family Papers, 1738–1958, Vault A45 Hoar Unit 1, Box 2, Series II. Ebenezer Rockwood Hoar Papers, [182-]–1895, Concord Free Public Library. Used by permission.

Oliver Wendell Holmes Additional Papers (MS Am 1234.1–.2, 1234.4–.11). Houghton Library, Harvard University.

Oliver Wendell Holmes Letters from Various Correspondents, 1820–1894 (MS Am 1241.1). Houghton Library, Harvard University.

Oliver Wendell Holmes (1809–1894) Papers (MSS26377), Manuscript Division, Library of Congress, Washington, D.C.

Houghton, Mifflin and Company Contracts (MS Am 2346). By permission of the Houghton Library, Harvard University.

Houghton Mifflin Company Correspondence and Records (MS Am 1925–1925.4). By permission of the Houghton Library, Harvard University.

Houghton Mifflin Company Records (MS Am 2030–2030.4). By permission of the Houghton Library, Harvard University.

Alexander Ireland Collection, Manchester Central Library, Manchester, England.

Alexander Ireland Collection, Special Collections Library, University of Michigan.

Local Studies Division, Manchester Central Library, Manchester, England.

Macmillan Archives, Add 55256, Correspondence, Vol CDLXXI, British Library.

O. C. McCulloch Papers, Mss L363, Manuscript Section, Indiana State Library.

Miscellaneous Autograph Letters, Add 34813, Section D, British Library.

Record Book Social Circle in Concord, Deposit Collection, Concord (Massachusetts) Free Public Library. Used by permission.

Records of the Third Parish, Dedham, courtesy of the Dedham Historical Society, Dedham, Massachusetts.

John O. Sargent Papers, 1831–1893, microfilm edition, 4 reels (Boston: Massachusetts Historical Society, 1978), Massachusetts Historical Society. Used by permission.

Jabez T. Sunderland Papers, Bentley Historical Library, University of Michigan. 86485 Aa; UAm. Used by permission.

Charles Dudley Warner Papers, Courtesy of the Watkinson Library, Trinity College, Hartford, CT.

INDEX

marriages, 43, 50; and Holmes, 94–95; and John Camden Hotten, 47–50; ideas about biography, 53–54, 56–59, 72; impact of writings on Emerson's reputation, 126–127; *In Memoriam. Ralph Waldo Emerson: Recollections of his Visits to England in 1833, 1847-8, 1872-3, and Extracts from Unpublished Letters,* 51–55; later years and death of, 122; library of, 50, 122; and Manchester, 41–43; and *Manchester Examiner,* 42–43, 122; meetings with authors, 40; meetings with Emerson, 39–40; political ideas, 41–43; publication, reception, and sales of writings, 53, 54, 57–58, 72; *Ralph Waldo Emerson: His Life, Genius, and Writings,* 54–57; sources for writings, 54–55; support for Public Libraries and Museums Act, 42–43; and Transcendentalism, 56
Ireland, Anne, 50, 122
Ireland, Eliza Mary Blithe, 41
Ireland, John Nicholson, 50

James, Henry, Jr., 9, 46
James, Henry, Sr., 2, 94
James R. Osgood publishers, 28, 34, 36, 48, 57, 64–65, 71, 78, 80, 122–123
Jefferson Liberal Institute, 14, 18
Jefferson, Thomas, 128
Johnson, Samuel, 5, 85
Jones, Jenkin Lloyd, 15–16

Kendall, Paul Murray, 4, 6
Keyes, John Shepard, 108
Kleinfield, H. L., xiv

Landor, Walter Savage, 39
Langtry, Lillie, 53
Larcom, Lucy, 78
Leggett, Mary, 36
Lewes, George Henry, 34
Lincoln, Abraham, 26, 46, 104
Literary World magazine, 4, 21, 130
Liverpool-to-Manchester Railway, 41

Longfellow, Henry Wadsworth, 7, 46, 79
Lowell, James Russell, 46, 81, 94

Manchester, England, 40–43
Manchester Examiner newspaper, 42–43, 122
Martin, Frederick, 61
Mason, J. M., 46
McCulloch, Oscar Carleton, 16–17
McGann, Jerome J., xxiv
McMillin, T. S., xix, 30, 88, 92
Melville, Herman, 6
Meredith, George, 46
Mifflin, George H., 126
Mill, John Stuart, 46, 67
Milton, John, 62, 66, 97
Mitchell, Charles E., xviii–xix, 88
Mitchell, S. Wier, 78
Mitchell's Newspaper Press Directory, 42
Monaco, James, 127, 129
Morley, John, 64
Morse, John Torrey, Jr., 74, 78, 92
Motley, John Lathrop, 97
Myerson, Joel, 125

New Thought, 91
Norton, Andrews, 67
Norton, Charles Eliot, 53, 111; editing of Emerson-Carlyle correspondence, 57–58, 61–62, 65, 71, 105, 124; on Froude, 5–6

Oliphant, Margaret O. W., xvii, 58
O'Neill, Bonnie Carr, 128
Ostrander, Dempster, 18

Paine, Thomas, 123, 128
Palfrey, John Gorham, 45
Parker, Theodore, 44, 67, 116
Peabody, Elizabeth Palmer, 22, 53, 58, 66–67, 102
Perry, Bliss, 103
photography, xvii, xxi, xxiii, 7–8, 128–129
Pinel, Philippe, 93
psychiatry, 92–94